I0020073

Texts in Computing

Volume 17

Acts of the Programme
Semantics and Syntax

Isaac Newton Institute for the Mathematical Sciences,

January to July 2012

Texts in Computing Series Editor
Ian Mackie   mackie@lix.polytechniqu

Acts of the Programme
Semantics and Syntax
Isaac Newton Institute for the
Mathematical Sciences,

January to July 2012

Edited by
Arnold Beckmann
and
Benedikt Löwe

ISBN 978-1-84890-080-6

College Publications
Scientific Director: Dov Gabbay
Managing Director: Jane Spurr
Department of Computer Science
King's College London, Strand, London WC2R 2LS, UK

http://www.collegepublications.co.uk

Original cover design by Richard Fraser
Cover produced by Laraine Welch
Printed by Lightning Source, Milton Keynes, UK

Table of Contents

SAS Seminar Week 2.

SAS Seminar Week 3.

SAS Workshop "Is Cryptographic Theory Practically Relevant?".

SAS Seminar Week 5.

SAS Seminar Week 6.

Special PUAI evening lecture.

SAS Workshop "Turing in Context @ King's".

SAS Seminar Week 7.

SAS Seminar Week 8.

SAS Seminar Week 9.

SAS Seminar Week 10.

SAS Satellite Workshop "Pattern Formation: The inspiration of Alan Turing".

SAS Seminar Week 11.

SAS Workshop "Logical Approaches to Barriers in Complexity II".

SAS Special Evening Lecture.

SAS Seminar Week 13.

SAS Seminar Week 22.

SAS Satellite Workshop "The Incomputable".

Preface

Acts of the Programme
Semantics and Syntax: A Legacy of Alan Turing

Isaac Newton Institute for Mathematical Sciences,
Cambridge, UK, 9 January – 6 July 2012

The research programme *Semantics and Syntax* was one of the central activities of the *Alan Turing Year 2012*, the world-wide celebration of the life and work of the exceptional scientist *Alan Mathison Turing* (1912–1954). It took place during the first six months of the *Alan Turing Year* in Cambridge, included Turing's 100th birthday on 23 June 2012 at King's College, and combined the character of an intensive high-level research semester with outreach activities as part of the centenary celebrations. The programme had almost 200 visiting fellows and programme participants (Appendix A lists them), as well as several hundred additional workshop participants, many of which were leaders of their respective fields. It was organised by Arnold Beckmann (Swansea), S. Barry Cooper (Leeds), Benedikt Löwe (Amsterdam & Hamburg), Elvira Mayordomo (Zaragoza), and Nigel Smart (Bristol).

Due to the embedding of the programme in the *Alan Turing Year*, the programme had a large number of workshops and events. Some of the workshops doubled as the major international events of the relevant sub-communities. The heart of the research programme was the *SAS Seminar*,

FIGURE 1. Four of the organisers (Cooper, Löwe, Beckmann, Mayordomo) in the Old Combination Room at *Corpus Christi College* during the conference *Computability in Europe 2012*. (Picture taken by Sara J. Wilkinson).

a series of 30-minute informal lectures in which the new fellows presented open problems they intended to work on to the rest of the visiting fellows in form of "teaser talks". Beyond the immediate activity at the INI, there was a number of other Cambridge events that were intertwined with the research activity at the INI and brought more researchers in contact with the fellows. The international conferences *EuroCrypt 2012* and *CiE 2012* brought several hundreds of the leading thinkers of our fields to Cambridge.

This volume documents the presentations that were given as part of the programme *Semantics and Syntax* in chronological order. These include the abstracts of the teaser talks given in the *SAS Seminar* and abstracts of the talks given at five of the seven workshops, as well as written versions of two open problem sessions (pp. 85–95 and pp. 210–215.)

Workshops related to the SAS Programme

The Mathematical Legacy of Alan Turing (Organiser: Benedikt Löwe). The first day of the programme was one of the *Spitalfields Days* funded by the *London Mathematical Society*. The *Spitalfields Days* present the subject matter of a research programme to the wider academic public, in order to get them interested in the programme. Hugh Woodin, George Barmpalias, Nigel Smart, and Anuj Dawar gave research introductions to their respective research areas. The abstracts for this event can be found on pp. 1–7.

Is Cryptographic Theory Practically Relevant? (Organisers: Kenny Paterson, Nigel Smart). This workshop bridged the divide between theoretical cryptography and cryptography as practised in industry. The event was highly successful with around one hundred participants from around the globe. The talks ranged from talks about the challenges phased by the banking industry, via car security (both car locks, and the security of the electronic control systems), to smart metering systems in the energy supply market. A number of new research directions arose from the workshop, including collaboration between academics and Cryptomathic on a system for securing messaging between HSMs (Hardware Security Modules) used in various banking applications. The abstracts for this event can be found on pp. 30–52.

Turing in Context @ King's College (Organisers: Liesbeth De Mol, Benedikt Löwe, Ken Moody, Giuseppe Primiero). This workshop was not directly part of the SAS Programme, but was associated to it. The workshop highlighted the many contributions of Alan Turing for a general academic audience, in particular for undergraduate and postgraduate students of all fields, and put these contributions in a historical context. The event was hosted by Turing's former college in Cambridge, King's College. The abstracts for this event can be found on pp. 67–83.

Pattern Formation: The inspiration of Alan Turing (A Satellite Meeting at St. John's College, Oxford; organisers: Bernold Fiedler, Benedikt Löwe, Philip Maini). Morphogenesis, one of the fields that Alan Turing had worked on, was not included in the main focus of the programme *Semantics and Syntax*. In order to compensate for that, the organisers arranged for a satellite workshop for the morphogenesis community at St. John's College in Oxford. The workshop bridged the gap between the theoretical work of the mathematical biologist and the laboratory work that confirms or refutes the predictions of the theoretical model. The participants of this conference were from mathematics, biology and chemistry and emphasised the importance of including both theoretical and empirical research in the future agenda of morphogenesis. The abstracts for this event can be found on pp. 121–151.

Logical Approaches to Barriers in Complexity II (Organisers: Arnold Beckmann, Anuj Dawar). This workshop brought together leading researchers from the communities working on logical descriptions of complexity, i.e., descriptive complexity, propositional proof complexity and bounded arithmetic. It especially focused on work that draws on methods from the different areas which appeal to the whole community. It was considered as a follow-up workshop to *Logical Approaches to Barriers in Computing and Complexity* held at the *Alfried-Krupp-Wissenschaftskolleg* in Greifswald in February 2010. The abstracts for this event can be found on pp. 160–192.

Formal and Computational Cryptographic Proofs (Organisers: Nigel Smart, Shafi Goldwasser). This workshop aimed to bridge the gap between Formal Methods based approaches to verifying the security of cryptographic protocols and those based on complexity theory. For over a two decades the complexity theoretic approach has been considered the *de facto* standard way of performing such verification; with the approach via formal methods being considered almost fatally flawed. In recent years various researchers have found ways of repairing these flaws and the advent of automatic complexity theoretic verification of protocols via tools based on formal methods is becoming a reality. Highlights of this workshop included a number of talks on the world leading work in this area being performed by Microsoft Research in Cambridge, as well as work on automatic verification from researchers in France. A number of talks focused on the current hot topic of *fully homomorphic encryption*, with many of the main players in the field visiting the Newton Institute in this period. Different application domains were considered, including the use of these techniques to verify the secure dismantling of nuclear weapons. The abstracts for this event are not part of this book.

The Incomputable (A Satellite Meeting at Chicheley Hall, Newport Pagnell; organisers: S. Barry Cooper, Mariya I. Soskova). This workshop was bridging another gap: that between the mathematical theory of computability and its relevance for the real world. This is a core aspect of Turing's scientific legacy, and this meeting for the first time reunited (in)computability theory and 'big science' in a way not attempted since Turing's premature passing. *The Incomputable* was generously supported by the John Templeton Foundation and the venue at

Chicheley Hall made the event particularly attractive. The abstracts for this event can be found on pp. 243–298.

7th Conference on Computability, Complexity and Randomness

(Organisers: Elvira Mayordomo, Wolfgang Merkle). This workshop constituted the 7th annual meeting of the active algorithmic randomness community. Its main added value was bringing together researchers from computer science and mathematics. The meeting successfully included long discussion periods every afternoon as well as 31 specialised talks, including one on the applications of information theory to biology. The informal proceedings of CCR 2012 can be found on the webpages of the Isaac Newton Institute under `http://www.newton.ac.uk/programmes/SAS/sasw04.html`.

As of May 2013, the programme *Semantics and Syntax* has produced 55 preprints that are stored on the preprint server of the Isaac Newton Institute and are openly accessible—see Appendix B for a list of those. We expect this number to grow in the next few years: these preprints complement the short abstracts in this volume as a documentation of the research done at the Isaac Newton Institute during the programme.

We should like to thank the Isaac Newton Institute for the generous financial support, the smooth organisation, and the warm hospitality; in particular, we should like to extend our thanks to the INI directors, Sir David Wallace and John Toland, the INI manager, Christine West, and to the INI staff, in particular Mustapha Amrani, Jonathan Chin, Esperanza de Felipe, Kathryn de Ridder, Almarie Ehlers, Sarah Fendt, Sue Gilbert, Steve Greenham, Robert Leonard, Jenny Mackay, Chie Sibley Obata, Sara Wilkinson, and Stephen Williams. We should also like to thank Churchill College, Girton College and Robinson College for their hospitality allowing our fellows to participate in their breakfasts, brunches, lunches and suppers. The editors of this book should like to extend special thanks to Corpus Christi College and Robinson College for granting Fellowships to them: Corpus Christi a Visiting Fellowship to Benedikt Löwe, and Robinson College a Bye-Fellowship to Arnold Beckmann. Further thanks go to King's College for hosting several of our events.

The Isaac Newton Institute also financially supported the production of this volume, for which we were assisted by Aadil Kurji (Amsterdam & Bristol) in typesetting. Of course, we thank our fellow organisers, S. Barry Cooper, Elvira Mayordomo, and Nigel Smart for their help in coordinating the scientific side of the programme, and all of the fellows and participants who were crucial for the success. In particular, we thank the scientific advisory committee of the SAS programme, Samson Abramsky (Oxford), Stephen A. Cook (Toronto), Jan Denef (Leuven), Martin Hyland (Cam-

bridge), Arjen Lenstra (Lausanne), Angus MacIntyre (London), Jacques
Stern (Paris), and Hugh Woodin (Berkeley).

Arnold Beckmann and Benedikt Löwe
Swansea and Amsterdam/Hamburg, May 2013

Ivan Nikolaev Soskov (23 September 1954 – 5 May 2013)

While finishing the Acts of the SAS Programme, the shocking news reached us that our
colleague Ivan Soskov had unexpectedly died.

Ivan Soskov studied at Sofia University
where he graduated in 1979 with a degree
in Mathematical Logic. He became a doctoral
student of Dimiter Skordev and defended his
Ph.D. thesis entitled *Computability in Partial
Algebraic Systems* in 1983. Ivan spent his career at Sofia University, first as Assistant Professor in the *Laboratory of Applied Logic*, and
later at the Faculty for Mathematics and Com-

puter Science. In 1991, he was promoted to Associate Professor and spent
two years at the University of California at Los Angeles (1991–1993). After he had obtained the higher doctorate (D.Sc.) in 2001, he was promoted
to Full Professor in 2005. He was head of the Department for Mathematical Logic and Applications from 2000 to 2007 and Dean of the Faculty of
Mathematics and Computer Science from 2007 until his death.

Ivan's research field was classical computability theory, in particular degree spectra and enumeration degrees. He has supervised fifteen Master
students in subjects related to his research expertise and had three doctoral
students, Stela Nikolova (1992), Vessela Baleva (2002), and Hristo Ganchev
(2009); three additional doctoral students were still working under Ivan's
supervision at the time of his death.

Ivan had been a visiting fellow of our programme, and also constributed
an abstract to this volume (p. 254). He will be missed.

Appendix A

List of visiting fellows and programme participants.

Samson Abramsky (Oxford, 3 Apr. to 31 May),

Peter Aczel (Manchester, 15 Jan. to 26 Mar., and 29 Apr. to 29 May),

Jesse Alama (Lisbon, 15 Jan. to 15 Apr.),

Klaus Ambos-Spies (Heidelberg, 1 to 31 Mar., and 11 to 16 Jun.),

Marat Arslanov (Kazan, 1 to 27 Mar., and 11 to 16 Jun.),

Albert Atserias (Barcelona, 11 Jan. to 21 Feb., and 26 to 30 Mar.),

Jeremy Avigad (Pittsburgh PA, 23 to 31 May),

Liliana Badillo-Sanchez (Leeds, 12 to 16 Mar., 4 to 24 Jun., and 5 to 6 Jul.),

Gilles Barthe (Madrid, 8 to 21 Apr.),

George Barmpalias (Beijing, 9 Jan. to 19 Feb., and 2 to 6 Jul.),

Arnold Beckmann (Swansea, 9 Mar. to 6 Jul.),

Veronica Becher (Buenos Aires, 17 Jun. to 6 Jul.),

Christian Becker-Asano (Freiburg, 8 to 15 Mar.),

Ulrich Berger (Swansea, 15 Mar. to 14 Jun.),

Bruno Blanchet (Paris, 9 to 14 Apr.),

Lenore Blum (Pittsburgh PA, 17 to 25 Jun.),

Elette Boyle (Cambridge MA, 9 to 16 Jun.),

Vasco Brattka (Cape Town, 9 Jun. to 6 Jul.),

Douglas Bridges (Christchurch, 22 to 30 Jan.),

Andrew Brooke-Taylor (Kobe, 2 to 9 Feb., and 27 to 29 Apr.),

Sam Buss (La Jolla CA, 25 Mar. to 1 Apr.),

Christian Calude (Auckland, 4 Jun. to 6 Jul.),

Luca Cardelli (Cambridge, 9 Jan. to 6 Jul.),

Merlin Carl (Konstanz, 11 to 29 Feb.),

Stefano Cavagnetto (Prague, 31 Jan. to 13 Feb.),

Douglas Cenzer (Gainesville FL, 14 Jan. to 2 Feb., and 11 to 16 Jun.),

Maurice Chiodo (Melbourne, 16 Jan. to 6 Jul.),

Peter Cholak (Notre Dame IN, 15 Jun. to 6 Jul.),

S. Barry Cooper (Leeds, 9 Jan. to 6 Jul.),

Stephen A. Cook (Toronto, 1 May to 13 Jun.),

Marcos Cramer (Bonn, 25 to 31 Mar.)),

Stefan Dantchev (Durham, 19 Mar. to 20 Apr.),

Martin Davis (Berkeley CA, 1 Feb. to 1 Mar.),

Anuj Dawar (Cambridge, 9 Jan. to 6 Jul.),

Liesbeth De Mol (Gent, 13 to 24 Jun.),

Gregorio de Miguel Casado (Zaragoza, 24 Feb. to 9 Mar.),

Yevgeniy Dodis (New York NY, 9 to 20 Apr.),

Rod Downey (Wellington, 14 Jan. to 6 Jul.),

Martin Escardo (Birmingham, 28 May to 28 Jun.),

Kousha Etessami (Edinburgh, 9 to 13 Apr.),

Michael Fellows (Darwin NT, 28 Jun. to 7 Jul.),

Bernhard Fisseni (Amsterdam & Essen, 15 Jan. to 25 Feb., and 25 Mar. to 5 Apr.),

Cédric Fournet (Cambridge, 31 Jan. to 6 Jul.),

Cameron Freer (Cambridge MA, 5 to 26 Feb., and 12 to 15 Jun.),

Sy-David Friedman (Vienna, 12 to 16 Mar., and 11 to 15 Jun.),

Michal Garlik (Prague, 2 to 25 May),

Rainer Glaschick (Paderborn, 12 to 19 Apr.),

Shafi Goldwasser (Cambridge MA, 9 to 13 Apr., and 9 to 23 Jun.),

Andrew Gordon (Cambridge, 10 Jan. to 6 Jul.),

Christian Greiffenhagen (Manchester & Nottingham, 23 to 27 Jan., and 14 to 19 May),

Noam Greenberg (Wellington, 16 Jun. to 6 Jul.),

Jens Groth (London, 11 Jan. to 6 Jul.),

Joel David Hamkins (New York NY, 21 Mar. to 20 Apr., and 11 to 24 Jun.),

Juris Hartmanis (Ithaca NY, 18 to 23 Jun.),

Ian Herbert (Berkeley CA, 12 Feb. to 10 Mar., and 1 to 7 Jul.),

Andrew Hodges (Oxford, 27 to 28 Mar.),

Mark Hogarth (Cambridge, 9 Jan. to 6 Jul.),

Bjarki Holm (Cambridge, 9 Jan. to 6 Jul.),

Martin Hyland (Cambridge, 9 Jan. to 6 Jul.),

Tanmay Inamdar (Amsterdam, 9 to 30 Jan.),

Emil Jeřábek (Prague, 26 Mar. to 12 Apr.),

Valetine Kabanets (Vancouver BC, 23 Apr. to 6 Jul.),

Iskander Kalimullin (Kazan, 1 to 27 Mar.),

Julia Knight (Notre Dame IN, 29 May to 4 Jun.),

Peter Koepke (Bonn, 12 Feb. to 9 Apr., and 13 to 22 Jun.),

Phokion Kolaitis (Santa Cruz CA, 29 Mar. to 25 Apr.),

Antonina Kolokolova (St. John's NF, 23 Apr. to 6 Jul.),

Shigeyuki Kondo (Osaka, 13 to 17 Mar., and 18 to 26 Jun.),

Jan Krajíček (Prague, 19 Mar. to 13 Jun.),

Hugo Krawczyk (Yorktown Heights NY, 29 Jan. to 3 Feb.),

Karen Lange (Wellesley MA, 16 to 27 May),

Steffen Lempp (Madison WI, 11 to 26 Feb.),

Carlos Léon (Hamburg, 9 to 25 Jan.),

Andy Lewis (Leeds), 15 to 28 Feb., 21 Apr. to 7 May, and 19 May to 6 Jul.),

Angsheng Li (Beijing, 9 Jan. to 9 Feb.),

Zhenhao Li (Amsterdam, 9 Jan. to 29 Feb., and 30 Apr. to 15 Jun.),

Benedikt Löwe (Amsterdam & Hamburg, 9 Jan. to 6 Jul.),

Robert Lubarsky (Boca Raton FL, 10 May to 28 Jun.),

Jack Lutz (Ames IA, 29 Feb. to 18 May, and 26 Jun. to 6 Jul.),

Ian Mackie (Paris, 9 to 20 Jan.),
Anotida Madzvamuse (Brighton, 18 to 26 Jun.),
Yuri Matiyasevich (St. Petersburg, 9 Jan. to 15 Feb. and 11 to 16 Jun.),
Ueli Maurer (Zürich, 9 to 13 Apr.),
Elvira Mayordomo (Zaragoza, 29 Apr. to 6 Jul.),
Alexander Melnikov (Nanyang, 30 Apr. to 20 May, and 23 to 27 Jun.),
Wolfgang Merkle (Heidelberg, 11 to 15 Jun., and 1 to 6 Jul.),
Russell Miller (New York NY, 19 Jan. to 2 Feb., 12 to 27 Feb., and 12 to
     15 Jun.),
Ruth Millikan (Storrs CT, 12 to 23 Jun.),
Antonio Montalban (Chicago IL, 11 to 23 Feb., and 11 to 24 Jun.),
Ken Moody (Cambridge, 9 Jan. to 6 Jul.),
Anthony Morphett (Parkville VIC, 9 to 31 Jan.),
Sebastian Müller (Prague, 1 to 31 May),
Niall Murphy (Madrid, 12 to 18 Apr.),
David Naccache (Paris, 29 to 31 Jan.),
Raja Nararajan (Mumbai, 30 Apr. to 1 Jun.),
Turlough Neary (Zürich, 13 to 18 Apr.),
Bernhard Nebel (Freiburg, 8 to 15 Mar.),
André Nies (Auckland, 3 Jun. to 6 Jul.),
Dag Normann (Oslo, 25 May to 25 Jun.),
Grant Passmore (Cambridge, 9 Jan. to 6 Jul.),
Dirk Pattinson (London, 3 to 30 Apr.),
Kenny Paterson (London, 30 Jan. to 2 Feb., and 10 Apr. to 31 May),
Rehana Patel (Middletown CT, 12 to 30 Jun.),
Arno Pauly (Cambridge, 14 Feb. to 6 Jul.),
Jan Pich (Prague, 1 Mar. to 11 May),
David Pointcheval (Paris, 10 to 19 Apr.),
Giuseppe Primiero (Gent, 3 Feb. to 7 Mar., and 6 Jun. to 2 Jul.),
Pavel Pudlák (Prague, 25 Mar. to 20 Apr.),
R. Ramanujam (Chennai, 20 May to 13 Jun.),
Michael Rathjen (Leeds, 9 to 18 Jan.),
Jean Razafindrakoto (Swansea, 26 to 30 Mar., and 20 to 22 May),
Søren Riis (London, 9 Jan. to 11 May),
Phillip Rogaway (Davis CA, 27 Mar. to 6 May),
Dan Roy (Cambridge, 31 Jan. to 6 Jul.),
Mark Ryan (Birmingham, 23 to 26 Apr.),
Nicole Schweikardt (Frankfurt, 25 Mar. to 2 Apr.),
Helmut Schwichtenberg (Munich, 20 Feb. to 17 Mar., and 4 to 30 Jun.),
Peter Schuster (Leeds, 9 to 18 Jan.),
Monika Seisenberger (Swansea, 15 May to 14 Jun.),
Anton Setzer (Swansea, 9 Jan. to 18 Mar., and 26 Apr. to 2 Jun.),

Richard Shore (Ithaca NY, 15 to 21 Jun.),

Tom Shrimpton (Portland OR, 30 Jan. to 3 Feb.),

Ted Slaman (Berkeley CA, 11 Feb. to 10 Mar., and 11 to 24 Jun.),

Nigel Smart (Bristol, 9 to 10 Jan., 30 Jan. to 17 Feb., and 26 Mar. to
27 Apr.),

Paul Smolensky (Baltimore MD, 18 to 23 Jun.),

Bob Soare (Chicago IL, 20 Mar. to 6 Jul.),

Andrea Sorbi (Siena, 11 Feb. to 3 Mar., and 11 to 16 Jun.),

Ivan N. Soskov (Sofia, 1 to 18 Jun.),

Alexandra A. Soskova (Sofia, 25 May to 25 Jun.),

Mariya I. Soskova (Sofia, 13 to 27 Feb., 16 to 20 Apr., and 25 May to
26 Jun.),

Mike Stannett (Sheffield, 28 May to 6 Jul.),

Graham Steel (Paris, 26 Jan. to 2 Feb.),

Sourav Tarafder (Kolkata, 21 Apr. to 27 May),

Stefano Tessaro (Cambridge MA, 10 to 13 Apr., and 9 to 16 Jun.),

Niel Thapen (Prague, 9 Jan. to 6 Jul.),

John Tucker (Swansea, 11 to 16 Jun.),

Jouko Väänänen (Helsinki & Amsterdam, 9 to 27 Jan.),

Les Valiant (Cambridge MA, 20 to 23 Jun.),

Moshe Y. Vardi (Houston TX, 1 to 31 Mar.),

Serge Vaudenay (Lausanne, 29 Jan. to 1 Feb.),

Steen Vermeeren (Leeds, 18 Jun. to 6 Jul.),

Stan Wainer (Leeds, 20 Feb. to 18 Mar., and 4 to 30 Jun.),

Zi Wang (Prague, 2 to 28 May),

Yanjing Wang (Beijing, 10 to 17 Mar.),

Bogdan Warinschi (Bristol, 9 Apr. to 25 May),

Andreas Weiermann (Gent, 10 to 15 Jan.),

Philip Welch (Bristol, 1 Feb. to 3 Apr., and 1 May to 30 Jun.),

Linda Westrick (Berkeley CA, 9 to 23 Jan.),

Glynn Winskel (Cambridge, 18 to 19 Feb., and 17 Jun.),

Andreas Witzel (New York NY, 8 to 18 Mar.),

Hugh Woodin (Berkeley CA, 9 to 14 Jan.),

Damien Woods (Pasadena CA, 12 to 18 Apr.),

Shengyang Zhong (Amsterdam, 9 to 31 Jan.).

Appendix B

List of INI preprints resulting from the SAS programme until May 2013.

NI12010-SAS J Alama, L Mamame and J Urban. Dependencies in formal mathematics: applications and extraction for Coq and Mizar.

NI12011-SAS C Bylinski and J Alama. New developments in parsing Mizar.

NI12017-SAS J Alama. Tipi: A TPTP-based theory development environment emphasizing proof dependencies.

NI12018-SAS J Alama, T Heskes, D Kühlwein, E Tsivtsivadze and J Urban. Premise selection for mathematics by corpus analysis and Kernel methods.

NI12019-SAS J Alama and R Kahle. Checking proofs.

NI12020-SAS U Andrews, S Lempp, JS Miller, Keng Meng Ng and L San Mauro et Al. Universal computably enumerable equivalence relations.

NI12021-SAS B Kjos-Hassen, A Taveneaux and N Thapen. How much randomness is needed for statistics?

NI12022-SAS D Doty, JH Lutz, MJ Patitz, RT Schweller and SM Summers et Al. The tile assembly model is intrinsically universal.

NI12025-SAS J Alama. Escape to Mizar from ATPs.

NI12026-SAS G Primiero. Intuitionistic logic of proofs with dependent proof terms.

NI12027-SAS X Gu, JH Lutz, E Mayordomo and P Moser. Dimension spectra of random subfractals of self-similar fractals.

NI12030-SAS RR Lutz, JH Lutz, JI Lathrop, TH Klinge and D Mathur et Al. Requirements analysis for a product family of DNA Nanodevices.

NI12031-SAS P Aczel. Some open (?) problems concerning dependent type theories.

NI12032-SAS P Aczel, H Ishihara, T Nemoto and Y Sangu. Generalized geometric theories and set-generated classes.

NI12033-SAS P Aczel. Rudimentary and arithmetical constructive set theory.

NI12035-SAS J Avigad and V Brattka. Computability and analysis: the legacy of Alan Turing.

NI12036-SAS V Brattka, S Le Roux and A Pauly. Connected choice and the Brouwer Fixed Point Theorem.

NI12037-SAS R Downey. Randomness, computation and mathematics.

NI12038-SAS R Downey, A Dediu and C Martin-Vide. A parameterized complexity tutorial.

NI12039-SAS RG Downey, CG Jockusch Jr. and PE Schupp. Asymptotic density and computably enumerable sets s.

NI12040-SAS R Downey. The birth and early years of parameterized complexity The Multivariate Algorithmic Revolution and Beyond. Essays Dedicated to Michael R Fellows on Occasion of 60th Birthday.

NI12041-SAS R Downey, H Bodlaender, F Fomin and D Marx. A basic parameterized complexity primer The Multivariate Algorithmic Revolution and Beyond, Essays Dedicated to Michael R Fellows on the Occasion of His 60th Birthday.

NI12042-SAS G Barmpalias and R Downey. Exact pairs for the ideal of the K-trivial sequences in the turing degrees.

NI12043-SAS R Downey, A Kach, S Lempp and D Turetsky. Computable categoricity versus relative computable categoricity.

NI12044-SAS R Downey, KM Ng and R Solomon. On minimal wtt-degrees and computably enumerable Turing degrees.

NI12046-SAS EJ Spoors and SS Wainer. A hierarchy of ramified theories below PRA.

NI12047-SAS R Downey and KM Ng. Lowness for bounded randomness.

NI12048-SAS R Bod, B Fisseni, A Kurji and B Löwe. Objectivity and reproducibility of proppian narrative annotations.

NI12049-SAS B Fisseni and B Löwe. Which dimensions of narratives are relevent for human judgments of story equivalence?

NI12050-SAS PD Welch. G-games.

NI12051-SAS PD Welch. Global reflection principles.

NI12052-SAS JM Hitchcock and E Mayordomo. Base invariance of feasible dimension.

NI12053-SAS AA Abbott, CS Calude, J Conder and K Svozil. Kochen-Specker theorem revisited and strong incomputability of quantum randomness.

NI12055-SAS JD Hamkins, G Leibman and B Löwe. Structural connections between a forcing class and its modal logic.

NI12056-SAS JD Hamkins. Every countable model of set theory embeds into its own constructible universe.

NI12059-SAS JD Hamkins and B Löwe. Moving up and down in the generic multiverse.

NI12060-SAS E Mayordomo. Effective dimension in some general metric spaces.

NI12061-SAS R Glaschick. A size index for multitape Turing Machines.

NI12063-SAS TA Slaman and A Sorbi. A note on initial segments of the enumeration degrees.

NI12064-SAS V Becher and S Grigorieff. Wadge hardness in Scott spaces and its effectivization.

NI12065-SAS V Becher and PA Heiber. Normal numbers and finite automata.

NI12066-SAS V Becher and S Grigorieff. Borel and Hausdorff hierarchies in topological spaces of Choquet games and their effectivization.

NI12067-SAS V Becher and PA Heiber. Normality and differentiability.

NI12068-SAS V Becher. Turing's normal numbers: towards randomness.

NI12069-SAS RA Shore. The Turing degrees below generics and randoms.

NI12070-SAS G Barmpalias, R Hölzl, AEM Lewis and W Merkle. Analogues of Chaitin's omega in the computably enumerable sets.

NI12071-SAS G Barmpalias and A Li. Kolmogorov complexity and computably enumerable sets.

NI12072-SAS G Barmpalias and RG Downey. Resolute sequences in initial segment complexity.

NI12073-SAS G Barmpalias. Algorithmic randomness and measures of complexity.

NI12081-SAS A Beckmann and SR Buss. Improved witnessing and local improvement principles for second-order bounded arithmetic.

NI12082-SAS A Beckmann, SR Buss and S-D Friedman. Safe recursive set functions.

NI12088-SAS Y Matiyasevich. New conjectures about zeroes of Riemann's zeta function.

NI13004-SAS AG Melnikov and A Nies. The classification problem for compact computable metric spaces.

NI13005-SAS M Lauria, P Pudlák, V Rödl and N Thapen. The complexity of proving that a graph is Ramsey.

NI13012-SAS M Garlík. Ajtai's completeness theorem for nonstandard finite structures.

Opening Workshop "The Mathematical Legacy of Alan Turing" (Spitalfields Day) 9 January 2012

Benedikt Löwe

University of Amsterdam, Amsterdam, The Netherlands and Universität Hamburg, Hamburg, Germany

E-mail: b.loewe@uva.nl

On 9 January 2012, the programme "Semantics & Syntax" was officially opened with the workshop "The mathematical legacy of Alan Turing". In addition to being the official opening of the programme, this event provided the general mathematical public (with strong emphasis on postgraduate students) a glimpse of the current state of the art and explain what was going to happen during the six months at Cambridge.

The day was one of the *Spitalfields Days* of the London Mathematical Society, named in honour of the Spitalfields Mathematical Society, a precursor of the London Mathematical Society which flourished from 1717 to 1845. Spitalfields Days provide survey lectures aimed at a general mathematical audience.

The workshop had four invited speakers whose abstracts are included in this book: George Barmpalias (Chinese Academy of Sciences, China), Anuj Dawar (University of Cambridge, U.K.), Nigel Smart (University of Bristol, U.K.), and Hugh Woodin (UC Berkeley, U.S.A.).

(Picture courtesy of The Isaac Newton Institute)

In addition to the abstracts in this booklet, slides and videos of some of the talks can be found at

http://www.newton.ac.uk/programmes/SAS/sasw05.html

Arnold Beckmann, Benedikt Löwe (*eds.*). *Acts of the programme "Semantics and Syntax"*. Isaac Newton Institute for the Mathematical Sciences, January to July 2012.

SAS Opening Workshop "The Mathematical Legacy of Alan Turing" (Spitalfields Day).

The Global Structure of the Turing Degrees

Hugh Woodin

University of California, Berkeley CA, United States of America
E-mail: woodin@math.berkeley.edu

I surveyed joint work with Slaman. This included first a discussion of the Coding Theorem stated here for the partial order,

$$\mathcal{D} = (\mathcal{D}, \leq_{\mathrm{T}}),$$

of the Turing degrees. The theorem actually holds in a wide class of degree structures.

Theorem 1. *Fix $n < \omega$. There is a formula $\varphi(x_0, \ldots, x_n, y_0, \ldots, y_m)$ such that if $\mathcal{R} \subset \mathcal{D}^n$ is countable then there exist degrees $d_0, \ldots, d_m$ such that*

$$\mathcal{R}^n = \{(a_0, \ldots, a_n) \in \mathcal{D}^n \mid (\mathcal{D}, \leq_{\mathrm{T}}) \models \varphi[a_0, \ldots, a_n, d_0, \ldots, d_m]\}.$$

As an easy corollary one obtains Simpson's Theorem:

Theorem 2. *The first order theory of*

$$(\mathcal{P}(\omega), \omega, +, \cdot, 0, 1)$$

is recursively reducible to the first order theory of

$$(\mathcal{D}, \leq_{\mathrm{T}}).$$

The key definition of a persistent automorphism of a countable ideal $\mathcal{I} \subset \mathcal{D}$ was inspired by the Shore-Odifreddi Theorem. This allows one to prove using meta-mathematical methods from Set Theory combined with constructions from Recursion Theory, our main theorem concerning the existence of an automorphism of the structure, $(\mathcal{D}, \leq_{\mathrm{T}})$. A survey of this methodology was the main part of the talk.

Arnold Beckmann, Benedikt Löwe (eds.). *Acts of the programme "Semantics and Syntax"*.
Isaac Newton Institute for the Mathematical Sciences, January to July 2012.

Talk given at the SAS Opening (Spitalfields Day), 9 January 2012, 11:30–12:30.

Theorem 3. *Suppose that*

$$\pi : (\mathcal{D}, \leq_{\mathrm{T}}) \to (\mathcal{D}, \leq_{\mathrm{T}})$$

is an automorphism. Then the following hold.

(1) *For all $d \geq_{\mathrm{T}} 0''$, $\pi(d) = d$.*

(2) *π is uniquely determined by $\pi(g)$ where g is any 5-generic degree.*

(3) *π is represented by an arithmetic function.*

This allows one to use the Coding Theorem to prove the following characterization of when a relation

$$\mathcal{R} \subset \mathcal{D}^n$$

is definable without parameters.

Theorem 4. *Fix $n < \omega$ and suppose*

$$\mathcal{R} \subset \mathcal{D}^n.$$

Then the following are equivalent.

(1) *$\mathcal{R}$ is definable in $(\mathcal{P}(\omega), \omega, +, \cdot, 0, 1)$ without parameters.*

(2) *$\mathcal{R}$ is definable in $(\mathcal{D}, \leq_{\mathrm{T}})$ without parameters and $\mathcal{R}$ is invariant under all automorphisms of $(\mathcal{D}, \leq_{\mathrm{T}})$.*

I ended with a discussion of the Biinterpretability Conjecture which in light of Theorem 4 reduces to the conjecture that there are no nontrivial automorphisms of $(\mathcal{D}, \leq_{\mathrm{T}})$.

Modern Cryptography for Non-cryptographers

Nigel Smart

University of Bristol, Bristol, United Kingdom
E-mail: nigel@compsci.bristol.ac.uk

In this talk we presented a rapid introduction to the prevailing approach in modern cryptography; namely that of Provable Security. In this paradigm security for a system is shown by providing a complexity theoretic reduction to certain assumptions. Systems are built in a modular way; with security reducing from one layer to the other; until at the bottom we reach a hard mathematical problem such as factoring or discrete logarithms. The talk discussed syntax and security models for symmetric encryption, asymmetric encryption and key-encapsulation mechanisms. It was then (informally) demonstrated that a hybrid encyrption scheme is secure as long as the KEM and DEM components are themselves secure.

At the end of the talk the Random Oracle Model was discussed, by showing that RSA-KEM is a secure KEM as long as the RSA problem is hard. A discussion was presented as to the merits and pitfalls of this approach compared to more symbolic approachs based on Formal Methods. Finally, as a precursor to other events in the program Zero-Knowledge was presented via means of the Schnorr identification protocol.

Arnold Beckmann, Benedikt Löwe (eds.). Acts of the programme "Semantics and Syntax". Isaac Newton Institute for the Mathematical Sciences, January to July 2012.

Talk given at the SAS Opening (Spitalfields Day), 9 January 2012, 14:00–15:00.

Measures of Relative Complexity

George Barmpalias[*]

Chinese Academy of Sciences, Beijing, People's Republic of China
E-mail: barmpalias@gmail.com

One of the main methodologies in the theory of computation is the use of reducibilities for analyzing and comparing problems. Turing reducibility was introduced by Post in order to model the notion of an infinite binary sequence X being computable from another Y. This notion of relative computation is very general (assuming infinite time and memory resources) and was introduced by Turing in 1939. Post also introduced a number of stronger reducibilities, like truth-table and many-one reducibility, mainly because they were easier to study than Turing reducibility. Analogues of these pre-orders have been studied in the area of feasible computation (e.g., polynomial time reductions). The logical and algebraic study of the induced degree structures has been a major if technical part of computability theory. A renewed interest in the theoretical study of algorithmic randomness (originally introduced by Kolmogorov and Solomonoff in the 1960s) in the last ten years motivated researchers in computability theory to introduce a number of pre-orders for the study of algorithmic randomness and complexity. An important feature of most of these measures $\leq_*$ of relative randomness is that, strictly speaking, they are not reducibilities. In other words, if $X \leq_* Y$ we no longer necessarily have that X is related to Y in some algorithmic way. Equivalently, such a relation does not necessarily entail the 'definability' of X from Y. Thus the link between definability and reducibility that is so prominent in the reducibilities from classical computability theory is broken; this is why these new pre-orders are often branded 'weak reducibilities'.

For example, the K-reducibility gives a formal way to express the notion that a stream Y is more random than X; in symbols $X \leq_K Y$. This means that its initial segments have higher complexity than those of X. The LK-reducibility measures the oracle power of streams when they are used for the compression of finite programs. There are a number of facts that relate these two notions of relative complexity. For example, if X, Y are random then $X \leq_K Y$ implies that $Y \leq_{LK} X$. In other words, if one stream is more random than another (and both are random) then it has less compressing power. Another rather deep connection is that the notions of triviality with respect to $\leq_K$ and $\leq_{LK}$ are identical. In other words, a stream cannot

[*]Barmpalias acknowledges support from the Newton institute, a research fund for international young scientists No. 611501-10168 and an *International Young Scientist Fellowship* number 2010-Y2GB03 from the Chinese Academy of Sciences.

Arnold Beckmann, Benedikt Löwe (*eds.*). *Acts of the programme "Semantics and Syntax".* Isaac Newton Institute for the Mathematical Sciences, January to July 2012.

Talk given at the SAS Opening (Spitalfields Day), 9 January 2012, 15:15–16:15.

compress programs more than an oracle-free machine if and only if its initial segments can be described as easily as 0000. . . .

The study of relative algorithmic randomness and complexity via weak reducibilities is a considerable part of the recent research on this topic. The fact that they do not constitute reducibilities in the traditional sense is the reason why a lot of the classical methods are not applicable to their study. A number of new tools and techniques have been introduced for this reason, while some of the classical methods continue to be useful in some cases. A considerable number of open problems and questions continues to motivate active research on reducibilities in algorithmic randomness and triviality.

On Syntactic and Semantic Complexity Classes

Anuj Dawar

University of Cambridge, Cambridge, United Kingdom

E-mail: Anuj.Dawar@cl.cam.ac.uk

The title of the Newton Institute programme "Semantics and Syntax: A Legacy of Alan Turing" invites us to think about the many meanings of the terms "syntax" and "semantics" in the context of logic, computability and theoretical computer science. Semantics is about interpreted structure, syntax about symbol manipulation and Turing's notion of computability often elucidates when semantics can be reduced to syntax. In this talk, I investigate one use, in computational complexity theory, of the terms. Complexity classes are often described as either syntactic or semantic. However, these terms do not have a precise mathemtical definition for the reason that a "complexity class" is not itself a well-defined term. Instead, we have a zoo of complexity classes. In the talk, I explore the distinction between syntactic and semantic complexity classes through some specific examples, focussing on the question of the existence of a computable enumeration of witnesses for all members of the class. P and NP are examples of syntactic classes while BPP and NP intersect co-NP are examples of semantic classes. The classification is also tied up to the existence of complete problems. Classes which admit complete problems are generally syntactic. The converse statement holds for a wide-range of classes, including BPP and NP intersect co-NP. Finally, I relate this distinction to the fundamental open question of descriptive complexity theory: the existence of a logic for expressing the polynomial time properties of graphs.

Arnold Beckmann, Benedikt Löwe (*eds.*). *Acts of the programme "Semantics and Syntax".* Isaac Newton Institute for the Mathematical Sciences, January to July 2012.

Talk given at the SAS Opening (Spitalfields Day), 9 January 2012, 16:30–17:30.

Diophantine Machines

Yuri Matiyasevich

Russian Academy of Sciences, St. Petersburg, Russia
E-mail: yumat@pdmi.ras.ru

Non-Deterministic Diophantine Machine (NDDM for short) were introduced by Leonard Adleman and Kenneth Manders. Syntactically, they are just Diophantine equations

$$P(a, x_1, \ldots, x_m) = 0$$

with, say, one parameter a. An NDDM gets a value of this parameter as input and guesses the values of the unknowns, and a is accepted provided that the polynomial P vanishes.

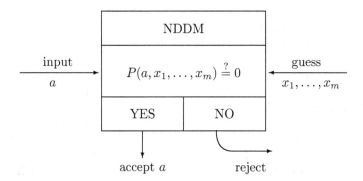

Theorem (The DPRM-theorem). *NDDMs are as powerful as, say, Turing machines, i.e., every set acceptable by a Turing machine is accepted by some NDDM, and, of course, vice versa*

Respectively, the existence of universal Turing machine implies the existence of universal NDDM, or, equivalently, *universal Diopnantine equation.* In its turn this implies that the traditional number-theoretical hierarchy of Diophantine equations of degree 1, 2, ... with 1, 2 , ... unknowns collapses at some level. In particular, solving an arbitrary parametric Diophantine equation with any number of parameters can be reduced to solving another Diophantine equation (with the same parameters) of degree D in M unknowns where $\langle D, M \rangle$ is any of the following pairs: $\langle 4, 58 \rangle$, $\langle 8, 38 \rangle$, $\langle 12, 32 \rangle$, $\langle 16, 29 \rangle$, $\langle 20, 28 \rangle$, $\langle 24, 26 \rangle$, $\langle 28, 25 \rangle$, $\langle 36, 24 \rangle$, $\langle 96, 21 \rangle$, $\langle 2668, 19 \rangle$, $\langle 2 \times 10^5, 14 \rangle$, $\langle 6.6 \times 10^{43}, 13 \rangle$, $\langle 1.3 \times 10^{44}, 12 \rangle$, $\langle 4.6 \times 10^{44}, 11 \rangle$, $\langle 8.6 \times 10^{44}, 10 \rangle$, $\langle 1.6 \times 10^{45}, 9 \rangle$.

These bounds are uniform with respect to the number of parameters provided that D is the degree with respect to unknowns *only.*

Arnold Beckmann, Benedikt Löwe (*eds.*). *Acts of the programme "Semantics and Syntax".* Isaac Newton Institute for the Mathematical Sciences, January to July 2012.

Talk given at the SAS Seminar, 11 January 2012, 17:00–17:30.

Open Problem. *Are there similar uniform bounds with respect to the total (both in the parameters and unknowns) degree?*

Definition. A purely existential representation

$$a \in \mathfrak{M} \iff \exists x_1 \ldots x_m T(a, x_1, \ldots, x_m)$$

is called *single-fold* if for given value of the parameter a there exists at most one choice of the values of $x_1, \ldots, x_m$.

Theorem (Matiyasevich). *Every effectively enumerable set $\mathfrak{M}$ has a single-fold exponential Diophantine representation*

$$a \in \mathfrak{M} \iff \exists x_1 \ldots x_m [E(a, x_1, x_2, \ldots, x_m) = 0]$$

where E is an exponential polynomial, an expression constructed by combining the variables and particular integers using the traditional rules of addition, multiplication and exponentiation.

Open Problem. *Does every effectively enumerable set $\mathfrak{M}$ have a single-fold Diophantine representation*

$$a \in \mathfrak{M} \iff \exists x_1 \ldots x_m [P(a, x_1, x_2, \ldots, x_m) = 0]$$

Singlefold representations find numerous interesting application. For example, let

$$a \in \mathfrak{M} \iff \exists x_1 \ldots x_m [E(a, x_1, x_2, \ldots, x_m) = 0]$$

be a single-fold exponential Diophantine representation of an undecidable set $\mathfrak{M}$. Then we have:

- *For every value of a the exponential Diophantine equation*

$$E(a, x_1, x_2, \ldots, x_m) = 0$$

  has at most one solution in $x_1, x_2, \ldots, x_m$;

- *For every total computable function α there is a value of a such that the above equation has a (unique) solution $x_1, x_2, \ldots, x_m$ and*

$$\max\{x_1, x_2, \ldots, x_m\} > \alpha(a)$$

Open Problem. *Can this result be improved for the case of genuine Diophantine equations?*

Gregory Chaitin, using singlefold representations, showed the existence of computational chaos in the theory of exponential Diophantine equations; the question about the existence of similar computational chaos in the theory of genuine Diophantine equations remains open.

For more details see [1, 2] and references in these papers.

Bibliography

[1] Y. Matiyasevich. Computation paradigms in light of Hilbert's tenth problem. In S. B. Cooper, B. Löwe, and A. Sorbi, editors, *New computational paradigms*, pages 59–85. Springer, New York, 2008.

[2] Y. V. Matiyasevich. What can and cannot be done with Diophantine problems. *Proceedings of the Steklov Institute of Mathematics*, 275(1):118–132, 2011.

Conservation of Data

Ian Mackie

École Polytechinque, Palaiseau, France
E-mail: iancmackie@gmail.com

There are a number of fundamental laws of nature: conservation of energy, conservation of momentum, conservation of mass, and numerous others from physics, chemistry and biology. In addition, in the 1960's, Rolf Landauer discovered that energy is needed to erase data. All of this motivated an investigation into an approach to computation where data is conserved: programs do not erase or copy data (i.e., the program inputs are not copied or erased).

We review some of the work on reversible and quantum computation to avoid erasing data, and put forward other approaches such as linearity and directly conserving data by defining new models. We suggest an approach where syntax and semantics are developed hand-in-hand so that data conservation is also reflected in the syntax.

The work is parametrised on what we take as the data that we conserve: bits, memory locations, data structures, programs, etc., and also which kind of computational model we wish to use. We briefly review the appropriateness of term rewriting systems, lambda calculus, interaction nets, geometry of interaction, chemical abstract machine, as well as suggesting some directions for new models.

To justify that the general ideas can work, we give some examples of models of computation that conserve data, and show several programming examples (sorting algorithms, Dijkstra's partition algorithm). In these examples the syntax and semantics both reflect the use of data in the program, and thus we obtain a visually appealing syntax for in-place algorithms.

We conclude the talk with some suggestions of adapting existing models of computation and developing new models and syntax. Developing a programming language syntax at the same time as understanding the problem semantically seems fruitful, and programming directly with the computational model avoids the potential distinction as to what is conserved. Much of the effort is currently being applied in these areas, where we envisage applications to topics such as in-place algorithm design, and compiler technology for optimising these algorithms.

Arnold Beckmann, Benedikt Löwe (*eds.*). *Acts of the programme "Semantics and Syntax"*.
Isaac Newton Institute for the Mathematical Sciences, January to July 2012.

Talk given at the SAS Seminar, 11 January 2012, 17:30–18:00.

Extended Goodstein Sequences

Andreas Weiermann

Ghent University, Ghent, Belgium

E-mail: weierman@cage.ugent.be

The Goodstein sequence for a natural number m is a sequence of natural numbers starting with m and then forming successively a new number in step k by subtracting first a one from the number obtained so far and then changing the base $k+2$ in the complete base $k+2$ representation of the intermediate result by $k+3$. This sequence always hits zero but PA is unable to show this. In our talk we extend the Goodstein process to allow branches of the Ackermann function in the description of a given number. To avoid ambiguity we develop an appropriate term rewriting framework and show that termination of the new sequences requires the well orderedness of $\varphi\omega 0$. We indicate how to extend the construction to higher branches of the Schwichtenberg Wainer hierarchy so that independence results for the impredicative theories ID_n of iterated inductive definitions can be obtained. Also phase transitions for the new principles can be obtained (joint work with Michiel De Smet, Gunnar Wilken and Frederik Meskens). Similar results can be obtained for Hydra games.

Arnold Beckmann, Benedikt Löwe (*eds.*). *Acts of the programme "Semantics and Syntax"*. Isaac Newton Institute for the Mathematical Sciences, January to July 2012.

Talk given at the SAS Seminar, 11 January 2012, 18:00–18:30.

Promptness, Randomness and Degrees

Anthony Morphett

University of Melbourne, Parkville VIC, and Australian Catholic University, Fitzroy VIC,
Australia

E-mail: awmorp@gmail.com

Computably enumerable (c.e.) sets range, in information content, from the trivially computable up to those with complete information of the halting problem. There are several ways to assess the information content of a c.e. set $A \subseteq \mathbb{N}$. One is to examine the jump A' of A. The set A is *low* if $A' \leq_T 0'$; that is, if its jump has no more information than the (unrelativised) halting problem. The set A is *superlow* if in fact $A' \leq_{tt} 0'$; in this case, A' can be computed from $0'$ with a pre-determined sequence of oracle queries. Superlowness implies lowness but not the converse.

Other ways of assessing information content arise from the c.e. Turing degrees. A c.e. set A is *low cuppable* if there is a low set B such that $A \oplus B \equiv_T 0'$. Such a set, although perhaps not capable of computing the halting problem alone, requires only low additional information to achieve this. Another property is non-cappability: A is non-cappable if for all non-computable c.e. sets B there is a non-computable c.e. set X such that $X \leq_T A$ and $X \leq_T B$. Such a set has some non-trivial information in common with any other non-trivial c.e. set. These properties are particularly notable as they are definable in the language of the c.e. Turing degrees.

The two properties of low cuppability and non-cappability were unified by work of Ambos-Spies, Jockusch, Shore and Soare [1], who showed them both to be equivalent to the 'dynamic' property of prompt permitting. The c.e. set A is *promptly permitting* if there is a computable function p such that, for any c.e. set W,

$$|W| = \infty \Rightarrow \exists x, s : x \text{ enters } W \text{ at stage } s \text{ and } A[s] \upharpoonright x \neq A[p(s)] \upharpoonright x. \quad (1)$$

It was shown in [1] that A is promptly permitting iff it is low cuppable iff it is non-cappable. Prompt permitting can be considered a strengthening of incomputability; if we drop the requirement in (1) that p be computable, then (1) becomes true exactly if A is incomputable.

Recent work has examined another lowness property, namely *low-for-randomness*. An infinite binary sequence X is *random* if

$$\exists c \forall n \, K(X \upharpoonright n) > n - c;$$

such a sequence is incompressible in the sense that no initial segment has a short algorithmic description. Recall that $K(\sigma)$ is the prefix-free Kolmogorov complexity of σ: the length of the shortest program (in a fixed

Arnold Beckmann, Benedikt Löwe (*eds.*). *Acts of the programme "Semantics and Syntax".*
Isaac Newton Institute for the Mathematical Sciences, January to July 2012.

Talk given at the SAS Seminar, 12 January 2012, 16:00–16:30.

universal self-delimiting programming language) which outputs σ. If we add an oracle A to our universal programming language, we obtain a notion of *randomness relative to A*: X is A-random if

$$\exists c \forall n\ K^A(X \upharpoonright n) > n - c.$$

In general, access to the information from a non-trivial oracle A will improve compression, and thus A-randomness will be stronger than unrelativised randomness. However, there is a non-trivial class of sets for which this is not the case. A set A is *low-for-random* if, for all sequences X,

$$X \text{ is random } \Rightarrow X \text{ is } A\text{-random.}$$

Being computable implies being low-for-random, which implies being super-low, and these implications cannot be reversed. Hence the low-for-random c.e. sets form a proper subclass of the (super)low c.e. sets.

Using the notion of low for randomness, we can strengthen the properties of low cuppability and non-cappability. Say that a c.e. set A is *low-for-random cuppable* if there is a low-for-random c.e. set B such that $A \oplus B \equiv_T 0'$. Such sets exist; however, not all low cuppable, nor even all superlow cuppable, c.e. sets are low-for-random cuppable. Say that A is *non-cappable to low-for-randoms* if for each non-low-for-random c.e. set B there is a non-low-for-random c.e. set X such that $X \leq_T A$ and $X \leq_T B$. We can also strengthen the notion of prompt permitting. The property of *prompt non-low-for-randomness* was defined in [2], and shown to give a proper, non-trivial subclass of the class of promptly permitting sets. My recent work has focussed on connections between these properties. I have shown that prompt non-low-for-randomness is implied by both low-for-random cuppability and non-cappability to low-for-randoms, however the converse of both implications are open. Several other variations of capping and cupping properties also suggest themselves for future investigation.

Bibliography

[1] K. Ambos-Spies, C. G. Jockusch, Jr., R. A. Shore, and R. I. Soare. An algebraic decomposition of the recursively enumerable degrees and the coincidence of several degree classes with the promptly simple degrees. *Trans. Amer. Math. Soc.*, 281(1):109–128, 1984.

[2] A. Morphett. Prompt enumerations and relative randomness. *J. Logic Comput.*, 22(4):877–897, 2012.

From Narratology to Formal Narrative Structures: What is Relevant in a Story?

Carlos León

Universität Hamburg, Hamburg, Germany

E-mail: carlos.leon@uni-hamburg.de

We use narratives every day. They are a crucial form of communication ranging from simple tales to complex explanations of laws. Narratives play a fundamental role in knowledge representation, management, retrieval and understanding.

Finding a way to produce and understand narratives is a long term Artificial Intelligence challenge. In order to achieve it, strong focus has been put on the structural study of narrations from a formal point of view. Much of this research has been influenced by narratology.

However, narratology uses concepts that are too complicated to be currently processed by machines. Our current knowledge representation techniques do not allow for creating computer programs that able to handle the very complex characteristics of objects as apparently simple as every day narratives.

In this talk, our current research on *computational models of narrative* is presented. In particular, we are working on trying to find out which structural properties of narratives define them in such a way that these narratives can be compared in terms of their similarity.

From this point of view, the syntax-semantics duality plays a very important role. The extent to which the similarity of narrations can be found out through its structural characteristics heavily constraints what can be done by basic computer processes. The more semantical this similarity is, the more knowledge based the computational method will be.

Since similarity of narrations is necessarily linked to human criteria at different levels of granularity, evaluation of human behaviour is a promising way of finding out what parts of a narration are considered important by humans. The talk also describes the ongoing research on designing and running several experiments in which we want to find out how people summarize and formalize, the extent to which they can be trained or how they tag narrative texts regarding among others.

Arnold Beckmann, Benedikt Löwe (*eds.*). *Acts of the programme "Semantics and Syntax".*
Isaac Newton Institute for the Mathematical Sciences, January to July 2012.

Talk given at the SAS Seminar, 12 January 2012, 16:30–17:00.

Homophyly Law of Networks: Principles, Methods and Experiments

Angsheng Li

Chinese Academy of Sciences, Beijing, People's Republic of China

E-mail: angsheng@ios.ac.cn

I introduce a mathematical definition of communities of networks, and the small community phenomenon of networks, a notion defined by a triple (alpha,beta,gamma) of constants alpha, beta and gamma, called local dimension of networks. Our new results that networks from some classical models do satisfy the small community phenomenon, while others, including the well-known ER model and PA model fail to satisfy the small community phenomenon. Our experiments show that most real networks satisfy a small comunity phenomenon. A fundamental question is thus: What are the mechanisms of community structures of real networks? To answer this question, I introduce our new model of networks, the homophyly model.

It was shown a homophyly theorem that, for a network, G say, generated from the homophyly model, with probability $1 - o(1)$, G satisfies simultaneously the following properties:

1. (power law) the degrees of the network follow a power law,

2. (small world) the small diameter of the network is $O(\log n)$,

3. (small community) nodes of the same color form naturally a community of size $\text{poly}(\log n)$,

4. (small community phenomenon) a significant fraction of nodes are contained in some small communities,

5. (interpretability of community) nodes within a small community share some common features, the same color in our model,

6. (internal centrality) a small community has a small set dominating internal links within the community. In fact, nodes within a small community satisfy the power law degree distribution,

7. (external centrality) a community has a small set dominating the external links of the community, and

8. (local communication law) local communications within the same community have length $O(\log \log n)$.

Arnold Beckmann, Benedikt Löwe (eds.). Acts of the programme "Semantics and Syntax". Isaac Newton Institute for the Mathematical Sciences, January to July 2012.

Talk given at the SAS Seminar, 12 January 2012, 17:00–17:30.

The homophyly model explores that homophyly is the mechanism of community structures of real networks.

The homophyly theorem implies that there is a homophyly law of networks that homophyly ensures that real networks satisfy the small community phenomenon, that a small community is interpretable, and that the small communities of a network follow a number of local laws characterised by the homophyly theorem.

The homophyly law has been validated by experiments on real world networks. The homophyly law starts the new direction of local theory of networks, and leads to a new searching system with new properties such as searching, interpreting, discovering and predicting (SIDP) in networks.

Induction in Algebra: A First Case Study

Peter M. Schuster

University of Leeds, Leeds, United Kingdom

E-mail: pschust@maths.leeds.ac.uk

Many a concrete theorem of abstract algebra admits a short and elegant proof by contradiction but with Zorn's Lemma (ZL). A few of these theorems have recently turned out to follow in a direct and elementary way from the Principle of Open Induction (OI) distinguished by Raoult. A proof of the latter kind may be extracted from a proof of the former sort. If the theorem has finite input data, then a finite partial order carries the required instance of induction, which thus—unlike OI in general—is provable by fairly elementary means.

This approach is intended as a contribution to the partial realisation of Hilbert's Programme in algebra started by Coquand and Lombardi, and was motivated by related work of Berger, Coquand in infinite combinatorics, and by the rise of dynamical algebra and formal topology. The ideal objects characteristic of any invocation of ZL are eliminated, and it is made possible to work with finite methods only, e.g., to pass from classical to intuitionistic logic.

A typical example is the well-known theorem "every nonconstant coefficient of an invertible polynomial is nilpotent." This theorem can be reduced to the case, which in turn is readily settled, of polynomials over an integral domain. The reduction is usually done by a universal quantification over prime ideals, which are ideal objects in Hilbert's sense. One in fact invokes the contrapositive KL of a variant of Krull's Lemma, which contrapositive can notably be deduced from ZL by a proof by contradiction. Along this reduction proof via KL one virtually looses the computational information contained in the hypothesis of the theorem. In particular the proof fails to provide an algorithm for computing an exponent under which the nilpotent indeed vanishes. All this notwithstanding, we can extract a proof that is based on induction over a finite partial order; and the tree one can grow in an obvious way alongside the induction encodes an algorithm which computes the exponent.

Arnold Beckmann, Benedikt Löwe (eds.). Acts of the programme "Semantics and Syntax". Isaac Newton Institute for the Mathematical Sciences, January to July 2012.

Talk given at the SAS Seminar, 17 January 2012, 16:00–16:30.

The Logic of Dependence and Independence

Jouko Väänänen*

University of Helsinki, Helsinki, Finland and University of Amsterdam, Amsterdam, The Netherlands

E-mail: jouko.vaananen@helsinki.fi

The goal in dependence logic, introduced in [2], is to establish a basic theory of dependence and independence underlying seemingly unrelated subjects such as causality, random variables, bound variables in logic, database theory, the theory of Social Choice, and Quantum Mechanics. There is an wealth of new results in this field demonstrating remarkable convergence. The concepts of (in)dependence in the different fields of science and humanities have surprisingly much in common and a common logic is starting to emerge.

The monograph [2] introduced the concept of a *dependence atom* $=(\vec{x}, \vec{y})$ with the meaning that the attributes $\vec{x}$ totally (functionally) determine the attributes $\vec{y}$ in a given data, as well as **dependence logic**, the extension of first order logic with the atoms $=(\vec{x}, \vec{y})$. The corresponding *independence atom* $\vec{x} \perp_{\vec{z}} \vec{y}$, the attributes $\vec{x}$ and $\vec{y}$ are totally independent of each other, if $\vec{z}$ is kept fixed, was introduced in [1].

The attributes $\vec{x}, \vec{y}$ and $\vec{z}$ depend on the application area. In database theory they could be "salary", "telephone number", "department", or "boss". In scientific experiments they can be readings of a gauge, or measurements of a magnitude. In logic they are variables that can be bound by quantifiers, in social choice theory they are voting results, and finally, in statistics that are random variables. There is a great variety of applications for this simple concept.

The fundamental properties of $=(\vec{x}, \vec{y})$ and $\vec{x} \perp \vec{y}$ have been axiomatized independently in different contexts. The approach to treat $= (\vec{x}, \vec{y})$ and $\vec{x} \perp_{\vec{z}} \vec{y}$ as part of elementary logic, is an approach that unifies the different application areas.

It would be a mistake to think that $=(\vec{x}, \vec{y})$ is mathematically trivial. It is just the contrary: some of the most difficult questions of computer science and mathematics, such as P=NP and the Continuum Hypothesis, are within the reach of $=(\vec{x}, \vec{y})$. In fact, the results in [2], based on earlier results by Ehrenfeucht, Enderton and Walkoe, show that the expressive power of dependence logic is closely entangled with the power of existential second order logic. Thus on finite models we are talking about NP, non-deterministic polynomial time, and on infinite domains we are blocked away, by results of Gödel, Turing and Church, from any kind of meaningful

---

*Research partially supported by grant 40734 of the Academy of Finland.

Arnold Beckmann, Benedikt Löwe (*eds.*). *Acts of the programme "Semantics and Syntax".* Isaac Newton Institute for the Mathematical Sciences, January to July 2012.

Talk given at the SAS Seminar, 17 January 2012, 16:30–17:00.

complete axiomatization of validity in the full language. So there is a sharp contrast between considering the mere atoms $=(\vec{x},\vec{y})$ (axiomatizable) and considering full first order logic with $=(\vec{x},\vec{y})$ (badly non-aximatizable). We are in the process of trying to penetrate deeper into quantificational first order logic with the atoms $=(\vec{x},\vec{y})$ without losing axiomatization.

The main methodological innovation behind dependence logic is that of **team semantics**. The basic idea, due to Hodges, is that phenomena such as dependence and independence, can only be manifested in a multitude of examples. A token observation or row of data cannot indicate dependence or independence. Based on this, the bold idea of team semantics, developed systematically in [2] is to base the semantics of first order (or other) logic on the concept of a *set* of assignments satisfying a formula. Such sets are called **teams**. In contrast, the traditional Tarski semantics is based on the concept of a *single* assignment satisfying a formula. The arising team semantics is slightly more complex than the Tarski semantics, but the upshot is that it can be used to give exact mathematical meaning to dependence and independence. For example, we say that a team X of assignments satisfies $=(\vec{x},\vec{y})$ if for any two assignments from X it holds that if they agree about $\vec{x}$, they agree about $\vec{y}$. More exactly,

$$\forall s, s' \in X(s(\vec{x}) = s'(\vec{x}) \rightarrow s(\vec{y}) = s'(\vec{y})).$$

Similarily, we say that a team X of assignments satisfies $\vec{x}\perp_{\vec{z}}\vec{y}$ if

$$\forall s, s' \in X \exists s'' \in X(s(\vec{z}) = s'(\vec{z}) \rightarrow$$
$$(s''(\vec{z}) = s(\vec{z}) \wedge s''(\vec{x}) = s(\vec{x}) \wedge s''(\vec{y}) = s'(\vec{y}))).$$

Team semantics can be extended to entire first order logic and indeed to many other logics as well, including modal logic. Suddenly a vast literature of dependence and independence concepts, until now scattered in far away fields, can be treated in a uniform way, and as part of predicate logic. The powerful techniques developed in predicate (and other kinds of) logic over the last 100 years can be unleashed to investigate dependencies and independencies as if they were nothing more than equations and inequalities. Naturally, the emerging theory is much more involved than traditional logic, but on the other hand, it reaches areas not covered by the latter.

Bibliography

[1] E. Grädel and J. Väänänen. Dependence and independence. *Studia Logica*, to appear.

[2] J. Väänänen. *Dependence logic*, volume 70 of *London Mathematical Society Student Texts*. Cambridge University Press, Cambridge, 2007.

Slow Consistency

Michael Rathjen

University of Leeds, Leeds, United Kingdom

E-mail: rathjen@maths.leeds.ac.uk

The fact that "natural" theories, i.e., theories which have something like an "idea" to them, are almost always linearly ordered with regard to logical strength, has been called one of the great mysteries of the foundation of mathematics. However, one easily establishes the existence of theories with incomparable logical strengths using self-reference (Rosser-style). As a result, PA+Con(PA) is not the least theory whose strength is greater than that of PA. But still we can ask: is there a sense in which PA+Con(PA) is the least "natural" theory whose strength is greater than that of PA? In the talk I shall exhibit natural theories in strength strictly between PA and PA+Con(PA) as well as incomparable theories by introducing a notion of slow consistency. This is joint work with Sy-David Friedman and Andreas Weiermann.

Arnold Beckmann, Benedikt Löwe (*eds.*). *Acts of the programme "Semantics and Syntax".* Isaac Newton Institute for the Mathematical Sciences, January to July 2012.

Talk given at the SAS Seminar, 17 January 2012, 17:00–17:30.

Sherali-Adams Relaxations and Graph Indistinguishability

Albert Atserias

Universitat Politècnica de Catalunya, Barcelona, Spain.

E-mail: atserias@lsi.upc.edu

The direct linear programming relaxation of the integer program for the vertex cover problem has integrality gap 2. This means that the worst-case ratio between the optimum of the integral program over its relaxation can always be bounded by 2, but no better. Stronger linear programming relaxations of the vertex cover problem can be obtained by adding linear inequalities that remain valid for the convex hull of the integral solutions. Typical examples include the "triangle constraints," saying that in every valid vertex cover, at least two out of the three points of any triangle in the graph must be covered. A systematic method to produce all valid linear inequalities for an arbitrary integer program was suggested by Sherali and Adams. Their method produces a hierarchy of relaxations that get tighter as a certain parameter k ranges from 0, where we get the direct linear programming relaxation, to the dimension of the program n, where we get exactly the convex hull of the integral solutions. Using some recent results that link together the levels of the Sherali-Adams hierarchy for the linear programming relaxation of graph isomorphism with indistinguishability by first-order logic with counting quantifiers and a bounded number of variables, we suggest an approach towards proving strong integrality gaps for vertex cover and other problems that survive many rounds of the Sherali-Adams hierarchy. The goal would be to re-prove some of the known integrality gap results for problems of interest by different means, and wishfully improve upon them.

Arnold Beckmann, Benedikt Löwe (*eds.*). *Acts of the programme "Semantics and Syntax".*
Isaac Newton Institute for the Mathematical Sciences, January to July 2012.

Talk given at the SAS Seminar, 19 January 2012, 16:00–16:30.

Decision Methods over Real and Algebraically Closed Fields

Grant Olney Passmore

University of Cambridge, Cambridge, and The University of Edinburgh, Edinburgh, United Kingdom

E-mail: grant.passmore@cl.cam.ac.uk

Tarski's theorem that the elementary theory of real closed fields (RCF) admits effective elimination of quantifiers is one of the longstanding hallmarks of mathematical logic. From this result, the decidability of elementary algebra and geometry readily follow, and a most tantalising situation arises: In principle, every elementary arithmetical conjecture over finite-dimensional real and complex spaces may be decided simply by formalising the conjecture and asking a computer of its truth. So why then do we still not know how many unit hyperspheres may kiss in five dimensions? Is it 41? 42?

The issue is one of complexity. Though decidable, RCF is fundamentally infeasible. Due to Davenport-Heinz, it is known that there exist families of n-dimensional RCF formulas of length $O(n)$ whose only quantifier-free equivalences must contain polynomials of degree $2^{2^{\Omega(n)}}$ and of length $2^{2^{\Omega(n)}}$. Nevertheless, there are countless examples of difficult, high-dimensional RCF problems solved in mathematical and engineering practice. What is the disconnect?

1. RCF problems solved in practice are most often solved using an ad hoc combination of methods, *not* by a general decision method.

2. RCF problems arising in practice commonly have structural properties dictated by the application domain from which they originated. Such structural properties can often be exploited making such problems more amenable to analysis and pushing them within the reaches of restricted, more efficient variants of known decision methods.

With this in mind, many researchers have in recent years proposed proof procedures, some complete, some heuristic and incomplete, for various fragments of RCF. Many of these procedures have proved their worth in both mathematical and engineering practice. This situation gives rise to many interesting research questions of both theoretical and applied character. In this talk, we give a broad overview of the goals of those of us working on decision methods over real and algebraically closed fields, highlighting some interesting recent results and ongoing challenge problems.

Arnold Beckmann, Benedikt Löwe (*eds.*). *Acts of the programme "Semantics and Syntax".*
Isaac Newton Institute for the Mathematical Sciences, January to July 2012.

Talk given at the SAS Seminar, 19 January 2012, 16:30–17:00.

Computability Questions about Fields

Russell Miller[*]

Queens College, Flushing NY, and City University of New York, New York NY, United States of America

E-mail: Russell.Miller@qc.cuny.edu

Many of the concepts standard in computable model theory today trace back to the 1956 paper *Effective Procedures in Field Theory*, by Fröhlich and Shepherdson. There the authors used Turing's definition of a partial computable function to show that many procedures simply could not be carried out in an arbitrary field F, even assuming one knows the elements of F and can compute the field operations on those elements. For example, they formalized van der Waerden's intuitive notion that it is not in general decidable whether a polynomial from $F[X]$ has a root in F, or whether it is reducible within the polynomial ring $F[X]$. Indeed, they showed that these two questions about polynomials (having a root, and being reducible) are equicomputable: one can be done by a Turing machine if and only if the other can. Their proof generalizes easily to show that the set of reducible polynomials and the set of polynomials with roots are Turing-equivalent, and Rabin capitalized on these notions in his 1960 paper investigating effective algebraic closures of fields.

In this talk we will review these notions and then present recent refinements. The result of Turing-equivalence between the two sets described above was surprising: it is readily seen that decidability of irreducibility allows one to decide whether a polynomial has a root, but the reduction in the opposite direction is by no means apparent. Fröhlich and Shepherdson gave one such reduction, while another is implicit in Rabin's paper. A third reduction, which holds provided that the computable field has a computable transcendence basis over its prime subfield, was presented by the speaker in a 2010 paper. This new one has the stronger property of being a 1-reduction: the irreducibility of a polynomial $p \in F[X]$ is reduced to the single question of whether another polynomial $q \in F[X]$, computed effectively from p, has a root in F. In the same paper, the author constructed a computable field, algebraic over the rationals (and thus trivially having a computable transcendence basis), for which there is no 1-reduction in the opposite direction. Therefore, the two questions are indeed of distinct degrees of difficulty, although distinguishing them requires the notion of a 1-reduction, which is finer than Turing reducibility but nevertheless absolutely standard in computability theory. This theorem was recently strengthened by the speaker's

[*]The author was partially supported in this work by Grant # DMS – 1001306 from the National Science Foundation, by Grant # 13397 from the Templeton Foundation, and by many sequential grants from The City University of New York PSC-CUNY Research Award Program.

Arnold Beckmann, Benedikt Löwe (*eds.*). *Acts of the programme "Semantics and Syntax"*. Isaac Newton Institute for the Mathematical Sciences, January to July 2012.

Talk given at the SAS Seminar, 24 January 2012, 16:00–16:30.

Ph.D. student Rebecca Steiner, who produced a computable algebraic field in which there is not even any wtt-reduction from having a root to being reducible. Steiner has established exactly the property necessary for such a wtt-reduction to exist, and the result has been known to surprise algebraists as well as computable model theorists.

Fröhlich and Shepherdson also gave the first example of a computable structure which is not *computably categorical*. The modern version of this concept holds of those computable structures $\mathcal{A}$ with the property that, for every computable structure $\mathcal{B}$ which is classically isomorphic to $\mathcal{A}$, there exists a computable isomorphism from $\mathcal{A}$ onto $\mathcal{B}$. Thus, for this $\mathcal{A}$, the property of being isomorphic to $\mathcal{A}$ is always witnessed effectively. We will remind our listeners of this and several related definitions. Fröhlich and Shepherdson gave two distinct examples of pairs of computable fields which were classically isomorphic to each other, but not computably isomorphic, and to the speaker's knowledge, this is the first instance of this concept anywhere in the literature. However, the concept proved to be more accessible for several other types of structures than for fields. Structural characterizations of computable categoricity are known for linear orders, for instance, and also for Boolean algebras and for trees (viewed as partial orders), due to work by many researchers since about 1980; yet there is no known structural characterization of computable categoricity for computable fields. We will survey the current state of affairs in this area, including several recent results by the speaker (some joint with Schoutens, others joint with Shlapentokh, and still others joint with Hirschfeldt, Kramer, and Shlapentokh). For computable algebraic fields, the situation is by now fairly well understood, and the lack of a nice characterization is justified to some extent by the discovery that, even when the field is algebraic, the property of being computably categorical is still Π_4^0-complete, whereas for the other classes above it was always a Σ_3^0-property.

Constructive Thoughts on Operator Algebras

Douglas Bridges

University of Canterbury, Christchurch, New Zealand

E-mail: `d.bridges@math.canterbury.ac.nz`

Operator algebra theory, in its classical form, is developed in about as nonconstructive a manner as one could imagine: typical existence proofs use contradiction arguments and applications of Zorn's lemma. Finding a viable constructive development of, or perhaps alternative to, operator algebra theory would seem to be a major test of Bishop-style constructive mathematics (or, indeed, of any other approach to extracting the computational content of a classical theory). In my talk I shall present some of the background, some recent progress, and some of the major problems that lie at the very start of such a development.

Arnold Beckmann, Benedikt Löwe (*eds.*). *Acts of the programme "Semantics and Syntax".* Isaac Newton Institute for the Mathematical Sciences, January to July 2012.

Talk given at the SAS Seminar, 24 January 2012, 16:30–17:00.

Automated and Human Proofs in General Mathematics: An Initial Comparison

Jesse Alama

New University of Lisbon, Lisbon, Portugal
E-mail: jesse.alama@gmail.com

First-order translations of large mathematical repositories allow discovery of new proofs by automated reasoning systems. Large amounts of available mathematical knowledge can be re-used by combined AI/ATP systems, possibly in unexpected ways. But in this setting automated systems can be also more easily misled by irrelevant knowledge, and finding deeper proofs is typically more difficult. Both large-theory AI/ATP methods, and translation and data-mining techniques of large formal corpora, have significantly developed recently, providing enough data for an initial comparison of the proofs written by mathematicians and the proofs found automatically. In this talk we present highlights of such an initial experiment and comparison conducted over the 50000 mathematical theorems from the Mizar Mathematical Library.

Arnold Beckmann, Benedikt Löwe (eds.). Acts of the programme "Semantics and Syntax".
Isaac Newton Institute for the Mathematical Sciences, January to July 2012.

Talk given at the SAS Seminar, 24 January 2012, 17:00–17:30.

The "Million Message Attack" in 15 Thousand Messages

Graham Steel

École Normale Supérieure de Cachan, Cachan, France

E-mail: graham.steel@lsv.ens-cachan.fr

In this talk, we will first take a look at a classic piece of cryptanalysis, namely Bleichenbacher's chosen-ciphertext attack on RSA encryption using PKCS#1 v1.5 padding (the so-called "million message attack"). We will then show some original optimisations that allow the attack to be performed using a median of just $15,000$ messages, and explain why this is relevant to currently deployed cryptographic systems.

Arnold Beckmann, Benedikt Löwe (*eds.*). *Acts of the programme "Semantics and Syntax".* Isaac Newton Institute for the Mathematical Sciences, January to July 2012.

Talk given at the SAS Seminar, 26 January 2012, 16:00–16:30.

Reuniting the Antipodes: Bringing Together Nonstandard Analysis and Constructive Analysis

Sam Sanders

Ghent University, Ghent, Belgium

E-mail: sasander@cage.ugent.be

Constructive Analysis was introduced by Errett Bishop to identify the 'computational meaning' of mathematics. In the spirit of intuitionistic mathematics, notions like 'algorithm,' 'explicit computation,' and 'finite procedure' are central. The exact meaning of these vague terms was left open, to ensure the compatibility of Constructive Analysis with several traditions in mathematics. Constructive Reverse Mathematics (CRM) is a spin-off of Harvey Friedman's famous Reverse Mathematics program, based on Constructive Analysis. Bishop famously derided Nonstandard Analysis for its lack of computational meaning. In this talk, we introduce 'Ω-invariance': a simple and elegant definition of 'finite procedure' in (classical) Nonstandard Analysis. Using an intuitive interpretation, we obtain many results from CRM, thus showing that Ω-invariance is quite close to Bishop's notion of 'finite procedure.'

Arnold Beckmann, Benedikt Löwe (eds.). Acts of the programme "Semantics and Syntax".
Isaac Newton Institute for the Mathematical Sciences, January to July 2012.

Talk given at the SAS Seminar, 26 January 2012, 16:30–17:00.

Is Cryptographic Theory Practically Relevant?
31 January – 2 February 2012

Kenny Paterson[1] and Nigel Smart[2]

[1]Royal Holloway, University of London, Egham, United Kingdom
[2]University of Bristol, Bristol, United Kingdom
E-mail: kenny.paterson@rhul.ac.uk,nigel@compsci.bristol.ac.uk

The workshop brought together researchers who work in theoretical aspects of cryptography (principally, provable security of protocols) with people working on applied aspects of cryptography, particularly people involved in standardization and in industrial deployment of cryptography. The main goal of the workshop was to strengthen the dialogue between these two groups of people, which is currently perceived to be quite weak. Ultimately, we aimed to make a start on bridging the divide between what academic cryptographers believe should be the goals of cryptographic protocol design and what is actually deployed in the real world. The potential benefits of doing so were

- to bring a better understanding of real-world cryptographic issues to the theoretical community, helping to inform their research and set new research challenges for the theoretical community;
- enabling practitioners to develop a clearer view of the current state-of-the-art in cryptographic research and what it offers to practice;
- providing a forum for exchanging ideas and building relationships between researchers from the different communities.

The list of speakers consisted of John Beric (Mastercard International), Mike Bond (Cryptomathic), Christian Cachin (IBM Zurich), Liqun Chen (HP Labs), Cas Cremers (ETH Zurich), George Danezis (Microsoft Research), George French (Barclays/UK Cabinet Office), Jens Groth (University College London), Richard Horne (Barclays/UK Cabinet Office), Aggelos Kiayias (University of Connecticut), Hugo Krawczyk (IBM Research), David McGrew (Cisco Systems), David Naccache (ENS Paris), Christof Paar (Ruhr University, Bochum), Bart Preneel (Katholieke Universiteit Leuven), Thomas Ristenpart (University of Wisconsin), Hovav Shacham (UCSD), Tom Shrimpton (Portland State University), Graham Steel (ENS Cachan), Serge Vaudenay (EPFL, Switzerland), Mike Ward (Mastercard International), and Douglas Wikström (Kungliga Tekniska Högskolan).

Arnold Beckmann, Benedikt Löwe (eds.). Acts of the programme "Semantics and Syntax". Isaac Newton Institute for the Mathematical Sciences, January to July 2012.

SAS Workshop "Is Cryptographic Theory Practically Relevant?".

(Picture courtesy of The Isaac Newton Institute)

In addition to the abstracts in this booklet, slides and videos of some of the talks can be found at

http://www.newton.ac.uk/programmes/SAS/sasw07.html

Privacy in Deniable Anonymous Concurrent Authentication with Setup is Impossible: Do We Care?

Serge Vaudenay

École Polytechnique Fédérale Lausanne, Lausanne, Switzerland

E-mail: serge.vaudenay@epfl.ch

In this talk we review three stories about theoretical cryptography and their impact in practice. This includes a recent analysis of RC4, the notion of deniable interactive proof, and the impossibility of strong privacy in RFID protocols.

To follow up our analysis of RC4 at Eurocrypt 2011, which was purely theoretical, we compare the results with practical experiments and identify several flaws which could have been avoided by carefully checking all assumptions. This illustrates how practice could help theory in cryptanalysis.

Deniable authentication can be done using zero-knowledge. More efficient protocols are available with setup assumptions such as a CRS or a random oracle. However, deniability is no longer implied by zero-knowledge. Even worse: using tamper resistance as setup assumption, regular zero-knowledge protocols are no longer deniable. This shows that some cryptographic notions such as deniability are very fragile and may be hard to achieve in practice, even though the theory inspires efficient protocols.

Finally, our model for privacy in RFID protocols identified some protocols based on public-key cryptography achieving the maximal feasible level of privacy, but the strongest one was impossible. By revisiting the impossibility proof, we realize that we can slightly update the model to better capture the intuitive notion and privacy and make the strongest level achievable, ... with exactly the same protocol as before. Although we had to fight with the theory, this had no impact on the practical protocol.

Bibliography

[1] K. Ouafi and S. Vaudenay. Strong privacy for RFID systems from plaintext-aware encryption. In J. Pieprzyk, A.-R. Sadeghi, and M. Manulis, editors, *Cryptology and Network Security, 8th International Conference CANS'12, Darmstadt, Germany*, volume 7712 of *Lecture Notes in Computer Science*, pages 247–262. Springer Berlin Heidelberg, 2012.

[2] P. Sepehrdad, S. Vaudenay, and M. Vuagnoux. Statistical attack on RC4. In *Advances in Cryptology - EUROCRYPT 2011 - 30th Annual International Conference on the Theory and Applications of Cryptographic*

Arnold Beckmann, Benedikt Löwe (eds.). Acts of the programme "Semantics and Syntax". Isaac Newton Institute for the Mathematical Sciences, January to July 2012.

Talk given at the SAS Workshop "Is Cryptographic Theory Practically Relevant?", 31 January 2012, 09:45–10:30.

Techniques, Tallinn, Estonia, May 15-19, 2011, volume 6632 of *Lecture Notes in Computer Science*, pages 343–363. Springer, 2011.

[3] S. Vaudenay. Deniable RSA signature. In D. Naccache, editor, *Cryptography and Security: From Theory to Applications - Essays Dedicated to Jean-Jacques Quisquater on the Occasion of His 65th Birthday*, volume 6805 of *Lecture Notes in Computer Science*, pages 132–142. Springer, 2012.

Storage Encryption and Key Management

Christian Cachin

IBM Research - Zurich, Rüschlikon, Switzerland

E-mail: cca@zurich.ibm.com

Data encryption has become a key requirement for enterprise storage systems. As a consequence of this I have looked into storage encryption methods and contributed to several storage security products at IBM. Research has formulated the notion of tweakable encryption modes, which specifically address a requirement of storage encryption. On the other hand, practitioners have used specific key-wrapping modes for a long time before researchers came up with a formal notion. We highlight where and how they are used.

The biggest concern in storage encryption are cryptographic keys, which must be maintained securely and reliably. Users struggle with the key-management problem because operating procedures and formats differ across systems. When multiple users access a key server, its interface must be designed with special consideration for cryptographic relations among keys. Cryptographic hardware-security modules (HSMs) face the same problem. Some logical attacks through the key-management operations of HSMs have been reported in the past, which allowed to expose keys merely by exploiting their interfaces in unexpected ways. We show how to model the security of key-management systems formally and protect them from interface attacks. This work originates in the context of creating the OASIS Key Management Interoperability Protocol (KMIP), a new open standard for enterprise-level key management.

Arnold Beckmann, Benedikt Löwe (eds.). Acts of the programme "Semantics and Syntax". Isaac Newton Institute for the Mathematical Sciences, January to July 2012.

Talk given at the SAS Workshop "Is Cryptographic Theory Practically Relevant?", 31 January 2012, 11:00–11:45.

Mathematical and Practical Security Problems not Directly Related to Cryptography

David Naccache

École Normale Supérieure Paris, Paris, France

E-mail: david@naccache.fr

Bored by random oracles, lattices, security reductions and games? This talk is for you! We will describe a number of practical security problems (some of which very mathematical) met while designing security systems. Subjet to available time, we will address the efficient spatial scattering of secrets, the geometrical properties of protective chip wire-meshes, a new breed of system fault protections requiring combinatorial tools, the optimal placement of scramblers, quick pre-identification and the use of secure devices to... attack other secure devices

Arnold Beckmann, Benedikt Löwe (*eds.*). *Acts of the programme "Semantics and Syntax".*
Isaac Newton Institute for the Mathematical Sciences, January to July 2012.

Talk given at the SAS Workshop "Is Cryptographic Theory Practically Relevant?", 31 January 2012, 11:45–12:30.

Efficient Verification of ElGamal Ciphertext Shuffles

Jens Groth

University College London, London, United Kingdom

E-mail: j.groth@ucl.ac.uk

A shuffle is a permutation and rerandomization of a set of ciphertexts. This means that the input ciphertexts and the output ciphertexts contain the same set of plaintexts but in permuted order. Furthermore, due to rerandomization of the ciphertexts the permutation is hidden. Mix-nets often use a sequence of random shuffles performed by different mix-servers to hide the link between senders and plaintexts. A common use is found in voting schemes, where a mix-net uses random shuffles to anonymize a set of encrypted votes.

To protect against malicious mix-servers it is necessary to verify that the shuffles are correct. Otherwise, a bad mix-server could for instance substitute encrypted votes cast by honest voters with encrypted votes for another candidate. Zero-knowledge proofs can be used to guarantee the correctness of a shuffle without revealing the underlying permutation or anything else. By providing such a zero-knowledge proof the mix-server can prove that it has not substituted any ciphertexts or in any other way deviated from the protocol; but at the same time the link between input ciphertexts and output ciphertexts remains secret.

Zero-knowledge proofs for correctness of a shuffle are complicated beasts but we will present a construction that is both efficient and where the required communication is much smaller than the size of the shuffle itself. We have implemented the zero-knowledge proof and will provide concrete performance measurements for verifying shuffles of ElGamal ciphertexts.

Arnold Beckmann, Benedikt Löwe (eds.). Acts of the programme "Semantics and Syntax".
Isaac Newton Institute for the Mathematical Sciences, January to July 2012.

Talk given at the SAS Workshop "Is Cryptographic Theory Practically Relevant?", 31 January 2012, 14:00–14:45.

A Long Answer to the Simple Question, "Is TLS Provably Secure?"

Tom Shrimpton

Portland State University, Portland OR, United States of America
E-mail: teshrim@cs.pdx.edu

TLS is perhaps the Internet's most widely used security protocol, and at its heart is a subprotocol for providing data privacy and integrity, called the TLS Record Protocol. Is the TLS Record Protocol provably secure? A series of papers starting in 2000 delivered the answers (roughly): no, not for all possible underlying encryption schemes; yes, for some of the specific encryption schemes that TLS uses, but only under some impractical assumptions; yes, under less restrictive assumptions, but for a definition of "secure" that is hard to understand; yes, as long as your integrity-providing "tag" isn't too short. We'll explore this line of papers, as well as some interesting attacks that helped to guide the provable-security results. In the end, we'll argue that the answer is still "it depends on how you use it" by discussing new results on using secure authenticated encryption (e.g., TLS) as a tunnel between a user and a proxy, through which webpages are requested and downloaded. We'll see that it is surprisingly easy to determine which webpage was visited, even in the presence of some sophisticated efforts to fragment and pad the webpage data prior to entering the provably-secure encryption tunnel.

Arnold Beckmann, Benedikt Löwe (*eds.*). *Acts of the programme "Semantics and Syntax"*.
Isaac Newton Institute for the Mathematical Sciences, January to July 2012.

Talk given at the SAS Workshop "Is Cryptographic Theory Practically Relevant?", 31 January 2012, 14:45–15:30.

Analysis of Cryptographic Security APIs

Graham Steel

École Normale Supérieure de Cachan, Cachan, France

E-mail: gsteel@ens-cachan.fr

In practice, many developers use cryptography via an application program interface (API) either to a software library or a hardware device where keys are stored and all cryptographic operations take place. Designing such interfaces so that they offer flexible functionality but cannot be abused to reveal keys or secrets has proved to be extremely difficult, with a number of published vulnerabilities in widely-used APIs appearing over the last decade. This talk will discuss recent research on the use of formal methods to specify and verify such interfaces in order to either detect flaws or prove security properties. We will focus on the example of RSA PKCS#11, the most widely used interface for cryptographic devices. We will demonstrate a tool, Tookan, which can reverse engineer the particular configuration of PKCS#11 in use on some device under test, construct a model of the device's functionality, and call a model checker to search for attacks. If an attack is found, it can be executed automatically on the device. We will comment on design principles for the next generation of APIs.

Arnold Beckmann, Benedikt Löwe (eds.). Acts of the programme "Semantics and Syntax".
Isaac Newton Institute for the Mathematical Sciences, January to July 2012.

Talk given at the SAS Workshop "Is Cryptographic Theory Practically Relevant?", 31 January 2012, 16:00–16:45.

Scaling Cryptographic Deployments

Richard Horne and George French

Barclays and UK Cabinet Office/Barclays, United Kingdom
E-mail: rbdhorne@btinternet.com

As use of cryptography has exploded in recent years, so has the vulnerability to exploitation of the multitude of implementations. Organisations such as banks who critically depend on cryptography on a massive scale (both in terms of volume of keys under management and number of different implementations) need: 1. Solutions that enable standardised, central service provision of cryptography, and 2. Implementations of cryptographic standards and protocols that are demonstrably secure. This talk will discuss the requirements and illustrate how research is required to meet them. It will illustrate the real-world applicability of current research to identify weaknesses in implementations of cryptographic protocols.

Arnold Beckmann, Benedikt Löwe (eds.). Acts of the programme "Semantics and Syntax".
Isaac Newton Institute for the Mathematical Sciences, January to July 2012.

Talk given at the SAS Workshop "Is Cryptographic Theory Practically Relevant?", 31 January 2012, 16:00–16:45.

Recent Advances in Computational Extractors

Hugo Krawczyk

IBM Research, Yorktown Heights NY, United States of America
E-mail: Hugo@ee.technion.ac.il

Randomness extractors are algorithms that map sources of sufficient min-entropy to outputs that are statistically close to uniform. Randomness extraction has become a central and ubiquitous notion in complexity theory and theoretical computer science with innumerable applications and surprising and unifying connections to other notions. Cryptography, too, has greatly benefited from this notion. Cryptographic applications of randomness extractors range from the construction of pseudorandom generators from one-way functions to the design of cryptographic functionality from noisy and weak sources (including applications to quantum cryptography) to the more recent advances in areas such as leakage- and exposure-resilient cryptography, circular encryption, fully homomorphic encryption, etc.

Randomness extractors have also found important cryptographic uses in practical applications, particularly for the construction of key derivation functions. In many of these applications, the defining property of randomness extractors, namely, statistical closeness of their output to a uniform distribution, can be relaxed and replaced with computational indistinguishability. Extractors that provide this form of relaxed guarantee are called "computational extractors".

In this talk I will cover some recent advances in the understanding and applicability of computational extractors with particular focus on their role in building key derivation functions.

See http://tools.ietf.org/html/rfc5869 for a connection between this talk and the question "Is Cryptographic Theory Practically Relevant?"

Arnold Beckmann, Benedikt Löwe (eds.). Acts of the programme "Semantics and Syntax".
Isaac Newton Institute for the Mathematical Sciences, January to July 2012.

Talk given at the SAS Workshop "Is Cryptographic Theory Practically Relevant?", 1 February 2012, 09:00–09:45.

The Practical Application of Cryptography to International Card Payments

John Beric and Mike Ward

MasterCard Worldwide, London, United Kingdom

E-mail: John_Beric@mastercard.com

The presentation will explore chip card payment systems based on the EMV specifications and their use of and reliance on cryptography. The presentation will begin by reviewing from first principles the heuristics of payments and the fundamental security requirements of card payments. It will then motivate the choice (made in the mid-1990s) of EMV cryptographic algorithms and standards and the experience gained in the intervening years regarding cryptanalytic research and practical impact. It will then conclude by presenting plans for additional cryptographic algorithms that might be included in EMV in the near future.

Arnold Beckmann, Benedikt Löwe (eds.). Acts of the programme "Semantics and Syntax". Isaac Newton Institute for the Mathematical Sciences, January to July 2012.

Talk given at the SAS Workshop "Is Cryptographic Theory Practically Relevant?", 1 February 2012, 09:45–10:30.

Cryptography with Work-based Corruptions and the Combinatorics of Anonymity

Aggelos Kiayias

University of Athens, Athens, Greece

E-mail: aggelos@cse.uconn.edu

In the setting of cryptographic protocols, the corruption of a party has been viewed as a simple, uniform and atomic operation, where the adversary decides to get control over a party and this party immediately gets corrupted. In this talk, motivated by the fact that different players may require different resources to get corrupted, we introduce the notion of resource-based corruptions, where the adversary must invest some resources in order to perform corruptions. If the adversary has full information about the system configuration then resource-based corruptions would provide no fundamental difference from the standard corruption model. However, in the 'anonymous' setting (where anonymity is in the sense that such configuration is hidden from the adversary), much is to be gained in terms of efficiency and security. We showcase the power of anonymity in the setting of secure multiparty computation with resource-based corruptions and prove that anonymity can effectively be used to circumvent impossibility results. Regarding efficiency gains, we show that anonymity can be used to force the corruption threshold to drop from $1/2$ to $1/3$, in turn allowing the use of more efficient cryptographic protocols in various settings. This presentation reported on joint work with Juan Garay, David Johnson (AT&T), Moti Yung (Google).

Arnold Beckmann, Benedikt Löwe (*eds.*). *Acts of the programme "Semantics and Syntax".* Isaac Newton Institute for the Mathematical Sciences, January to July 2012.

Talk given at the SAS Workshop "Is Cryptographic Theory Practically Relevant?", 1 February 2012, 11:00–11:45.

HSM Portal—Practical Tools Built on Theory

Mike Bond

Cryptomathic Ltd., Cambridge, United Kingdom

E-mail: Mike.Bond@cryptomathic.com

Cryptomathic has been working on a new approach to applications cryptography, inspired by the need to give useful and sound building blocks to applications developers, rather than flexible but dangerous tools. This is partly based on some ideas and work by George French, Senior Security Architect, Barclays. The talk describes novel features of our "M portal"—a cryptographic service which offers high-level primitives to applications, and abstracts away dirty detail of hardware security module and software cryptography and key management. Using a high-level approach allows the service to offer primitives closer to the theoretical models of black box cryptography than are ordinarily provided by a simple crypto library. Our talk will discuss why we believe the gap between applications developers requiring cryptography and security engineers/theorists is ever widening. We believe new tools are needed and proposed theoretical ideas need to be brought to life to bridge this gap, lest practice become totally disconnected from theory in the future.

Arnold Beckmann, Benedikt Löwe (*eds.*). *Acts of the programme "Semantics and Syntax".*
Isaac Newton Institute for the Mathematical Sciences, January to July 2012.

Talk given at the SAS Workshop "Is Cryptographic Theory Practically Relevant?", 1 February 2012, 11:45–12:30.

Theory and Practice for Hash Functions

Bart Preneel

Katholieke Universiteit Leuven, Leuven, Belgium
E-mail: bart.preneel@esat.kuleuven.be

In the last seven years we have witnessed a surge in the cryptanalysis of hash functions. The most visible result was the cryptanalysis of MD5 and SHA-1 by Wang et al., but there have been other results including multi-collision attacks, long message second preimage attacks, and rebound attacks. There has also been substantial progress in understanding security definitions and models (e.g., indifferentiability) and a large number of security reductions has been proven. In 2007, NIST has launched the call for the SHA-3 competition. In 2008 more than 60 submissions were received, which makes this the largest open cryptographic competition to date. In this talk we will discuss the impact of the research on hash functions on practice and the interaction between theory and practice in the SHA-3 competition.

Arnold Beckmann, Benedikt Löwe (eds.). Acts of the programme "Semantics and Syntax".
Isaac Newton Institute for the Mathematical Sciences, January to July 2012.

Talk given at the SAS Workshop "Is Cryptographic Theory Practically Relevant?", 1 February 2012, 14:00–14:45.

Lessons Learned from Four Years of Implementation Attacks against Real-World Targets

Christof Paar

Ruhr-Universität Bochum, Bochum, Germany

E-mail: cpaar@crypto.rub.de

Over the last few years we were able to break various real-world security systems using various flavours of physical attacks. About three years ago we were able to break KeeLoq, which is a 64 bit block cipher that is popular for remote keyless entry (RKE) systems. Even though the attack seems almost straightforward in hindsight, there were many practical and theoretical problems to overcome. More recently we were able to break certain types of the DESFire contactless smart card, which are widely used, e.g., for payment application. We also completely broke the bit stream encryption used in Xilinx FPGAs. In all cases we were able to recover the keys for either 3DES or AES using power analysis attacks. In contrast to KeeLoq, both 3DES and AES are considered very secure from a classical cryptanalytical point of view. Interesingly, the real-world implications of these key-extraction attacks are highly dependend on the system design (and not on the cipher used).

In addition to summarizing the above mentioned work, I will try to draw some meaningful conclusions. This includes the often considerable practial hurdles an attacker has to overcome and the important role that system design plays.

Arnold Beckmann, Benedikt Löwe (eds.). Acts of the programme "Semantics and Syntax".
Isaac Newton Institute for the Mathematical Sciences, January to July 2012.

Talk given at the SAS Workshop "Is Cryptographic Theory Practically Relevant?", 1 February 2012, 14:45–15:30.

Privacy for Smart Meters: From Theory to Running Meter Code

George Danezis

Microsoft Research, Cambridge, United Kingdom

E-mail: gdane@microsoft.com

Over that past year our team has developed a portfolio of technologies to address privacy issues in smart metering. These were inspired by cryptographic techniques well established in research, but unheard of in the domain of embedded systems security. In this talk I chart our journey from the design of the techniques, to our experiences implementing them to be part of a real smart meter. Considerations such as memory footprint, stateless interfaces, and compatibility with communications protocols, not mere security properties, ended up being the deciding factor.

Arnold Beckmann, Benedikt Löwe (eds.). Acts of the programme "Semantics and Syntax". Isaac Newton Institute for the Mathematical Sciences, January to July 2012.

Talk given at the SAS Workshop "Is Cryptographic Theory Practically Relevant?", 1 February 2012, 16:00–16:45.

Practice-driven Cryptographic Theory

Tom Ristenpart

University of Wisconsin, Madison WI, United States of America
E-mail: rist@cs.wisc.edu

Cryptographic standards abound: TLS, SSH, IPSec, XML Encryption, PKCS, and so many more. In theory the cryptographic schemes used within these standards solve well understood problems, yet a parade of damaging attacks leave us with the question: What gives? Theoreticians often suggest (at least in private) that the problems are well-understood and attacks arise because standardizers misunderstand cryptographic theory. I'll use some of my recent work which uses provable-security techniques to analyze important standards (including TLS, HMAC, and PKCS#5) to argue that, just as often, it is the theoreticians who don't have all the answers: analyzing practically-useful cryptography requires pushing models and proof techniques in never-before-considered directions. We'll see how (what I'll call) practice-driven cryptographic theory can lead to new understanding and improved confidence in cryptographic practice.

This talk covered joint work with Mihir Bellare, Yevgeniy Dodis, Kenneth Paterson, Thomas Shrimpton, Neils Fergeson, John Steinberger, and Stefano Tessaro.

Arnold Beckmann, Benedikt Löwe (eds.). Acts of the programme "Semantics and Syntax".
Isaac Newton Institute for the Mathematical Sciences, January to July 2012.

Talk given at the SAS Workshop "Is Cryptographic Theory Practically Relevant?", 2 February 2012, 09:00–09:45.

Cars and Voting Machines: Embedded Systems in the Field

Hovav Shacham

University of California, San Diego, La Jolla CA, United States of America
E-mail: hovav@cs.ucsd.edu

How well are the tools of modern cryptography employed in fielded embedded systems? How are the common tasks of communication and authentication, key storage and distribution, and firmware update and verification performed? In this talk, we describe evidence gathered from several studies of deployed embedded systems: a modern mass-market automobile and two electronic voting machines. These studies consisted of substantial reverse-engineering efforts by large teams of researchers. We find that in many cases the designers of the systems we studied are getting simple cryptographic tasks wrong. These failures suggest a lack of engagement with the cryptography and security research community. We consider some reasons for the status quo, and some ways that it might be improved. This presentation reported on joint work with Danny Anderson, Stephen Checkoway, Alexei Czeskis, Ariel Feldman, Edward Felten, J. Alex Halderman, Srinivas Inguva, Brian Kantor, Tadayoshi Kohno, Karl Koscher, Damon McCoy, Shwetak Patel, Eric Rescorla, Franziska Roesner, Stefan Savage, and Dan Wallach.

Arnold Beckmann, Benedikt Löwe (*eds.*). *Acts of the programme "Semantics and Syntax".*
Isaac Newton Institute for the Mathematical Sciences, January to July 2012.

Talk given at the SAS Workshop "Is Cryptographic Theory Practically Relevant?", 2 February 2012, 09:45–10:30.

From Cryptographer's Cryptography to Engineer's Crypto

Liqun Chen

Hewlett-Packard Laboratories, Bristol, United Kingdom
E-mail: liqun.chen@hp.com

Cryptography has become an increasingly important subject, not only for cryptographers but also for computer engineers. Having been involved for many years in research and industrial consultation in cryptography and its practical applications, I have become very aware of the huge gap between the cryptographer's and the engineer's point of view regarding cryptography. In this talk, I would like to share my experiences with the workshop participants, and will take cryptographic functionalities of a TPM (trusted platform module), as an interesting example, to discuss how to create a healthy life circle in cryptography. This will include a smooth link between academic research, international standards, industrial products and real usages.

Arnold Beckmann, Benedikt Löwe (*eds.*). *Acts of the programme "Semantics and Syntax".*
Isaac Newton Institute for the Mathematical Sciences, January to July 2012.

Talk given at the SAS Workshop "Is Cryptographic Theory Practically Relevant?", 2 February 2012, 11:00–11:45.

Verificatum—An Efficient and Provably Secure Mix-net

Douglas Wikström

Kungliga Tekniska Högskolan, Stockholm, Sweden

E-mail: dog@csc.kth.se

A common component in electronic election schemes is a so called 'mix-net'. This is a protocol executed by a group of servers that takes a list of ciphertexts and outputs the plaintexts in sorted order without revealing anything about the correspondence between input ciphertexts and output plaintexts. Thus, a mix-net can securely perform the tabulation in an electronic election where voters submit encrypted votes. Verificatum is an open source implementation of an efficient and provably secure mix-net (see http://www.verificatum.org). In its simplest form it is a Java application that is easy to install and use, but it can also exploit optimized C code, it can be configured in many ways, and it is a perfect platform for implementing more advanced election schemes. It has already been used successfully in the Wombat voting project. We will present Verificatum and describe the work we have done so far and what lies ahead.

Arnold Beckmann, Benedikt Löwe (eds.). Acts of the programme "Semantics and Syntax". Isaac Newton Institute for the Mathematical Sciences, January to July 2012.

Talk given at the SAS Workshop "Is Cryptographic Theory Practically Relevant?", 2 February 2012, 11:45–12:30.

Key Exchange: Security Models and Automatic Analysis

Cas Cremers

Eidgenössische Technische Hochschule Zürich, Zürich, Switzerland
E-mail: cas.cremers@inf.ethz.ch

During the last 20 years many game-based security models have been proposed for the analysis of Key Exchange protocols. The intent of these models is to prove Key Exchange protocols secure in the presence of increasingly powerful adversaries. In this talk, we present the main ingredients of these models, and relate them to practical threat models. We highlight both benefits and drawbacks of the way in which these security models are currently defined. Additionally, we present to what extent we can currently provide automatic analysis for Key Exchange protocols. We show how we use automatic analysis for evaluating existing security models as well as for developing alternative security models.

Arnold Beckmann, Benedikt Löwe (eds.). Acts of the programme "Semantics and Syntax".
Isaac Newton Institute for the Mathematical Sciences, January to July 2012.

Talk given at the SAS Workshop "Is Cryptographic Theory Practically Relevant?", 2 February 2012, 14:00–14:45.

Problems in Cryptographic Standards and Implementations

David McGrew

Cisco Systems, Herndon VA, United States of America

E-mail: mcgrew@cisco.com

In theory, we understand how to provide security through cryptography, yet too often practice does not live up to this promise. In standards, cryptographic imperatives compete with other pragmatic needs. This work seeks to understand those non-cryptographic needs and shed light on how they impact cryptographic security. We survey security failures in cryptographic standards and implementations, and analyze common problems. For standards, we consider the example of problems with authentication and the slow but steady adoption of authenticated encryption. For implementations, we review reported vulnerabilities and assess typical misuses and failure modes. Lastly, we suggest some ways that the research and standards communities can collaborate.

Arnold Beckmann, Benedikt Löwe (eds.). Acts of the programme "Semantics and Syntax".
Isaac Newton Institute for the Mathematical Sciences, January to July 2012.

Talk given at the SAS Workshop "Is Cryptographic Theory Practically Relevant?", 2 February 2012, 14:45–15:30.

Homotopy Type Theory and the Structure Identity Principle

Peter Aczel

The University of Manchester, Manchester, United Kingdom
E-mail: petera@cs.man.ac.uk

Vladimir Voevodsky and Steve Awodey were the independent originators, around 2005/06, of the ideas at the basis of Homotopy Type Theory (HoTT), an amalgam of Higher dimensional groupoid/category theory, Homotopy theory and Type theory. Vladimir Voevodsky's Univalence Axiom (UA) is a fundamental axiom, to be added to Per Martin-Löf's (intensional dependent) type theory, for a proposed Univalent Foundations of mathematics. My talk will focus on an application of UA, pointed out by Vladimir Voevodsky and Thierry Coquand, to a strong version of a Structure Identity Principle (SIP). This principle states that isomorphic mathematical structures are structurally identical; i.e., have the same structural properties:

$$A \cong B \ \Rightarrow \ A =_{\text{str}} B,$$

where, for structures A, B of the same signature, $A =_{\text{str}} B$ states that $P(A) \Leftrightarrow P(B)$ for all structural properties P of structures of that signature.

The axiom UA is an axiom about a type universe $\mathbb{U}$, that expresses in a strong way, in type theory, that isomorphic types in $\mathbb{U}$ are identical. It implies the strong form of SIP in type theory that $\mathbb{U}$-based isomorphic structures are identical; i.e., have the same properties (all properties expressible in type theory being structural).

Voevodsky has shown that type theory, with the Univalence axiom, has a model using the category of simplicial sets. The proof uses the metatheory of ZFC with a Grothendieck universe. Among the issues that need investigating is to what extent a more constructive proof can be found and to what extent UA increases the logical strength of type theory.

Arnold Beckmann, Benedikt Löwe (eds.). Acts of the programme "Semantics and Syntax".
Isaac Newton Institute for the Mathematical Sciences, January to July 2012.

Talk given at the SAS Seminar, 7 February 2012, 16:00–16:30.

A Logicians Approach to Network Coding

Søren Riis

Queen Mary, University of London, London, United Kingdom
E-mail: soren.riis@eecs.qmul.ac.uk

The main part of the talk is a brief and basic introduction to network coding and guessing games. This research is very rich on problems and puzzles ranging from "recreational" to the "deep and fundamental." Novel approaches on network coding based on guessing games, logic, and information theory have led to new lines of research:

- Combinatorial representations (with Peter Cameron and Max Gadouleau, 2011),

- Memoryless computation (with Max Gadouleau, 2011),

- Dynamic communication networks (with Max Gadouleau, 2011),

- Graph entropy and non-shannon information inequalities (PhD Thesis Yun Sun and Riis 2008),

- Construction of new classes of communication networks (with Max Gadouleau, 2010),

- New max-flow min-cut theorem for multiuser communication (with Max Gadouleau, 2011).

Towards the end of the talk I briefly explain how quite diverse problems (hat-puzzles, guessing games, network coding, dynamic network coding etc. . .) can be viewed as instances of general types of questions about finite models. This work is collaborative and was developed during my visit at the Isaac Newton Institute.

Arnold Beckmann, Benedikt Löwe (eds.). Acts of the programme "Semantics and Syntax".
Isaac Newton Institute for the Mathematical Sciences, January to July 2012.

Talk given at the SAS Seminar, 7 February 2012, 16:30–17:00.

The Bousfield Lattice from a Set-theoretic Perspective

Andrew Brooke-Taylor

Kobe University, Kobe, Japan

E-mail: andrewbt@gmail.com

In algebraic topology, it is interesting to consider, for each generalised homology theory E, the class of *E-acyclic spectra*: those spectra X such $E_*(X) = 0$. Bousfield observed that under reverse subclass inclusion, these classes form a lattice, with the join $\bigvee$ of spectra representing the homology theories providing the least upper bound, and the smash product $\wedge$ providing a lower bound, albeit not in general the greatest lower bound. A major advance was Ohkawa's result that this lattice, now known as the *Bousfield lattice* $\mathbf{B}$, is in fact set sized. However, there is much that remains unknown about this lattice, including for example its cardinality: $|\mathbf{B}|$ lies between $2^{\aleph_0}$ and $2^{2^{\aleph_0}}$, but as yet no one has managed to rule out either endpoint, or indeed the possibility of it consistently lying strictly between these values.

There are a number of important sublattices of $\mathbf{B}$. There is a natural distributive sublattice $\mathbf{DL}$, consisting of those Bousfield classes with representing spectra X satisfying $X \wedge X = X$; in this sublattice, $\wedge$ does in fact yield the greatest lower bound. There is a further sublattice $\mathbf{BA}$ which is a Boolean algebra, and then intermediate between $\mathbf{BA}$ and $\mathbf{DL}$ a complete Boolean algebra $\mathbf{cBA}$. Our research has focused on the differences between these sublattices, providing lower bounds on the cardinality of the differences. Providing concrete examples of elements in $\mathbf{DL} \smallsetminus \mathbf{cBA}$ also remains an open question. As a step in this direction, we are able to exhibit for each prime p and subset S of ω a triple of elements of which at least one is in this complement.

The research presented in this talk is joint work with Benedikt Löwe and Birgit Richter.

Arnold Beckmann, Benedikt Löwe (*eds.*). *Acts of the programme "Semantics and Syntax".*
Isaac Newton Institute for the Mathematical Sciences, January to July 2012.

Talk given at the SAS Seminar, 7 February 2012, 17:00–17:30.

Practical Reasoning with Proofs and Types

Giuseppe Primiero

Universiteit Gent, Ghent, Belgium

E-mail: Giuseppe.Primiero@UGent.be

In his *Practical forms of Type Theory*, Turing presented a "theory of types with small use of type themselves, as it is the case in ordinary mathematical arguments." Besides the use of names for values of undefined functions (introduced to prevent bad typing), Turing accounted *interpretability of types under assumptions* as a crucial feature for the representation of practical (mathematical) reasoning. In this talk, I will mainly be concerned with an account of assumptions-based reasoning within a provability interpretation of the Brouwer-Heyting-Kolmogorov semantics.

I will introduce an extension of the Intuitionistic Logic of Proofs in terms of a notion of dependent evidence, in the style of dependent types. An additional proof polynomial $\ll s\gg$ is given, which is used to construct a dependent evidence of the form $\ll s\gg[\![t]\!]B[A]$, reading: "t is a proof term for B, whenever A has a proof term s". Our intention is to separate interpretations of A as actually or just potentially justified. Dependent evidences can be easily extended to account for multiple assumptions and are a safe way to construct the quantificational fragment of this language.

The next task is to introduce a corresponding natural deduction calculus dubbed $\text{LP}_{\text{nd}\Diamond}$. By this step, we provide a two-tier translation: unconditional evidences are given in the form of formulas derivable from valid (global) assumptions only, according to the schema $\Delta; \cdot \vdash A \mid s$; and, on the other hand, dependent evidences are given as formulas derived from true (local) assumptions, according to the schema $\Delta; \Gamma \vdash A \parallel s$. Rules for the connectives of this language are shown and then a modal-like fragment is introduced, with locally sound and complete operators $!, ?$ on terms induced from, respectively, unconditional and dependent evidences. The system enjoys structural properties, equivalence on terms and well-behaving operators. Current research focuses on normalization and confluence for this calculus, using a technique available for normal forms of dependent types.

Applications of such systems are foreseen in the modeling of problems in Distributed Knowledge, Programming and Trusted Networks.

Arnold Beckmann, Benedikt Löwe (*eds.*). *Acts of the programme "Semantics and Syntax".* Isaac Newton Institute for the Mathematical Sciences, January to July 2012.

Talk given at the SAS Seminar, 9 February 2012, 16:00–16:30.

Proof Complexity and Search Problems

Neil Thapen

Academy of Sciences of the Czech Republic, Prague, Czech Republic

E-mail: thapen@math.cas.cz

An NP search problem is given by a polynomial time relation $R(x, y)$, with the properties that (a) $R(x, y)$ implicitly bounds the length of y by some polynomial in the length of x, and (b) R is total, that is, for all x there is some y such that $R(x, y)$ holds. The search problem is to find such a y, given x.

Bounded arithmetic is a name for various fragments of Peano arithmetic, without exponentiation and in which induction only holds for certain Δ_0 formulas. The NP search problems provably total in such a theory T play the role of the provably recursive functions of T. An important problem in the area is to show that theories with stronger induction correspond to strictly stronger classes of search problems, at least in the case where everything is relativized to an oracle. This is closely connected with the problem of separating the strength of certain natural families of propositional proof systems.

This talk will be a brief introduction to the area. The main examples I will discuss are: the NP search problem PLS; the bounded arithmetic theory T_2^1, which has induction for formulas with one existential bounded quantifier (that is, for NP formulas); and the propositional proof system known as narrow resolution. I will sketch why the $\forall \Sigma_1^b$ sentences provable in T_2^1 correspond on one hand to the narrow CNFs with short refutations in narrow resolution, and on the other hand to the NP search problem PLS. If there is time I will mention recent work on characterizing the search problems and propositional proof systems corresponding to stronger theories.

Arnold Beckmann, Benedikt Löwe (*eds.*). *Acts of the programme "Semantics and Syntax"*. Isaac Newton Institute for the Mathematical Sciences, January to July 2012.

Talk given at the SAS Seminar, 9 February 2012, 16:30–17:00.

Finite Self-information

Ian Herbert

University of California, Berkeley CA, United States of America

E-mail: iherbert@math.berkeley.edu

The prefix-free Kolmogorov complexity K of a finite string σ is the length of the shortest program that outputs σ, and can be used as a measure of the information content of σ. The mutual information of two finite strings, σ and τ, can be given by $K(\sigma) + K(\tau) - K(\sigma, \tau)$, where $K(\sigma, \tau) = K(\langle \sigma, \tau \rangle)$ for some standard pairing function $\langle \cdot , \cdot \rangle$. Levin has proposed an extension of this concept to the infinite case: for A, $B \in 2^\omega$ the mutual information of A and B is

$$I(A : B) = \log_2 \sum_{\sigma, \tau \in 2^{<\omega}} 2^{K(\sigma) - K^A(\sigma) + K(\tau) - K^B(\tau) - K(\sigma, \tau)},$$

where $K^A(\sigma)$ and $K^B(\tau)$ are the prefix-free Kolmogorov complexities of σ using A as an oracle and τ using B as an oracle, respectively. In the case where A and B are finite, this coincides up to an additive constant with the previous definition. One way of thinking of this defintion is to treat $K(\sigma) - K^A(\sigma)$ as a measure of how much A 'knows' about σ; if σ has 10 bits of information, but A thinks σ has only 7 bits of information, then A has 3 bits of information about σ. Similarly, we can think of $K(\tau) - K^B(\tau)$ as a measure of how much B 'knows' about τ, and $K(\sigma, \tau)$ as a measure of how far σ is from τ. If we restrict the sum to only those pairs where $\sigma = \tau$ we get another notion, simplified mutual information, and it is open whether these notions coincide.

A real A is said to have *finite self-information* is $I(A : A) < \infty$. It is clear that any K-trivial real (which has $K^A(\sigma) \geq K(\sigma) - c$ for all σ and some c independent of σ) has finite self-information. In this talk we discuss a result of Hirschfeldt and Weber that there are non-K-trivial reals with finite self-information and an extension due to the speaker that shows the property of finite self-information is very far from K-triviality: there is a perfect Π_1^0 class of reals with finite self-information, and any real above $0'$ is the join of two such reals. Moreover, for a certain sense of 'reasonable', these results hold for all 'reasonable' weakenings of K-triviality. We end with some open questions about the application of these results to other lowness notions, and the extent to which K-triviality is somehow 'maximally weak' as a lowness notion with certain nice properties.

Arnold Beckmann, Benedikt Löwe (*eds.*). *Acts of the programme "Semantics and Syntax".*
Isaac Newton Institute for the Mathematical Sciences, January to July 2012.

Talk given at the SAS Seminar, 14 February 2012, 16:00–16:30.

Computable Structures of High Scott Rank

Antonio Montalban

The University of Chicago, Chicago IL, United States of America
E-mail: antonio@math.uchicago.edu

The computable structures of high Scott rank are exactly the ones that cannot be recognized by a computably infinitary formula. We ask a the following questions about these structures, originally due to Goncharov and Knight:

(A) Is it true that every computably-infinitary axiomatizable class of structures which has a computable structure of high Scott rank, has more than one?

(B) Is there a computable structure of high Scott rank whose index set is not Σ_1^1 complete?

(C) Is there a computably categorial structure of High Scott rank.

We observe that the relativized version of (A) implies Vaught's Conjecture, and we ask whether this can be reversed in any way. We also observe that (C) implies (B).

Arnold Beckmann, Benedikt Löwe (eds.). *Acts of the programme "Semantics and Syntax".*
Isaac Newton Institute for the Mathematical Sciences, January to July 2012.

Talk given at the SAS Seminar, 14 February 2012, 16:30–17:00.

Number Theoretic Consequences of Ramsey Theoretic Principles

Theodore A. Slaman

University of California, Berkeley CA, United States of America
E-mail: slaman@math.berkeley.edu

We investigate the properties of Ramsey's Theorem for Pairs in the context of subsystems of second order arithmetic.

Definition 1. For $X \subseteq \omega$, let $[X]^n$ denote the size n subsets of X. For $n, m > 0$ and $F : [\omega]^n \to \{0, \dots, m-1\}$, $H \subseteq \omega$ is *homogeneous for F* iff F is constant on $[H]^n$.

Theorem 2 (Ramsey, 1930, [2]). *For all $n, m > 0$ and all $F : [\omega]^n \to \{0, \dots, m-1\}$, there is an infinite set H such that H is homogeneous for F.*

If we fix n and m, then we represent that instance of Ramsey's Theorem by RT^n_m.

Definition 3. A *model* $\mathfrak{M}$ *of second-order arithmetic* consists of a structure $\mathfrak{N}$ for first-order arithmetic, called the *numbers* of $\mathfrak{M}$, and a collection of subsets of $\mathfrak{N}$, called the *reals* of $\mathfrak{M}$.

Definition 4. RCA_0 is the second-order theory formalizing the following.

- P^-, the axioms for the nonnegative part of a discretely ordered ring.

- $\mathrm{I}\Sigma_1$, for φ a Σ^0_1 predicate, if 0 is a solution to φ and the solutions to φ are closed under successor, then φ holds of all numbers.

- The reals are closed under join and relative Δ^0_1-definability.

Definition 5. In an ω-*model* $\mathfrak{M}$, $\mathfrak{N} = \omega$ and the reals of $\mathfrak{M}$ form an ideal in the Turing degrees.

We can decompose of RT^2_2 over RCA_0 into the two principles COH and SRT^2_2, defined as follows.

Definition 6. An infinite set X is *cohesive* for a family $R_0, R_1, \dots$ of sets iff for each i, one of $X \cap R_i$ or $X \cap \overline{R_i}$ is finite. COH is the principle stating that every family of sets has a cohesive set.

A partition $F : [\omega]^2 \to \omega$ is *stable* iff for all x, $\lim_{y \to \infty} F(x, y)$ exists. SRT^2_2 is the principle RT^2_2 restricted to stable partitions.

Arnold Beckmann, Benedikt Löwe (*eds.*). *Acts of the programme "Semantics and Syntax".*
Isaac Newton Institute for the Mathematical Sciences, January to July 2012.

Talk given at the SAS Seminar, 14 February 2012, 17:00–17:30.

Theorem 7 (Cholak, Jockusch, and Slaman, 2001, [1]). RCA_0 *proves the equivalence of* RT_2^2 *and* $SRT_2^2 \,\& \, COH$.

We settle a question from [1] about whether this decomposition is proper by showing that SRT_2^2 does not imply RT_2^2.

Theorem 8 (Chong, Slaman, and Yang). *There is a model* $\mathfrak{M}$ *of* RCA_0 *with the following properties.*

- $\mathfrak{M} \models SRT_2^2$

- $\mathfrak{M} \models \neg I\Sigma_2$

- *Every real in* $\mathfrak{M}$ *is low in* $\mathfrak{M}$.

However, we have been unable to determine whether every ω-model of $RCA_0 + SRT_2^2$ is also a model of RT_2^2, which we regard as an extremely interesting question.

Bibliography

[1] P. A. Cholak, C. G. Jockusch, and T. A. Slaman. On the strength of Ramsey's theorem for pairs. *J. Symbolic Logic*, 66(1):1–55, 2001.

[2] F. P. Ramsey. On a problem in formal logic. *Proc. London Math. Soc.*, 30:264–286, 1930.

Real Closed Fields and Models of Peano Arithmetic

Merlin Carl

Universität Konstanz, Konstanz, Germany

E-mail: Merlin.Carl@uni-konstanz.de

A real closed field (RCF) is a totally ordered field F that is elementary equivalent to the field of real numbers for the language of ordered rings. An integer part (IP) of a real closed field is a subring R, discretely ordered by the ordering relation of F, such that the smallest positive element of R is 1 and such that, for every $x \in F$, there is $k \in R$ such that $k \leq x < k + 1$.

Shepherdson proved that the non-negative parts IP's of real closed fields are exactly the models of IOpen, i.e., PA^- together with induction for quantifier-free formulas. This was used for proving several independence results for IOpen.

The topic of the talk will be generalizations of Shepherdson's theorem to larger fragments of PA, including PA itself. In particular: Which real closed fields have an integer part that is a model of PA?

This question was answered recently by D'Aquino, Knight and Starchenko, who proved that countable nonstandard models of PA are exactly the integer parts of countable, non-archimedean real closed fields that are recursively saturated.

However, by an example of Marker, recursive saturation is insufficient for the uncountable case. I will present some work with Salma Kuhlmann and Paola D'Aquino on the characterization of real closed fields F with an integer part that is a model of PA. In particular, it is necessary (but not sufficient) for such an F that its value group has a rank which is a dense linear ordering without endpoints.

Arnold Beckmann, Benedikt Löwe (eds.). *Acts of the programme "Semantics and Syntax".* Isaac Newton Institute for the Mathematical Sciences, January to July 2012.

Talk given at the SAS Seminar, 16 February 2012, 16:00–16:30.

The $\forall\exists$-theory of the Partial Ordering of the Σ_2^0-enumeration Degrees

Steffen Lempp

University of Wisconsin, Madison WI, United States of America

E-mail: lempp@math.wisc.edu

The first-order theory of the Σ_2^0-enumeration degrees is known to be undecidable by Slaman and Woodin, and indeed as complicated as first-order arithmetic by Ganchev and Soskova. An easy argument shows that the existential theory is decidable, while Kent showed that the $\exists\forall\exists$-theory is undecidable. The decidability of the $\forall\exists$-theory of this degree structure remains the object of intense investigation.

There are two subproblems of the $\forall\exists$-theory, the extension of embeddings problem and the lattice embeddings problem, which are known to be decidable by Lempp, Slaman and Sorbi, and by Lempp and Sorbi, resp. Some additional partial results by Andrews, Lempp, Ng and Sorbi will be discussed, with an eye toward ideas for a full solution.

Arnold Beckmann, Benedikt Löwe (eds.). Acts of the programme "Semantics and Syntax".
Isaac Newton Institute for the Mathematical Sciences, January to July 2012.

Talk given at the SAS Seminar, 16 February 2012, 16:30–17:00.

Formal Mathematics and Natural Language

Peter Koepke

Rheinische Friedrich-Wilhelms-Universität Bonn, Bonn, Germany

E-mail: koepke@math.uni-bonn.de

My research project at the Newton Institute is concerned with bridging the gap between "natural", ordinary mathematical language and argumentation on one side, and formal or symbolic language and formal derivations on the other.

Formal mathematics took off 100 years ago with Whitehead and Russell's Principia Mathematica. The basic principles were that every statement has to be completely formalised and that every claim has to be verified by a complete proof in a formal system. Complete formal proofs turned out however to be very long and very hard to understand. By the Gödel completeness theorem, formal mathematics is possible in principle. But it is not feasable to be fully carried out by humans.

With the advent of electronic computers, the complexity problem presented itself in a new light. Since the early days of computers, automatic provers and proof checkers have been developed. Nowadays a large body of basic mathematics, some specialised areas, and some remarkable theorems have been formalised and checked in formal mathematics systems like Mizar, Coq, or Isabelle.

On the other hand, formal mathematics is not widely known or used. According to Freek Wiedijk the reason is that "formal mathematics does not fit common mathematical practice."

My project is concerned with increasing the "naturalness" of formal mathematics. This concerns mainly input and output languages and formats, user interfaces, the logics and background theories available, and the degree of automation.

In my talk I indicated that standard linguistic techniques designed for natural language processing could rather straightforwardly be applied to mathematical texts. Established linguistic grammars are able to parse mathematical sentences. Discourse relation theory can capture the structure of mathematical proof texts.

This is the basis for the project Naproche (natural proof checking) that is being pursued at the universities of Bonn and Essen (for more information, see http://naproche.net/). The project encompasses:

— Theoretical studies of natural mathematical language

— Selection of adequate background theories like logics, set theories and type theories

Arnold Beckmann, Benedikt Löwe (eds.). Acts of the programme "Semantics and Syntax". Isaac Newton Institute for the Mathematical Sciences, January to July 2012.

Talk given at the SAS Seminar, 16 February 2012, 17:00–17:30.

- Software for automatic parsing of a controlled natural mathematical language into a first-order representation

- Proof checking using strong automatic theorem proving

A midterm challenge is to devise strong formal systems and to formulate substantial natural language mathematical texts, which are fully formal in that system. As an example we are working on a reformulation of Edmund Landau's, *Foundations of Analysis*, 1930.

The implemented system consists of some input editor, natural language processing to generate proof representation structures, logical processing to translate these into first-order predicate logic, and available state-of-the-art automatic theorem provers as proof checkers.

For a nontrivial initial segment of Laudau we were able to carry out the required formalisation, and there is virtually no textual blowup between the German original and the formalisation in the accepted language of the Naproche system.

In order to obtain further naturalness, the system will be enriched by several features:

- a weak but rich dependent type system

- a greater variety of proof schemes like "It suffices that ..."

- omission of redundant (obvious, trivial, recurrent) parts of texts

- optimization of the selection of premises given to the automatic theorem prover, using proximity, context, etc.

The omission of redundancy was demonstrated by a simple proof, in which a number of sentences were simply obvious.

We also discussed Wiedijk's idea of proof sketches, which look like direct translations of mathematical texts into the Mizar language but which are not complete Mizar texts.

IBM Watson from *Jeopardy!* to Healthcare. Could a Quiz-show Winning Computer Advise Your Doctor?

David Gondek, John Prager

IBM, Thomas J. Watson Research Center, Hawthorne NY, United States of America
E-mail: dgondek@us.ibm.com, jprager@us.ibm.com

David Gondek submitted the abstract for the lecture but was unable to come to Cambridge for personal reasons. John Prager was asked to take Gondek's place less that 24 hours before he had to leave from the East Coast to travel to Cambridge. We are very happy that he agreed to do so. A. Copestake, B. Löwe, G. Primiero

"Chronic kidney disease for $500 please!"

Although medical providers are unlikely to utter these words as they search for appropriate medical information and clinical guidelines to diagnose and manage patients, they may soon have an advanced computer system reading their notes and listening to their conversations with patients. Could IBM's automatic question-answering system Watson, which decisively bested the two greatest champions in the quiz show *Jeopardy!*, be reconfigured to gather evidence for professionals providing your health care? Could it answer questions about the latest medical knowledge, dig up hidden but crucial facts from your health record, and even help diagnose diseases that may have gone unrecognized? Challenges abound, from capturing the much deeper and subtler reasoning that medical reasoning demands, to identifying gaps of information in a patient's records, and ultimately to transform Watson from a system which competed against people on a quiz show to one which can interactively work with them to better care for your health.

Arnold Beckmann, Benedikt Löwe (*eds.*). *Acts of the programme "Semantics and Syntax".* Isaac Newton Institute for the Mathematical Sciences, January to July 2012.

Special PUAI evening lecture, 17 February 2012, 17:30–18:30.

Turing in Context
18 – 19 February 2012

Liesbeth De Mol[1], Benedikt Löwe[2,3], Ken Moody[4], Giuseppe Primiero[1]

[1]Universiteit Gent, Ghent, Belgium
[2]University of Amsterdam, Amsterdam, The Netherlands
[3]Universität Hamburg, Hamburg, Germany
[4]University of Cambridge, Cambridge, United Kingdom

E-mail: `Elizabeth.DeMol@UGent.be`, `b.loewe@uva.nl`, `km@cl.cam.ac.uk`, `Giuseppe.Primiero@UGent.be`

The event *Turing in Context* highlighted the many contributions of Alan Turing for a general academic audience, in particular for undergraduate and postgraduate students of all fields, and put these contributions in a historical context. The seven speakers consisted of Henk Barendregt (Radboud Universiteit Nijmegen), David Gondek (Thomas J. Watson Research Center, IBM), Jens Groth (University College London), Leslie Moran (Birkbeck College, University of London), Julian Richards (University of Buckingham), Raul Rojas (Freie Universität Berlin), and Angela Stevens (Westfälische Wilhelms-Universität Münster). They covered topics such as British war intelligence, discrimination laws, pattern formation in biological systems, artificial intelligence, as well as logic and foundations of computing.

The event Turing in Context was hosted by Turing's former college in Cambridge, King's College. It was sponsored by the King's College of our Lady and Saint Nicholas in Cambridge, the Isaac Newton Institute for the Mathematical Sciences, and the Society for the Study of Artificial Intelligence and Simulation of Behaviour (AISB).

Arnold Beckmann, Benedikt Löwe (*eds.*). *Acts of the programme "Semantics and Syntax".*
Isaac Newton Institute for the Mathematical Sciences, January to July 2012.

SAS Related Event "TiC@King's".

Zuse and Turing

Raul Rojas

Freie Universität Berlin, Berlin, Germany
E-mail: rojas@inf.fu-berlin.de

In my talk I will discuss Konrad Zuse's work and some interesting connections with Alan Turing's achievements. Konrad Zuse built several computers from 1936 to 1945, which he called "algebraic machines". He realized around 1941 that all of them could be reduced to a simpler one, the "logistic computer". He designed a high-level programming language based on predicate logic for this machine. It evolved into his "Plankalkül", the first high-level programming language, which remained unimplemented until we wrote an interpreter in 2000. Turing and Zuse were almost of the same age and started thinking about computing machines at about the same time. They both wrote the code or pseudocode for the first chess programs in the world. Zuse's work could appear, only superficially, as a series of disconected machines. What I intend to show is that they all fit in a general conception of computability.

Arnold Beckmann, Benedikt Löwe (eds.). Acts of the programme "Semantics and Syntax".
Isaac Newton Institute for the Mathematical Sciences, January to July 2012.

Talk given at the TiC@King's, 18 February 2012, 16:25–17:25.

The Laws Fascination with Homosexual Acts: Insights from the Wolfenden Review Archive

Leslie Moran

Birkbeck, University of London, London, United Kingdom

E-mail: L.Moran@bbk.ac.uk

Since the English reformation in the 16th century English law has inspired and fuelled a particular fascination with sexual relations between men. 20th century law reports offer a record of the intensity of this forensic scrutiny, mapping and generating the meaning of the minutiae of those relations. If for most the law operated as a distant but chilling threat, from time to time laws violence destroyed lives and provided a spectacle in the service of good order. Behind and operating through the law was an elaborate machine inciting speech about sexual relations between men. The archive of the Wolfenden review, that proposed the limited decriminalisation of certain homosexual acts in private, provides an incredible window into this forensic view of the world. In this paper I use that archive as a vehicle to examine how laws fascination with homosexual acts was operating at the time that Alan Turing experienced the violence of the law, to such devastating effect.

Arnold Beckmann, Benedikt Löwe (eds.). *Acts of the programme "Semantics and Syntax".*
Isaac Newton Institute for the Mathematical Sciences, January to July 2012.

Talk given at the TiC@King's, 18 February 2012, 17:40–18:40.

What Does Watson Understand? How Recent AI Activities Relate to Turing's Vision

John Prager

IBM, Thomas J. Watson Research Center, Hawthorne NY, United States of America
E-mail: jprager@us.ibm.com

In February of 2011, IBM's computer system called Watson participated in the US game show *Jeopardy!* on national television against two former champions—and won. *Jeopardy!* is a question-answering challenge, which despite including elements of speed and betting is at its core about finding answers to questions and having a good confidence estimate about those answers. Question-answering (QA) is a sub-field of Artificial Intelligence, and Watson is acknowledged to represent the current state-of-the-art. The Turing Test too employs a question-answering paradigm, and is often cast as the canonical test for intelligence or human-likeness in a machine. Thus it would seem appropriate to analyse Watson's performance for indications of intelligence, or the lack of it.

Watson is able to answer some obscure general-knowledge questions that average people have difficulty with, so in that very limited and technical sense is super-human. On the other hand it makes regular gaffes, usually in regard to questions about common sense or common human experience (of which it has none). In that sense, Watson is less intelligent than a child. For example, it would have no way to answer whether one can touch ones right elbow with ones right index finger—because this information is not provided explicitly in text or databases. We can extrapolate into the near future and expect more of the same: Watson, and/or other QA systems, will continue to improve in the depth and breadth of their knowledge of (or ability to extract from text) simple facts and relations, but will gain facility with common sense very much more slowly.

The inherent difficulty of QA for machines is not in the facts or the reasoning per se; to answer most general-knowledge questions does not require much in the way of formal logic, which can be easily built into software. The problem comes in the understanding of language. Language is inherently ambiguous, but even when it isn't its correct interpretation often requires much cultural understanding. That latter challenge is particularly difficult for machines to master, not only because of not experiencing the world as humans do, but because such social information is not written down or encoded in any easily accessible way, in contrast to a list of the plays of Shakespeare, for example.

Turing described his Test in terms of questions that involve problem-solving: mathematics and chess were problem areas that he and other early

Arnold Beckmann, Benedikt Löwe (*eds.*). *Acts of the programme "Semantics and Syntax".*
Isaac Newton Institute for the Mathematical Sciences, January to July 2012.

Talk given at the TiC@King's, 19 February 2012, 10:00–11:00.

computer pioneers spent much time on, but language processing was not on their radar. For obvious reasons, the field of computational linguistics did not exist prior to the electronic computer, so perhaps they may be forgiven for not giving much attention to the problem. That said, the Turing Test still stands as an excellent vehicle for testing intelligence, in the sense of being like a human. The only qualification is that discriminating questions might be rather more idiomatic and personal than originally thought.

From Mind to Turing to Mind

Henk Barendregt

Radboud University Nijmegen, Nijmegen, The Netherlands
E-mail: henk@cs.ru.nl

Using introspection as inspiration Turing came to a model of computability. In essence this is the model of the modern universal computer. Conversely Turing Machines form inspiration for a model of conscious cognition. The power of this model is that on the one hand it is simple and on the other hand it explains several phenomena known in cognitive neuropsychology.

Arnold Beckmann, Benedikt Löwe (eds.). Acts of the programme "Semantics and Syntax". Isaac Newton Institute for the Mathematical Sciences, January to July 2012.

Talk given at the TiC@King's, 19 February 2012, 11:15–12:15.

Pattern Formation and Turing Pattern in Developing Cell Systems

Angela Stevens

Westfälische Wilhelms-Universität Münster, Münster, Germany

E-mail: stevens@mis.mpg.de

With his seminal article on "The Chemical Basis of Morphogenesis" [1] Turing laid some of the foundations for the understanding of reaction-diffusion mechanisms and their connection to pattern formation in biology.

In this talk a short summary of his contribution and its mathematical and biological impact will be given, and further possible mechanisms for pattern formation in developmental cell systems will be discussed.

Bibliography

[1] A. M. Turing. The chemical basis of morphogenesis. *Philosophical Transactions of the Royal Society of London. Series B, Biological Sciences*, 237(641):37–72, 1952.

Arnold Beckmann, Benedikt Löwe (*eds.*). *Acts of the programme "Semantics and Syntax"*.
Isaac Newton Institute for the Mathematical Sciences, January to July 2012.

Talk given at the TiC@King's, 19 February 2012, 13:45–14:45.

Turing and Modern Cryptography

Jens Groth

University College London, London, United Kingdom

E-mail: j.groth@ucl.ac.uk

Turing played a crucial role in the British cryptanalytic efforts during the Second World War. We give an introduction to the workings of the Enigma machine that was one of the encryption devices used by Germany and discuss the role of Turing in breaking Enigma communication. However, due to his work being classified and not publicly available we argue Turing did not have much direct influence on modern day cryptographic practice.

The indirect influence of Turing on modern day cryptography is very significant though. In his famous 1937 paper "On computable numbers, with an application to the Entscheidungsproblem" Turing introduced a mathematical model of computation, which is now known as a Turing machine. Cryptographers today use Turing machines to model the capabilities of attackers and to reason about the security of cryptographic systems. We outline how a time-bounded Turing machine can be used to model the capabilities of an attacker and how it is used in mathematical security models.

Arnold Beckmann, Benedikt Löwe (eds.). Acts of the programme "Semantics and Syntax".
Isaac Newton Institute for the Mathematical Sciences, January to July 2012.

Talk given at the TiC@King's, 19 February 2012, 14:45–15:45.

The Contribution of Alan Turing to British Intelligence

Julian Richards

University of Buckingham, Buckingham, United Kingdom
E-mail: julian.richards@buckingham.ac.uk

If you were to select at random a rank-and-file member of the British intelligence services and ask them what contribution Alan Turing has made to their work today, the chances are that you would be met with a certain amount of vagueness. Of course, more than half a century after his untimely death, you would not expect Turing's name to be in the thoughts of everyone working in intelligence, but it is likely that his life of unfulfilled legacies and incomplete projects has had something to do with it, as did the rather shameful circumstances in which he fell from view in the early 1950s, not only from secret work but from this world altogether.

If Turing's general intellectual impact on the evolution of computing is now understood more clearly, albeit perhaps belatedly, his impact on the business of intelligence is—if I can phrase it this way—much more of an enigma. To try to address this question, it is necessary to briefly return to the huts at Bletchley Park during WW2 and consider the effect that the work of Turing and his colleagues had on the intelligence and war efforts.

As we know, Turing was fascinated by the question of solvable and unsolvable problems, and the challenges posed by Gödel's Theorem and Hilbert's *Entscheidungsproblem*, both dealing with the question as to whether mathematics can remain inherently consistent and solve every logical problem. As Turing himself concluded, "the fact of the matter is that there is no systematic method of testing puzzles to see whether they are solvable or not" [12, p. 1]. Faced with the problem of the German Enigma encryption during the war, the first question was whether the problem was solvable at all, and whether you could know if it was when you set out to try to build a system to solve it. Much of the work of Bletchley Park appears to have been conducted, initially at least, with no clue as to the likelihood of success. The pressure of war undoubtedly meant that the work had to go ahead anyway, but it is to the credit of Turing and his colleagues that they were not deterred and took on the challenge.

The upshot of Bletchley Park's efforts for the business of intelligence comprised a number of factors. From a military point of view, WW2 marked the ultimate marriage of technology with war, delivered to devastating effect in the shape of tanks, aircraft, rudimentary ballistic missiles and the atomic bomb. This was the industrialisation of war, and contributed heavily to WW2 being the most murderous conflict that human history has seen

Arnold Beckmann, Benedikt Löwe (*eds.*). *Acts of the programme "Semantics and Syntax".*
Isaac Newton Institute for the Mathematical Sciences, January to July 2012.

Talk given at the Turing in Context @ King's, 19 February 2012, 16:00–17:00.

before or since. At the same time, industrialisation and automation came
to define the intelligence realm. Interestingly, it had done so simultaneously
on both sides of the Channel, as Zuse constructed his elaborate mechanical
contraptions, and Turing and colleagues constructed machines to break the
Germans' communications.

The legacy clearly set the scene for the years that followed. The intelligence history of the Cold War, certainly as far as the West is concerned, is
characterised by the nature in which technical intelligence-gathering techniques (Techints) grew alongside general technological development in society to far outstrip the traditional human intelligence (Humint)-based techniques, although these continued as best they could. The Cold War became
the age of spy satellites and massive signals intelligence (Sigint) operations,
such that agencies like GCHQ in Britain and its much larger counterpart in
the US, the National Security Agency (NSA), became hubs for the largest
and most sophisticated computing complexes of any organisation in the
world. Rathmell notes how, over the slow decades of the Cold War, these
agencies became akin to an "intelligence factory", organised on the principles of "Fordist modes of production" to churn out a relentless flow of intelligence data on military dispositions and capabilities [10, p. 87]. In some
sections of the public, anxieties grew over the supposedly near-universal capabilities of such systems as the Echelon' satellite interception programme,
emerging in the 1970s, which critics described as a system for "indiscriminately intercepting" communications to such a level that it provided "the
US and its allies with the ability to intercept a large proportion of the
communications on the planet" [7].

The seeds of the Cold War had been sown in Bletchley Park in other
ways. We now know that, despite being allies during the war, Britain retained a healthy dose of scepticism about the intentions of its communist
friends towards the East. Aldrich asserts that, contrary to Churchill's claim
that work against Soviet traffic halted in 1941 on the advent of Russia finding itself on the side of the western Allies against Germany, Sigint work
against the Soviet target continued throughout the war [1, p.30].

Of course, we are in Cambridge today to celebrate the life and work
of Alan Turing, who walked these corridors many years ago. But another
group of people were also here at the same time, and their story is just as
central to the development of Cold War intelligence. The Cambridge Spies,
as they came to be known, comprised a group of at least five Cambridge
students[1] who were all recruited to spy for the Soviet Union through their

---

[1]The group is sometimes referred to as the Cambridge "ring of five", following a belief
held by many and encouraged by a Russian defector, Golitsyn, that groups of five are
significant in Russian and KGB lore and that the Cambridge group was a very specific
ring of spies. There has been some uncertainty as to the veracity of this claim, however,

sympathies for communism, and through the work of their KGB controller, Arnold Deutsch. Through this and other channels, it seems likely that the Soviets developed a fairly good idea of British techniques and activities on Sigint and decryption very early in the Cold War. The Cambridge historian Christopher Andrew notes the curious situation in which Stalin probably received more comprehensive monthly British intelligence assessments towards the end of the war than did Churchill, through the former's conduit to a key member of the Cambridge spies, Anthony Blunt. The latter prepared the monthly intelligence reports for Churchill in collaboration with Dick White, who would later become the head of MI5 and, subsequently, MI6 [3, pp. 289–290].

Another possibly key character amongst the Cambridge spies was John Cairncross, who worked at Bletchley Park between 1942 and 1943 when Turing was also there, and later dubbed himself "the Enigma Spy" [9, p. 254],[2] although Christopher Andrew describes his subsequent memoirs as "highly unreliable" [2, p. 327, fn. 17]. Whatever the truth, by the end of the war, we can be certain that the Soviets not only knew they were a key target for their erstwhile allies, but also knew a great deal about the West's Sigint capabilities. This, in turn, probably meant that the Soviet target, from a Sigint point of view, became an extremely secure system that was very difficult to penetrate.

Alan Turing was consulted by GCHQ in the first years after WW2, and that this was hardly surprising given his pivotal (if secret) role in the fields of computing and cryptanalysis at the time [8, p. 409]. Hodges also notes elsewhere that we do not know the precise nature of the work he was undertaking with GCHQ at this time. It is entirely reasonable to assume in general terms, however, that his expertise was sought in the areas of how to build a computer capable enough to industrialise the Sigint attack against the Soviet Union, and whether such technology could be successfully deployed against the mathematical problem of Soviet encryption. This challenge would have seemed every bit as unsolvable as did the Enigma challenge in the early part of WW2, and took on a similarly existential urgency when the Soviets detonated a nuclear bomb in 1949 (having obtained the technological know-how through spies working on the Manhattan Project in the US).

Turing's interest in whether machines could eventually think like humans drew him into an emerging field of enquiry called cybernetics, a term brought to academic attention with the publishing of a book by the same

---

and this has led to endless speculation about who else in the British hierarchy may have spied for the Soviet Union.

[2] There has been no suggestion from any quarter that Turing ever met any of the Cambridge spies, or that he ever came under suspicion of espionage.

name by an American mathematician, Norbert Wiener, in 1948 [8, p. 403].
In an interview for a newspaper in 1949, he observed:

> We have to have some experience with the machine [the Manchester
> computer] before we really know its capabilities. It may take years
> before we settle down to the new possibilities, but I do not see why it
> should not enter any one of the fields normally covered by the human
> intellect, and eventually compete on equal terms.[3]

We know that, at the same time in his life, he was also very interested in
certain patterns and processes he observed in the natural world, such as the
Fibonacci sequence of numbers. It is intriguing to ponder the meaning and
promise of one of the many half-finished and incomprehensible sets of plans
and computer programmes that were found in his house, called 'Fircones'
[8, p. 494].

Half a century later and long after Turing's death, developments in
robotics and the promise of previously unimagined advances in automation and biotechnology are indeed starting to realise Turing's predictions.
He was perhaps wrong, however, in his estimation that these would not be
controversial and that society would have adjusted in the intervening time
to receive such developments with a shrug of the shoulders.

On the question of the industrialisation of intelligence capability and
its moves into the realm of "thinking machines", there has clearly been a
mounting degree of public anxiety. In May 2009, GCHQ reflected public
sentiment by taking the unprecedented step of issuing a press release in
which it dened that it was planning to comprehensively monitor everyone's
communications.[4] The step was taken in the aftermath of a number of media headlines that had accused GCHQ of becoming a "Big Brother" and
the vanguard of a "police state". In its statement, GCHQ stressed both
the "necessity and proportionality" of all its operations—words relating to
the Human Rights Act provisions around invasions of privacy and the fact
that all of its activities are "meticulously" in accordance with ministerial
approval. "GCHQ does not target anyone indiscriminately", said the statement, and "does not spy at will".[5]

That GCHQ, an agency that very rarely comments on any operational
or technical matters publicly (and, indeed, was only placed formally on the
statute books in 1994) should choose to issue such an emphatic statement
about the justification for its activities and the scrupulously legal nature
of them, betrays a greatly heightened awareness of the moral and ethical
complexity surrounding the industrialisation of intelligence activities, and
the public's anxiety in these areas.

---

[3] Cited from [8, p. 406].

[4] "Government not planning to monitor all web use" (Daily Telegraph, 4 May 2009).

[5] From a 2009 GCHQ press release, accessed on the GCHQ website on 15 August 2009.

Meanwhile, in the area of technological advances in automation, the debates about unmanned aerial vehicles (UAVs) and their military and intelligence applications are already generating a great deal of disquiet in some quarters. Analysts such as Gregory bemoan the latest developments in the Revolution in Military Affairs (RMA), which allow for push-button warfare conducted with remotely controlled UAVs, reducing the "kill chain" from target identification to destruction, to under two minutes [6, p. 173]. Modern conflict in difficult and unfamiliar territory becomes, in Gregory's characterisation, little more than a "simulacrum of a video game" [6, p. 176].

Warfare that is easier to conduct, apparently causes significantly fewer casualties, and which alienates the perpetrator from the victims on the ground (video games, after all, are not real) may be more likely to happen than previous circumstances in which it was generally a riskier proposition. Despite the assurances from the users of such technology that it is "virtuous" in the sense that it greatly improves the precision of targeting and reduces collateral casualties, the technology is not seen that way in the countries on the receiving end. In Pakistan in particular, the use of unmanned drones for finding and eliminating high-value terrorist targets is seen as a gross transgression of sovereignty by a hegemonic power, to say nothing of the civilian casualties thought to number in the hundreds who have been amongst the dead. Potential further automation poses yet harder questions: what if UAVs are developed which could make automatic decisions about whether to fire a missile at a target based on intelligence that they have themselves collected? In some ways this would be a logical next step, but, as we have seen today in John Prager's presentation about IBM's 'Watson' computer, thinking machines can sometimes make bizarre mistakes. The growth of technological and information superiority that has underpinned the contemporary RMA has, so far, been a fundamentally asymmetric phenomenon. This is so in the sense that the best and most sophisticated intelligence and war-fighting capabilities have largely been the preserve of the US and her NATO allies, while insurgent and rogue-state foes have had to continue relying on largely Cold War or older technology. This may lead to a number of undesirable outcomes. These include decisions by those on the wrong side of the asymmetric equation to seek greater mass-casualty methods for striking back, to use terrorism and unconventional methods of attack, and to take the fight to civilians as the soldiers melt away from the battlefield to be replaced by robots and remotely-controlled devices [11, pp. 20–21]. Complaints from western militaries that their insurgent foes use "cowardly" tactics generally fall on deaf ears. Additionally, both states and non-state actors standing in opposition to the West, such as Iran and perhaps China to name but two, will increasingly seek to obtain and co-opt such technology themselves in order to balance the scales of power. The new global arms race in the twenty-first century is as much about UAVs and related technologies than about old-fashioned nuclear and ballistic missile capabilities. In the not too distant future, dominance by the most powerful actors in these areas may start to slip away as technology-transfer gathers pace.

The growth of cutting-edge new technologies in defence and intelligence spheres, such as bio- and nanotechnology, will surely encompass the same issues. As far as Turing is concerned, he could not really be held responsible for initiating the contemporary RMA and the ethical dilemmas it is increasingly posing. All he did was to foresee that such developments would be inevitable, and that those who doubted the technological likelihood of thinking machines' would probably be proved wrong.

Aside from technological legacies, Turing and his cohorts in Bletchley Park delivered a number of very significant cultural legacies to the British intelligence sector. One of the most significant, if not the most significant factor in post-war Western intelligence has been the unshakeable relationship between the US and its primary allies, and particularly the "special relationship" with the UK. As an NSA statement described it: "The bonds, forged in the heat of a world war and tempered by decades of trust and teamwork, remain essential to future intelligence successes".[6]

Again, it would be inappropriate to suggest that Turing was personally responsible for forging this relationship—the size of threat from a common Soviet enemy was much more significant—but the degree to which he recognised that mathematics is borderless was a very significant cultural legacy. In his life and work, Turing showed that he accorded with the sentiments of the great German mathematician, David Hilbert, who had said that "for mathematics, the whole cultural world is a single country".[7] It would not be unreasonable to suggest that the bedrock of the 'UKUSA' relationship, as it came to be known, is built very firmly on a notion of borderless cryptanalysis.

Even today, there is a cultural difference between intelligence agencies on both sides of the Atlantic, whereby the Humint agencies (MI5, MI6 and CIA) are very close and cordial, but do not match the unspoken and unchallenged collegiality that exists between GCHQ and NSA in the Sigint and cryptanalysis realms. In these agencies, the default position is to share just about everything.

Aside from working practices in which an unprecedented level of intelligence-sharing between the UK and the US was forged, Bletchley Park was also somewhat revolutionary in its working culture, and Turing was very

---

[6]NSA, UKUSA Agreement Release 1940–56.
[7]Cited from [8, p. 60].

much at the forefront of this change. Hodges notes that the military command of the intelligence services into whom the rapidly expanding Government Codes and Cipher School (GCCS) at Bletchley was plugged, was poorly equipped both physically, in terms of resources and personnel, and culturally in terms of an avowedly hierarchical structure which stifled creativity and flexibility. Almost by chance, since the academics were mostly not good administrators to say the least, Bletchley beat a new path through the forest [8, p. 203]. Turing, who to some extent was shielded from the labyrinth of government bureaucracy and hierarchy within his microcosmic Hut 8 environment, was reputedly the most disrespecting of hierarchy, not necessarily for any political reasons but because he was fundamentally a logician. It made no logical sense to him for somebody in the hierarchy to have power over someone else, unless that person was a superior intellect.[8]

A healthy disregard, if not contempt for traditional British hierarchy and pomposity may well have been forged through unhappy years in a British public school, and a subsequent experience of Cambridge in the 1930s, which was itself a small haven for liberal and anti-establishment ideas. (Indeed, it was here that the Cambridge spies grew out of an intellectual tolerance of communism to become Soviet spies.) As a homosexual living at a time when this was a criminal offence, Turing was already someone who had never quite fitted into the British standard order of things, and this undoubtedly fed his worldview. Once at Bletchley Park, this propensity for lateral thinking against the tide of tradition could deliver very positive effects. A striking example of this was Turing's decision to write a letter directly to Winston Churchill at the height of the code-breaking war to complain of a woeful lack of resources at Bletchley and the need to substantially increase the staffing. (The letter was co-signed by his colleagues Welchman, Alexander and Milner-Barry.) Such a letter would normally have needed to grind its way up through the government and military bureaucracy, but Turing was able to scythe through such procedures. Churchill, to his credit, took immediate note of the request and famously demanded "action this day".

At the same time, Turing was the complete antithesis of politically astute, and was never interested in or inclined to consider how best to interact with the hierarchy to achieve the best results. To many, he was also a rampant eccentric. Stories abound of odd behaviour, such as cycling through the streets in a gas mask to combat his hay fever, or arriving at a game of tennis dressed only in a raincoat. This set a cultural legacy that exists today, mainly in the Sigint agencies where the cryptanalysts reside, of a healthy respect for the wildest eccentricities of the mathematicians. To this day, visitors from the more cosmopolitan London-based intelligence agencies to GCHQ in Cheltenham will chuckle at the sight of long-haired and eccentrically-dressed mathematicians, playing complex card games or chess

---

[8]Cited from [8, p. 204].

in the corner, and largely left to their own devices by the other staff.

On a more serious note, it is the case that post-war intelligence in the UK and the US has recognised that mathematical geniuses must remain a protected and specially nurtured species. A fiercely merit-based notion of organisation is something that the Sigint agencies have attempted to adopt subsequently, and, as a result, are generally less hierarchical and formal than some of the other agencies. (NSA has a slightly different culture from GCHQ in that a large proportion of its staff are serving military officers, while GCHQ is an avowedly civilian organisation where military uniforms are very rarely seen.) There are also mechanisms in place for mathematicians and technologists to have separate, parallel career structures to other staff, within which they can reach higher levels of management and be paid more than their more "generalist" colleagues. It has to be said that the advent of New Public Management (NPM) philosophy, of which Sir David Omand was a strong advocate during his tenure as Director of GCHQ in 1996–1997 and which has seeped into all corners of government, may pose new challenges to such a culture. In the GCHQ of today (or indeed any government office), the need to undertake a fair amount of form-filling and administration alongside core work in order to maintain performance measures, would be an environment that Turing would have hated with a passion, and in which he would not have flourished.

These risks aside, if mathematicians became key intelligence players in the Cold War, today's rising stars are computer hackers and people who know their way around the internet and complex computer programmes with ease and confidence. Recruitment to the intelligence business today does not result from a tap on the shoulder and a strange conversation in a Cambridge college, but may be just as likely to come from a sequence within a video-game where GCHQ can advertise its wares.[9] In many ways, perhaps, the internet is the new Enigma' for British intelligence.

The long march of technology in defence and intelligence is starting to deliver what many are seeing as a complex and not entirely uncontroversial legacy. Following the strategic shock of the 9/11 attacks, some have accused Western intelligence of an unhealthy "infatuation with technology" that came to overshadow investment in traditional Humint [4]. While Western intelligence became star-struck with technologies such as spy satellites and massive computers, the mutating terrorist threat was able to turn the tables by adopting a different approach, and a new way of thinking in which massively complex problems of encryption did not feature at all.

Such issues of correctly prioritising intelligence responses to the rapidly changing post-war threats have been the subject of very extensive analysis

---

[9]GCHQ has recently arranged for the insertion of recruitment advertising bill-boards within the scenery of some popular video-games, and is thus clearly targeting a very specific section of the population with very specific skills.

in Intelligence Studies. There is no indication that Turing would necessarily have seen that anything had been done wrong here, however, just that these were new types of essentially logical problems that needed new mathematical and scientific thinking. Thus, while the Cold War target was "big and noisy", in Berkowitz's words, and was susceptible to the long development of industrialised intelligence responses, the fact that today's targets have "small signatures" and are more dynamic merely means that a different methodology and mindset are needed [5, pp. 291–292]. Turing would probably have taken to these challenges as willingly as he took to the challenge of Enigma, and would have seen that the use of computers and mathematical logic in creative new ways was just as apt today as it was then.

Bibliography

[1] R. J. Aldrich. *GCHQ: The uncensored story of Britain's most secret intelligence agency.* Harper Press, London, 2010.

[2] C. Andrew. Intelligence and international relations in the early cold war. *Review of International Studies*, 24:321–330, 1998.

[3] C. Andrew. *The Defence of the Realm: The Authorized History of MI5.* Penguin, London, 2010.

[4] C. Beal. Chronic underfunding of us humint plays role in intelligence failures, 2001.

[5] B. Berkowitz. Intelligence and the war on terrorism. *Orbis*, 46(2), 2002.

[6] D. Gregory. War and peace. *Transactions of the Institute of British Geographers*, 35(2):154–186, 2010.

[7] N. Hager. Exposing the global surveillance system. *Covert Action Quarterly*, 59:3–5, 1997.

[8] A. Hodges. *Alan Turing, the enigma.* Vintage, London, 1983.

[9] Z. J. Kapera. Summary report of the state of the soviet military sigint in november 1942 noticing 'enigma'. *Cryptologia*, 35(3):247–256, 2011.

[10] A. Rathmell. Towards postmodern intelligence. *Intelligence and National Security*, 17(3):87–104, 2002.

[11] N. Schörnig. Robot warriors: why the Western investment into military robots might backfire, 2010. PRIF Report No. 100.

[12] A. Turing. Solvable and unsolvable problems. *Science News*, 31:7–23, 1954.

Computability and Probabilistic Symmetries

Cameron Freer

Massachusetts Institute of Technology, Cambridge MA, United States of America
E-mail: freer@math.mit.edu

Probabilistic symmetries, especially aspects of exchangeability, give rise to representational results in probability theory for which computational questions are of particular interest. We will present two aspects of this theory, each with related open questions in computability and complexity theory.

De Finetti's theorem on exchangeability (1931, 1937) states that the distribution of a sequence of real random variables that is invariant to permutations of the coordinates (i.e., the sequence is exchangeable) can be written uniquely as a mixture of product measures. This representation makes conditional independence explicit, and is useful in applications within nonparametric Bayesian statistics and machine learning. We will describe a computable extension of de Finetti's theorem by Freer and Roy, which states that for a computable such distribution, the mixing measure is computable (uniformly in the original distribution). We will discuss complexity-theoretic aspects of this result, and state some open questions in the complexity theory of exchangeable sequences.

Aldous (1981) and Hoover (1979) generalized de Finetti's theorem to higher-dimensional arrays of random variables that are exchangeable in a suitable sense. In recent years, these results have been viewed through the theory of graph limits due to Lovász and Szegedy (2006) and others. We will describe several questions about computability corresponding to these representational results.

Arnold Beckmann, Benedikt Löwe (eds.). Acts of the programme "Semantics and Syntax".
Isaac Newton Institute for the Mathematical Sciences, January to July 2012.

Talk given at the SAS Seminar, 21 February 2012, 16:00–16:30.

Big Open Problems: A Discussion Session

The special research-oriented setting of the Isaac Newton Institute brings a large number of researchers together and places them in an environment conducive to joint research: no teaching or administrative duties, lots of blackboards and free coffee. This is the ideal environment to tackle some of the big problems of our field: problems that we normally don't dare to attack since we feel that we cannot commit enough research time for them. The Isaac Newton Institute is proud to report that programmes in the past have achieved such breakthroughs: the development of new techniques that shape the field, the solution to old and vexing problems, the start of new research programmes.

Aiming to continue this tradition, the organizers of "Semantics & Syntax" planned problem sessions during the SAS Seminar series. In these sessions, problems were collected whose solution would constitute a breakthrough in the above sense—in particular for problems that seem to be prone to be solvable in the special INI setting (taking into account the Semantics/Syntax divide and who is around as a Visiting Fellow).

1   Global Properties of Turing Equivalence and the Turing Degrees

The first set of open problems was presented by Theodore A. Slaman who would like to see the following problems resolved.

Definition 1. A Turing degree is the equivalence class of a subset of ω under equi-computability. The Turing degrees are ordered by relative computability.

One can vary the sets being considered, as when considering the Turing degrees of the recursively enumerable sets, or vary the notion of relative definability, as when considering the spectrum from many-one degrees, truth-table, Turing, enumeration, arithmetic, hyperarithmetic, constructible, and so forth.

A fundamental question, first raised by Sacks, is to characterize those operations on real numbers which are invariant under equi-definability, such as the Turing jump $X \mapsto X'$ or the function mapping X to the set of reals which are arithmetically definable from X. Sacks posed the following concrete question about a degree invariant solution to Post's Problem.

Arnold Beckmann, Benedikt Löwe (*eds.*). *Acts of the programme "Semantics and Syntax".* Isaac Newton Institute for the Mathematical Sciences, January to July 2012.

Talk given at the SAS Seminar, 21 February 2012, 16:30–17:30.

Question 2 (Sacks). *Is there an e such that the function $X \mapsto W_e^X$ satisfies the following conditions?*

1. *For all X, $X <_T W_e^X <_T X'$.*

2. *For all X and Y, if $X \equiv_T Y$ then $W_e^X \equiv_T W_e^Y$.*

More generally, excluding applications of the Axiom of Choice, all the known non-trivial examples come from notions of relative definability. Namely, there are the degree invariant functions from reals to reals that come from universal sets. Similarly, there are degree invariant functions from reals X to sets of reals containing X come from closures under relative definability.

Martin has conjectured that there are no other degree invariant functions, in the following sense.

Definition 3. A *cone of reals* is a set $\{X : X \geq_T B\}$, for some base B. A property P on the Turing degrees, D, *contains a cone* iff there is a cone of reals all of whose degrees satisfy P.

Theorem 4 (Martin, assuming the Axiom of Determinacy). *Suppose a set $A \subseteq 2^\omega$ is closed under $\equiv_T$. Then one of A or $2^\omega \setminus A$ contains a cone.*

Under AD, the cone filter is a $\{0, 1\}$-valued measure. Martin's conjecture is phrased in that context. For degree-invariant functions, we define order preserving on a cone, constant on a cone, and other notions, similarly. We define $F \geq_M G$ iff $F(X) \geq_T G(X)$ on a cone.

Conjecture 5 (Martin). *Assume ZF + AD + DC.*
   I. *If F is degree invariant and not increasing on a cone, then F is constant on a cone.*
   II. *The relation $\leq_M$ is a prewellordering of the set of degree invariant functions which are increasing on a cone. Further, if f has $\leq_M$-rank α, then f' has $\leq_M$-rank $\alpha + 1$, where $f' : x \mapsto f(x)'$ for all x.*

Martin's Conjecture is a particular realization of the view that all notions of relative definability extending relative computability appear in the logical hierarchy based on first order quantification over the finite sets. It is a recursion theoretic account of the apparent well-ordering among natural consistency strengths and among inner models of set theory.

One can also raise these issues for other notions of relative definability. For example, it is known that Martin's Conjecture fails if Turing equivalence is replaced by arithmetic equivalence $\equiv_A$. However, Sacks's question is open in that context.

Question 6. *Is there a Borel function F such that the following conditions hold?*
   1. For all X, $X <_A F(X) <_A X^\omega$.
   2. For all X and Y, if $X \equiv_A Y$ then $F(X) \equiv_A F(Y)$.

2   Natural Paths through Kleene's $\mathcal{O}$

The following open problem had been presented by Stan Wainer:

> Is there a "natural" path of ordinal notations going all the way through Kleene's constructive ordinals ?

Note 1. The question is admittedly vague, but Gödel himself apparently felt this to be a central problem.

Note 2. We seem able to distinguish natural ordinal notations from unnatural ones. The natural ones are constructed out of natural versions of ω such as $\omega = \sup_i(i)$ or $\omega = \sup_i(1 + i)$. An unnatural version would be $\omega = \sup_i g(i)$ where g is some wildly growing recursive function.

Note 3. Proof-theoretic ordinal notation systems are accepted as natural, though they may (and do) use strong diagonalization methods indexed by higher cardinal analogues from set theory. (Measuring consistency strength in one form or another).

Note 4. But these are small compared with ω_1^{CK}. Their corresponding subrecursive hierarchies of provably recursive functions appear very uniformly structured and quite different from the class of all recursive functions.

Note 5. Paths through Kleene's $\mathcal{O}$ do exist of course (cf., e.g., [1] for a variety of results on such things), but if their corresponding subrecursive hierarchies are Σ_1^1-definable then "boundedness" says that such paths cannot be inductively generated (i.e., Π_1^1).

Note 6. So what could "natural" mean? or (as Montalban asked) how would we ever decide that there isn't such a path. Perhaps **Note 5** already gives strong enough indication. Nevertheless, classifying the recursive functions is still an important issue.

3   Dependent Type Theories

This set of open problem had been presented by Peter Aczel. These problems concerning the logical strength of some dependent type theories are open, as far as the presenter is aware.

In § 3.1, the problems will be stated in a rather informal way and then two more precise versions concerning specific type theories are given. A selection of type theories will be described in §§ 3.2-3.6 and their rules will be presented in more detail in § 3.7.

3.1 The Problems

Q1: Is the type theory implemented in the Coq proof assistant logically weaker or stronger than ZF?

Q2: Does the addition of Voevodsky's Univalence Axiom and possibly other rules such as rules for higher dimenensional inductive definitions, to a standard dependent type theory increase the logical strength of the type theory?

We now state more precise versions of the problems using specific type theories which will be described in the rest of this note.

Q1′: Is MLWPSU$_{<\omega}$ logically weaker or stronger than ZF ?

Q2′: Is MLWU logically weaker than MLWU + $\mathbf{UA}(\mathbb{U})$, where $\mathbf{UA}(\mathbb{U})$ is Voevodsky's Univalence Axiom for the type universe $\mathbb{U}$.

In the rest of this note we first give an outline description of a selection of type theories obtained from a base type theory ML by adding a variety of additional forms of type. In our description we assume that the reader has some familiarity with the various forms of type in the literature. A more detailed presentation of the rules of the type theories has been placed in the appendix.

3.2 The Standard Forms of Judgement of a Dependent Type Theory

A type theory will be a system of rules for deriving judgements, each having the form

$$\Gamma \vdash \mathcal{B}$$

where Γ is its **context**

$$x_1 : A_1, \ldots, x_n : A_n$$

of $n \geq 0$ **variable declarations** $x_i : A_i$, for $i = 1, \ldots, n$, of distinct variables $x_1, \ldots, x_n$ and $\mathcal{B}$ is its **body**, which has one of the forms

$$A \text{ type} \quad A_1 = A_2 \quad a : A \quad a_1 = a_2 : A.$$

The body A type expresses that A is a type, $A_1 = A_2$ expresses that A_1, A_2 are judgementally equal types, $a : A$ expresses that a is a term of type A and $a_1 = a_2 : A$ expresses that a_1, a_2 are judgementally equal terms of type A.

When Γ is the empty context we will usually just write $\mathcal{B}$ rather than $\vdash \mathcal{B}$. Each rule will have instances, each of the form

$$\frac{J_1 \cdots J_m}{J}$$

where the $J_1, \ldots, J_m, J$ are forms of judgement. The $J_1, \ldots, J_m$ above the line are the **premisses** of the rule instance and J is its **conclusion**. The rules will be presented schematically, using conventions that we hope will mostly be obvious. Usually, a rule will allow a parametric list of variable declarations to appear in the premisses and conclusion of a rule. In presenting the rule the parametric list will be left implicit. For example a rule for forming function types $A \to B$ will be presented

$$\frac{A \text{ type} \quad B \text{ type}}{(A \to B) \text{ type}}$$

and will have instances

$$\frac{\Gamma \vdash A \text{ type} \quad \Gamma \vdash B \text{ type}}{\Gamma \vdash (A \to B) \text{ type}}.$$

where Γ can be any context.

A type theory will be presented by listing its rules, and the theorems of the type theory will form the smallest collection of judgements with the property that whenever the premisses of an instance of a rule are in the collection then so is the conclusion. We will first specify each theory by only presenting the rules that are relevent to the formation of the types of the type theory. A more detailed presentation of all the rules may be found in the appendix.

3.3 The Type Theories ML, ML⁻ and MLW

We start with the formation rules for the basic type theory ML. The theory ML⁻ is obtained from ML by leaving out the rules for the type N of natural numbers

<table>
<tr><td colspan="3" align="center">**Type Formation Rules for ML**</td></tr>
<tr>
<td>$\dfrac{}{N_n \text{ type}}$

for $n = 0, 1, \ldots$</td>
<td>$\dfrac{A \text{ type} \quad x : A \vdash B[x] \text{ type}}{(\Pi x : A)B[x] \text{ type}}$</td>
<td>$\dfrac{A \text{ type} \quad a_1, a_2 : A}{\text{Id}_A(a_1, a_2) \text{ type}}$</td>
</tr>
<tr>
<td>$\dfrac{}{N \text{ type}}$</td>
<td>$\dfrac{A \text{ type} \quad x : A \vdash B[x] \text{ type}}{(\Sigma x : A)B[x] \text{ type}}$</td>
<td>$\dfrac{A_1 \text{ type} \quad A_2 \text{ type}}{A_1 + A_2 \text{ type}}$</td>
</tr>
</table>

There are many more rules needed for the type theory. A complete set of rules is in the appendix. Here we offer the following remarks that may help reader's intuition. The type N_n is the n-element type having the n canonical elements $1_n, \ldots, n_n$ and N is the type of natural numbers, having the canonical elements 0 and $s(e)$ for $e : N$. The type $\mathrm{Id}_A(a_1, a_2)$ is the identity type. When $a_1 = a_2 = a : A$ then it has the canonical element $r_A(a)$. The Π and Σ types have, as special cases $A \to B = (\Pi- : A)B$ and $A \times B = (\Sigma- : A)B$, where $-$ indicates a variable that does not occur free in B. The type $(\Pi x : A)B[x]$ has canonical elements $(\lambda x : A)b[x]$ where $b[x] : B[x]$ for $x : A$ and $(\Sigma x : A)B[x]$ has the canonical elements $\mathsf{pair}(a, b)$ where $a : A$ and $b : B[a]$. Finally the sum type $A_1 + A_2$ has canonical elements $\mathsf{in}_1(a)$ for $a : A_1$ and $\mathsf{in}_2(a)$ for $a : A_2$.

We obtain the type theory MLW by adding the following rule.

$$\frac{A \text{ type} \quad x : A \vdash B[x] \text{ type}}{(Wx : A)B[x] \text{ type}}$$

This type $W = (Wx : A)B[x]$ is the inductive type whose canonical elements have the form $\mathsf{sup}\,(y : B[a])c[y]$ where $a : A$ and $c[y] : W$ for $y : B[a]$. Here it should be noted that free occurences of y in $c[y]$ become bound in the term $\mathsf{sup}\,(y : B[a])c[y]$.

3.4 Adding a Type Universe and an Impredicative Type of Propositions

Another possibility is to add a type universe to ML that reflects the forms of type of ML. Here, by a type universe we shall mean a type $\mathbb{U}$ whose elements are themselves types. So we add the following rules.

$$\frac{}{\mathbb{U} \text{ type}} \qquad \frac{A : \mathbb{U}}{A \text{ type}}$$

That $\mathbb{U}$ reflects the forms of type of ML is obtained by also adding the following rules.

$\mathbb{U}$ Term Formation Rules for ML$\mathbb{U}$		
$\dfrac{}{N_n : \mathbb{U}}\ (n = 0, 1, \ldots)$	$\dfrac{}{N : \mathbb{U}}$	$\dfrac{A : \mathbb{U} \quad a_1, a_2 : A}{\mathrm{Id}_A(a_1, a_2) : \mathbb{U}}$
$\dfrac{A : \mathbb{U} \quad x : A \vdash B[x] : \mathbb{U}}{(\Pi x : A)B[x] : \mathbb{U}}$	$\dfrac{A : \mathbb{U} \quad x : A \vdash B[x] : \mathbb{U}}{(\Sigma x : A)B[x] : \mathbb{U}}$	$\dfrac{A_1, A_2 : \mathbb{U}}{A_1 + A_2 : \mathbb{U}}$

By adding these rules to ML we obtain the type theory MLU. We obtain MLWU by adding to MLW the above rules together with the obvious rule to reflect the formation rule for W-types.

So far our type theories are generalised predicative and are well below the logical strength of full second order arithmetic. We get a fully impredicative type theory, MLℙ, by adding a calculus of constructions type universe ℙ having the following rules.

$$\frac{}{\mathbb{P} \text{ type}} \qquad \frac{A : \mathbb{P}}{A \text{ type}} \qquad \frac{A \text{ type} \quad x : A \vdash B[x] : \mathbb{P}}{(\Pi x : A)B[x] : \mathbb{P}}$$

The first two rules just express that ℙ is a type universe. The impredicativity comes in the third rule which allows the formation of the type $(\Pi x : A)B[x] : \mathbb{P}$ even though the type A might be ℙ itself or might be a type, such as $(N \to \mathbb{P}) \to \mathbb{P}$, that has been formed using ℙ.

We obtain the type theory MLℙU by combining the rules of MLℙ with those of MLU and adding the following reflection rules.

$$\frac{}{\mathbb{P} : \mathbb{U}} \qquad \frac{A : \mathbb{P}}{A : \mathbb{U}}$$

3.5 Adding a Hierarchy of Type Universes

Instead of adding just one type universe we can add an infinite increasing cumulative hierarchy of type universes $\mathbb{U}_1, \mathbb{U}_2, \ldots$, each reflecting the previous universes. So each $\mathbb{U}_n$ has all the rules we have given to U and in addition the rules

$$\frac{}{\mathbb{U}_n : \mathbb{U}_{n+1}} \qquad \frac{A : \mathbb{U}_n}{A : \mathbb{U}_{n+1}} \qquad (n = 1, 2, \ldots)$$

In this way we obtain the type theories $\text{MLU}_{<\omega}$ and $\text{MLWU}_{<\omega}$.

3.6 An Approximation to the Coq Type Theory

We now turn to a type theory close to the type theory implemented in the proof assistant Coq. This type theory is thoroughly impredicative. It is obtained from MLWℙ by adding a type universe $\mathbb{S}$ that also reflects MLW, and has the rule

$$\frac{A : \mathbb{P}}{A : \mathbb{S}}$$

but not the rule $\dfrac{}{\mathbb{P} : \mathbb{S}}$. and then adding a hierarchy of type universes $\mathbb{U}_0, \mathbb{U}_1, \ldots$ that reflects MLWPℙ𝕊, the resulting type theory being $\text{MLWℙ𝕊U}_{<\omega}$. In Coq the types ℙ and 𝕊 are called *Prop* and *Set* respectively.

3.7 Appendix

In this appendix we try to give a reasonably complete and accurate presentation of rules for the type theory MLW. Missing are the congruence rules for the constructors as they are very numerous and are determined according to a specific algorithm applied to the explicitly or implicitly given formation rule for each constructor. In fact the congruence rules for the constructors that do not bind any variables can be derived from the Subsitution rule below. Rather than try to precisely state the procedure for the constructors that bind variables we will illustrate it by giving the congruence rules for the constructors Σ and split. To understand the general pattern it should be noted that the expression $(\Sigma x : A)B[x]$ should be thought of as prefered notation for $\Sigma(A, (x)B[x])$ where it is indicated that free occurences of x in $B[x]$ become bound in $(\Sigma x : A)B[x]$. The formation rule for this type is

$$\frac{A \text{ type} \quad x : A \vdash B[x] \text{ type}}{(\Sigma x : A)B[x] \text{ type}}.$$

So its congruence rule is

$$\frac{A_1 = A_2 \quad x : A_1 \vdash B_1[x] = B_2[x]}{(\Sigma x : A_1)B_1[x] = (\Sigma x : A_2)B_2[x]}.$$

The formation rule for split is

$$\frac{\left\{\begin{array}{l} z : (\Sigma x : A)B[x] \vdash C[z] \text{ type} \\ x : A, y : B[x] \vdash c[x, y] : C[\text{pair}(x, y)] \end{array}\right.}{\left\{\begin{array}{l} z : (\Sigma x : A)B[x] \vdash \text{split}[z] : C[z] \\ x : A, y : B[x] \vdash \text{split}[\text{pair}(x, y)] = c[x, y] : C[\text{pair}(x, y)] \end{array}\right.}$$

where $\text{split}[e]$ abbreviates $\text{split}(e, (x, y)c[x, y])$. So its congruence rule is

$$\frac{\left\{\begin{array}{l} z : (\Sigma x : A)B[x] \vdash C[z] \text{ type} \\ x : A, y : B[x] \vdash c_1[x, y] = c_2[x, y] : C[\text{pair}(x, y)] \end{array}\right.}{z : (\Sigma x : A)B[x] \vdash \text{split}(z, (x, y)c_1[x, y]) = \text{split}(z, (x, y)c_2[x, y]) : C[z]}$$

3.7.1 Assumption and Substitution Rules

Assumption $\quad \dfrac{\Gamma \vdash \mathcal{B} \quad A \text{ type}}{x : A, \Gamma \vdash \mathcal{B}} \quad$ and $\quad \dfrac{\Gamma \vdash \mathcal{B} \quad A \text{ type}}{x : A, \Gamma \vdash x : A}$,

where it is assumed that x is not declared in Γ or in any implicit parametric context.)

Substitution $\quad \dfrac{x : A, \Gamma[x] \vdash \mathcal{B}[x] \quad a : A}{\Gamma[a] \vdash \mathcal{B}[a]}$

3.7.2 Equality Rules

$$\frac{A \text{ type}}{A = A} \qquad \frac{A_1 = A_2}{A_2 = A_1} \qquad \frac{A_1 = A_2 \quad A_2 = A_3}{A_1 = A_3}$$

$$\frac{a : A}{a = a : A} \qquad \frac{a_1 = a_2 : A}{a_2 = a_1 : A} \qquad \frac{a_1 = a_2 : A \quad a_2 = a_3 : A}{a_1 = a_3 : A}$$

$$\frac{a : A_1 \quad A_1 = A_2}{a : A_2} \qquad \frac{a_1 = a_2 : A_1 \quad A_1 = A_2}{a_1 = a_2 : A_2}$$

3.7.3 Finite Type Rules

For $n = 0, 1, 2, \ldots$ and $k = 1, \ldots, n$

$$\frac{}{N_n} \qquad \frac{}{k_n : N_n} \qquad \frac{\left\{ \begin{array}{l} z : N_n \vdash C[z] \text{ type} \\ c_i : C[i_n] \quad (i = 1, \ldots, n) \end{array} \right.}{\left\{ \begin{array}{l} z : N_n \vdash R_n(z) : C[z] \\ R_n(k_n) = c_k : C[k_n] \end{array} \right.}$$

where $R_n[e]$ abbreviates $R_n(e, c_1, \ldots, c_n)$.

3.7.4 Natural Number Rules

$$\frac{}{N \text{ type}} \qquad \frac{}{0 : N} \qquad \frac{e : N}{succ(e) : N}$$

$$\frac{\left\{ \begin{array}{l} z : N \vdash C[z] \text{ type} \\ c_0 : C[0] \\ z : N, x : C[z] \vdash d[z, x] : C[succ(z)] \end{array} \right.}{\left\{ \begin{array}{l} z : N \vdash R_N[z] : C[z] \\ R_N[0] = c_0 : C[0] \\ z : N, x : C[z] \vdash R_N[succ(z)] = d[z, R_N[z]] : C[succ(z)] \end{array} \right.}$$

where $R_N[e]$ abbreviates $R_N(e, c_0, (z, x)d[z, x])$.

3.7.5 Identity Type Rules

$$\frac{A \text{ type}}{x_1, x_2 : A \vdash Id_A(x_1, x_2)} \qquad \frac{a : A}{r_A(a) : Id_A(a, a)}$$

$$\frac{\left\{ \begin{array}{l} a : A \\ y : A, z : Id_A(a, y) \vdash C[y, z] \text{ type} \\ e : C[a, r_A(a)] \end{array} \right.}{\left\{ \begin{array}{l} y : A, z : Id_A(a, y) \vdash J(a, e, y, z) : C[y, z] \\ J(a, e, a, r_A(a)) = e : C[a, r_A(a)] \end{array} \right.}$$

3.7.6 Pi Type Rules

$$\frac{A \text{ type} \quad x : A \vdash B[x] \text{ type}}{(\Pi x : A)B[x] \text{ type}} \qquad \frac{f : (\Pi x : A)B[x] \quad a : A}{\mathsf{app}(f, a) : B[a]}$$

$$\frac{x : A \vdash b[x] : B[x]}{(\lambda x : A)b[x] : (\Pi x : A)B[x]} \qquad \frac{x : A \vdash b[x] : B[x] \qquad a : A}{\mathsf{app}((\lambda x : A)b[x], a) = b[a] : B[a]}$$

3.7.7 Sigma Type Rules

$$\frac{A \text{ type} \quad x : A \vdash B[x] \text{ type}}{(\Sigma x : A)B[x] \text{ type}} \qquad \frac{x : A \vdash B[x] \quad a : A \quad b : B[a]}{\mathsf{pair}(a, b) : (\Sigma x : A)B[x]}$$

$$\frac{\left\{ \begin{array}{l} z : (\Sigma x : A)B[x] \vdash C[z] \text{ type} \\ x : A, y : B[x] \vdash c[x, y] : C[\mathsf{pair}(x, y)] \end{array} \right.}{\left\{ \begin{array}{l} z : (\Sigma x : A)B[x] \vdash \mathsf{split}[z] : C[z] \\ x : A, y : B[x] \vdash \mathsf{split}[\mathsf{pair}(x, y)] = c[x, y] : C[\mathsf{pair}(x, y)] \end{array} \right.}$$

where $\mathsf{split}[e]$ abbreviates $\mathsf{split}(e, (x, y)c[x, y])$.

3.7.8 Binary Sum Rules

$$\frac{A_1 \text{ type} \quad A_2 \text{ type}}{A_1 + A_2 \text{ type}} \qquad \frac{A_1 \text{ type} \quad A_2 \text{ type} \quad a : A_i}{\mathsf{in}_i(a) : A_1 + A_2} \quad (i = 1, 2)$$

$$\frac{\left\{ \begin{array}{l} z : A_1 + A_2 \vdash C[z] \text{ type} \\ x : A_j \vdash d_j[x] : C[\mathsf{in}_j(x)] \quad (j = 1, 2) \end{array} \right.}{\left\{ \begin{array}{l} z : A_1 + A_2 \vdash \mathsf{case}[z] : C[z] \\ x : A_j \vdash \mathsf{case}[\mathsf{in}_j(x)] = d_j[x] : C[\mathsf{in}_j(x)] \quad (j = 1, 2) \end{array} \right.} \quad (i = 1, 2)$$

where $\mathsf{case}[e]$ abbreviates $\mathsf{case}(e, (x)d_1[x], (x)d_2[x])$.

3.7.9 W Type Rules

$$\frac{A \text{ type} \quad x : A \vdash B[x] \text{ type}}{(Wx : A)B[x] \text{ type}} \qquad \frac{a : A \quad y : B[a] \vdash c[y] : W}{(\sup y : B[a])c[y] : W}$$

where we use W to abbreviate $(Wx : A)B[x]$.

$$\frac{\left\{ \begin{array}{l} z : W \vdash C[z] \text{ type} \\ x : A, u : (B[x] \to W), v : C'[x, u] \vdash d[x, u, v] : C''[x, u] \end{array} \right.}{\left\{ \begin{array}{l} z : W \vdash \mathsf{R}_W[z] : C[z] \\ x : A, u : (B[x] \to W) \vdash \mathsf{R}_W[\sup'[x, u]] = d'[x, u] : C''[x, u] \end{array} \right.}$$

where we use the following abbreviations:

- $\mathsf{R}_W[e]$ abbreviates $\mathsf{R}_W(e, (x, u, v)d[x, u, v])$,
- $C'[x, u]$ abbreviates $(\Pi y : B[x])C[\mathsf{app}(u, y)]$,
- $d'[x, u]$ abbreviates $d[x, u, (\lambda y : B[x])\mathsf{R}_W[\mathsf{app}(u, y)]]$,
- $\mathsf{sup}\,'[x, u]$ abbreviates $(\mathsf{sup}\, y : B[x])\mathsf{app}(u, y)$, and
- $C''[x, u]$ abbreviates $C[\mathbf{sup}'[x, u]]$.

Bibliography

[1] S. Feferman. Classifications of recursive functions by means of hierarchies. *Trans. Amer. Math. Soc.*, 104:101–122, 1962.

Universality and Computation

Martin Davis

New York University, New York NY, United States of America

E-mail: martin@eipye.com

After a brief review of the Turing machine formalism and his notion of universal machine, the relevance of these matters to actual physical machines is discussed from a historical perspective. The significance of Turing's use of infinite memory and the implications for the importance of achieving very large RAM are discussed. Finally a few examples are given of a mistaken effort to confer universality anachronistically on devices (real and abstract) formulated before Turing's work.

Arnold Beckmann, Benedikt Löwe (*eds.*). *Acts of the programme "Semantics and Syntax".* Isaac Newton Institute for the Mathematical Sciences, January to July 2012.

Talk given at the SAS Seminar, 23 February 2012, 16:00–16:30.

Proofs and Computations

Helmut Schwichtenberg

Ludwig-Maximilians-Universität München, München, Germany

E-mail: schwicht@mathematik.uni-muenchen.de

A formal system TCF (theory of computable functionals) is described, which is similar to Heyting arithmetic in all finite types but with the Scott/Ershov partial continuous functionals as the domain of quantifiers. TCF has free type and predicate variables, to allow for abstract developments (groups, fields, real analysis). The underlying inference machinery is minimal logic (implication, universal quantification plus inductively and coinductively defined predicates). Computable functionals (of finite type, with free algebras at ground types) are given by their defining equations. Since the logic is constructive, program extraction by means of a realizability interpretation is possible. In fact, since the underlying term language is rather strong (a common extension T^+ of Gödel's system T and Plotkin's PCF), what one extracts is a term of T^+. A proof of the soundness theorem can therefore be carried out within the system. The soundness theorem says that whenever we have a proof M of a formula A, its extracted term $et(M)$ is realizer of A (in the sense of modified realizability of Kleene, Kreisel and Troelstra). Some case studies concerning exact real analysis and involving coinduction and corecursion are discussed.

Part of the presented material is based on a recent book by S.S. Wainer and the speaker [1].

Bibliography

[1] H. Schwichtenberg and S. S. Wainer. *Proofs and computations*. Perspectives in Logic. Cambridge University Press, Cambridge, 2012.

Arnold Beckmann, Benedikt Löwe (*eds.*). *Acts of the programme "Semantics and Syntax".*
Isaac Newton Institute for the Mathematical Sciences, January to July 2012.

Talk given at the SAS Seminar, 23 February 2012, 16:30–17:00.

The Structure of Weihrauch Degrees

Arno Pauly

University of Cambridge, Cambridge, United Kingdom

E-mail: Arno.Pauly@cl.cam.ac.uk

In [2], Brattka and Gherardi suggested a metamathematical research programme based upon a reducibility notion introduced by Weihrauch in [6]. A mathematical theorem of the form $\forall x \in X \; \exists Y \; P(x,y)$ is read as the computational task to provide a description of a suitable witness y given a description of $x \in X$. A comparison of theorems now is based on the question whether the computational task of one theorem is solvable using a single oracle call to another theorem. Here we wish to give a brief description of the resulting structure.

We recall that a *represented space* $\mathbf{X}$ is a pair (X, δ_X) where $\delta_X :\subseteq \{0,1\}^{\mathbb{N}} \to X$ is a partial surjection. A partial function $F :\subseteq \{0,1\}^{\mathbb{N}} \to \{0,1\}^{\mathbb{N}}$ is a *realizer* (symbolic: $F \vdash f$) of a partial multi-valued function $f :\subseteq \mathbf{X} \rightrightarrows \mathbf{Y}$, if for any $p \in \mathrm{dom}(f\delta_X)$ we find $\delta_Y(F(p))$ to be defined and $\delta_Y(F(p)) \in f(\delta_X(p))$.

Definition 1. For $f :\subseteq \mathbf{X} \rightrightarrows \mathbf{Y}$, $g :\subseteq \mathbf{U} \rightrightarrows \mathbf{V}$ let $f \leq_{\mathrm{W}} g$ hold, iff there are computable $H, K :\subseteq \{0,1\}^{\mathbb{N}} \to \{0,1\}^{\mathbb{N}}$ such that for any $G \vdash g$ we find $[p \mapsto H(\langle p, G(K(P))\rangle)] \vdash f$.

One readily verifies $\leq_{\mathrm{W}}$ to be a preorder, and we denote its partially ordered degrees (the Weihrauch degrees) by $\mathfrak{W}$. We let $\bot$ denote the degree of those multi-valued function where each $F :\subseteq \{0,1\}^{\mathbb{N}} \to \{0,1\}^{\mathbb{N}}$ is a realizer, and let $\top$ contain those without realizers. Finally, let 1 be the degree of $\mathrm{id}_{\{}0,1\}^{\mathbb{N}} : \{0,1\}^{\mathbb{N}} \to \{0,1\}^{\mathbb{N}}$.

Let $f + g$ denote the coproduct of multi-valued functions $f :\subseteq \mathbf{X} \rightrightarrows \mathbf{Y}$, $g :\subseteq \mathbf{U} \rightrightarrows \mathbf{V}$, and let $f \times g$ be the cartesian product. Furthermore let $f \oplus g :\subseteq \mathbf{X} \times \mathbf{U} \rightrightarrows \mathbf{Y} + \mathbf{V}$ be defined via $(0,y) \in (f \oplus g)(x,u)$ iff $y \in f(x)$ and $(1,v) \in (f \oplus g)(x,u)$ iff $v \in g(u)$.

Theorem 2 (Pauly [5], Brattka and Gherardi [3], Higuchi and Pauly [4]).

1. $+$, $\times$, $\oplus$ all induce operations on $\mathfrak{W}$.

2. $(\mathfrak{W}, \oplus, +)$ is a distributive lattice with top $\top$ and bottom $\bot$.

3. $(\mathfrak{W}, +, \times)$ is a commutative idempotent semiring with zero $\bot$ and one 1.

4. $(\mathfrak{W}, \oplus, +)$ is not a Heyting algebra.

5. 1 is join-irreducible but meet-reducible.

Arnold Beckmann, Benedikt Löwe (eds.). Acts of the programme "Semantics and Syntax". Isaac Newton Institute for the Mathematical Sciences, January to July 2012.

Talk given at the SAS Seminar, 23 February 2012, 17:00–17:30.

Both to contrast and to illuminate the formal structure given by the preceding theorem, the relative position of a few degrees originating from mathematical theorems is shown in the following diagram:

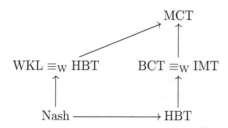

Here Nash refers to Nash's theorem that every finite two player game has a Nash equilibrium, HBT is Hilbert's Basis Theorem, WKL is Weak König's Lemma, HBT stands for the Hahn-Banach Theorem (for separable spaces), BCT abbreviates the Baire Category Theorem and IMT the Inverse Mapping Theorem. Finally, MCT is the Monotone Convergence Theorem. For references, see [1].

Bibliography

[1] V. Brattka, M. de Brecht, and A. Pauly. Closed choice and a uniform low basis theorem. *Ann. Pure Appl. Logic*, 163(8):986–1008, 2012.

[2] V. Brattka and G. Gherardi. Effective choice and boundedness principles in computable analysis. *Bull. Symbolic Logic*, 17(1):73–117, 2011.

[3] V. Brattka and G. Gherardi. Weihrauch degrees, omniscience principles and weak computability. *J. Symbolic Logic*, 76(1):143–176, 2011.

[4] K. Higuchi and A. Pauly. The degree-structure of Weihrauch-reducibility. arXiv 1101.0112, 2012.

[5] A. Pauly. On the (semi)lattices induced by continuous reducibilities. *Math. Log. Q.*, 56(5):488–502, 2010.

[6] K. Weihrauch. The TTE-interpretation of three hierarchies of omniscience principles. Informatik Berichte 130, FernUniversität Hagen, Hagen, 1992.

Predictably Terminating Computations

Stan S. Wainer

University of Leeds, Leeds, United Kingdom
E-mail: S.S.Wainer@leeds.ac.uk

Turing ("Checking a large routine", given at the inaugural conference on the EDSAC computer, Cambridge 1949) already saw the potential of transfinite induction as a method for proving program–termination.

But which inductions? Any would do for mere confirmation of termination, but proof-theoretic complexity should, in addition, provide program structure and measures of mathematical/computational complexity.

What is a "natural" computable ordinal? How can they be built up, from below?

Ordinal Presentations. A "presentation" of a countable ordinal α is a counting of it:

$$\alpha = \bigcup \{ \, \alpha[0] \subset \alpha[1] \subset \alpha[2] \subset \ldots \}$$

where each $\alpha[n]$ is finite and (for $\beta + 1 \prec \alpha$)

$$\beta + 1 \in \alpha[n] \to \beta \in \alpha[n] \quad \text{and} \quad \beta \in \alpha[n] \to \beta + 1 \in \alpha[n+1].$$

This defines a "rank functor" $G_\alpha : N_0 \to N$ where N is the category of natural numbers with all finite increasing maps between them, and N_0 has just one map i_{nm}, the injection of n into m, whenever $n \leq m$. On points, $G_\alpha(n) = |\alpha[n]|$ and on maps, $G_\alpha(i_{nm})$ is the map taking $G_\beta(n)$ to $G_\beta(m)$ for each $\beta \in \alpha[n]$. These are the very beginnings of Girard's Π^1_2 logic, but the context here is quite different. The point is that the presentation $(\alpha, [.])$ is (isomorphic to) $\lim_\to G_\alpha$, the direct limit of G_α. We thus regard G_α as α's "canonical" functorial representative.

Predictable Termination. Generate ever-larger ordinal presentations by starting with something small, e.g., ω with $\omega[n] = n$, and repeatedly applying the autonomy principle: allow new definitions of functors by α-recursions only if G_α has already (previously) been generated. With α-recursions, one might be able to define new functorial representatives of even greater ordinals, and so on. Where does this process end?

A suitable "normal form" for α-recursion is the fast growing hierarchy:

$$B_\alpha = \begin{cases} \text{successor} & \text{if } \alpha = 0 \\ B_\beta \circ B_\beta & \text{if } \alpha = \beta + 1 \\ \text{diag } (B_{\alpha_x}) & \text{if } \alpha \text{ is a limit.} \end{cases}$$

Arnold Beckmann, Benedikt Löwe (eds.). Acts of the programme "Semantics and Syntax". Isaac Newton Institute for the Mathematical Sciences, January to July 2012.

Talk given at the SAS Seminar, 28 February 2012, 16:00–16:30.

Theorem. If α is appropriately structured, it has a natural "lifting" to α^+ such that $B_\alpha = G_{\alpha^+}$ and hence $\alpha^+ \cong \lim_\rightarrow B_\alpha$.

Theorem. Let $\tau = \sup \tau_i$ where $\tau_0 = \omega$ and $\tau_{i+1} = \tau_i^+$. Then τ_{i+2} is the ordinal of ID_i and τ, the ordinal of $\Pi_1^1\text{-CA}_0$, is the "limit" of predictable termination in the sense above. The "accessible" (predictably terminating) recursive functions are therefore those provably recursive in $\Pi_1^1\text{-CA}_0$.

Bibliography

[1] H. Schwichtenberg and S. S. Wainer. *Proofs and computations.* Perspectives in Logic. Cambridge University Press, Cambridge, 2012.

Generalised Dynamical Systems

Philip Welch

University of Bristol, Bristol, United Kingdom

E-mail: p.welch@bristol.ac.uk

We should like to look at variants of dynamical systems with transfinitely repeated actions. With the assistance of transfinite machine models based on the usual versions of Turing, Register, Blum-Shub-Smale etc. machines) one can get some idea of the strengths of such systems. A start on this was effected in [4].

Let us give the following example: Suppose $f : \mathbb{N}^n \longrightarrow \mathbb{N}^n$. One may think of f acting on the points of an n-dimensional lattice torus where we identify '∞' (here ω) with 0. We set this up as follows. Given a point $r = (r_1, \ldots, r_n) \in \mathbb{N}^n$ set:

$$
\begin{aligned}
r^0 &= (r_1^0, \ldots, r_n^0) = (r_1, \ldots, r_n); \\
r^{\alpha+1} &= (r_1^{\alpha+1}, \ldots, r_n^{\alpha+1}) = f((r_1^\alpha, \ldots, r_n^\alpha)); \\
r^\lambda &= (r_1^\lambda, \ldots, r_n^\lambda) = (\text{Liminf}^*_{\alpha \to \lambda} r_1^\alpha, \text{Liminf}^*_{\alpha \to \lambda} r_2^\alpha, \ldots, \text{Liminf}^*_{\alpha \to \lambda} r_n^\alpha)
\end{aligned}
$$

where we define

$$
\text{Liminf}^*_{\alpha \to \lambda} r_1^\alpha = \text{Liminf}_{\alpha \to \lambda} r_1^\alpha
$$

if the latter is $< \omega$, and set it to 0 otherwise, thus:

$$
\begin{aligned}
r_i^\lambda &= \text{Liminf}_{\alpha \to \lambda} r_i^\alpha \quad \text{if the latter is } < \omega \\
&= 0 \quad\quad\quad\quad\quad\quad \text{otherwise.}
\end{aligned}
$$

One can ask: *"Which points get sent to the origin (at some stage)?"*

Definition 1. $Z_f =_{\text{df}} \{p \in \mathbb{N}^n \mid \exists \alpha p^\alpha = O\}$.

How hard is it to prove that such zero sets exist? Let GDS_Z be the statement: "$\forall n \forall f : \mathbb{N}^n \longrightarrow \mathbb{N}^n(Z_f \text{ exists})$."

Theorem 2 ([4]). *Over* ATR_0, *the statements* GDS_Z *and* $\Pi_1^1\text{-CA}_0$ *are equivalent.*

The proof of the above can be summarized as stating that it involves emulating the iteration function f as a program on an Infinite Time Register Machine of Koepke and Miller [2]. The halting or looping behaviour of an N-register such machine is determinate by the $(N{+}1)$'st admissible ordinal, and from this the bound is obtained of $\Pi_1^1\text{-CA}_0$, and incidentally shows that the *halting problem* for such machines is also only provable in a theory of this strength.

Arnold Beckmann, Benedikt Löwe (*eds.*). *Acts of the programme "Semantics and Syntax".* Isaac Newton Institute for the Mathematical Sciences, January to July 2012.

Talk given at the SAS Seminar, 28 February 2012, 16:30–17:00.

Suppose now $f : (\mathbb{Q} \cap [0,1])^n \longrightarrow (\mathbb{Q} \cap [0,1])^n$ and consider iterates of f on this *rational torus*. Such an f again can be coded by an oracle $Z \subseteq \mathbb{N}$ but now the Liminf* operation is somewhat more problematic:

(i) The Liminf values may not be rational;

(ii) Liminf, even when rational, is a Π_3^{KP} calculation.

Lemma 3. *Iterates of f, if always defined until γ, where γ is the least $\Pi_3(f)$-reflecting admissible ordinal will be defined, (and be looping) for ever.*

Question 4. *Is this upper bound best possible?*

Suppose now $f : (\mathbb{R} \cap [0,1])^n \longrightarrow (\mathbb{R} \cap [0,1])^n$ is continuous and consider iterates of f on this the *real torus*.

Then to determine whether, say iterations of f on starting real x go through the origin O requires Π_3^1-CA$_0$; again this can be seen by emulating the action of such an f on a Hamkins-Kidder ITTM [1].

A related question comes from Koepke and Seyfferth's analysis of an *iterated Blum-Shub-Smale machine* (ITBM) [3]. Here they only take *continuous limits* (the program crashes with no output if this cannot be done). To establish an upper bound, they simulate this on an ITTM, which needs large ordinals (beyond Π_2^1-CA$_0$) in their analysis. However the iterations they consider are short—only ω^ω length, so we show that their ITBM-machines can in fact be modelled by *Kleene recursion*.

However to show that, e.g., every real in L_{ω^ω} can be created one needs a *continuous* method of coding levels of L_α into such infinite time BSS-computations. However this again is practicable, and shows that their ITBM machines are, in effect, universal.

Bibliography

[1] J. D. Hamkins and A. Lewis. Infinite time Turing machines. *J. Symbolic Logic*, 65(2):567–604, 2000.

[2] P. Koepke and R. Miller. An enhanced theory of infinite time register machines. In *Logic and theory of algorithms*, volume 5028 of *Lecture Notes in Comput. Sci.*, pages 306–315. Springer, Berlin, 2008.

[3] P. Koepke and B. Seyfferth. Ordinal machines and admissible recursion theory. *Ann. Pure Appl. Logic*, 160(3):310–318, 2009.

[4] P. Koepke and P. D. Welch. A generalised dynamical system, infinite time register machines, and Π_1^1-CA$_0$. In *Models of computation in context*, volume 6735 of *Lecture Notes in Comput. Sci.*, pages 152–159. Springer, Heidelberg, 2011.

Model-comparison Games with Algebraic Rules

Bjarki Holm

University of Cambridge, Cambridge, United Kingdom

E-mail: bh288@cam.ac.uk

Variations of Ehrenfeucht-Fraïssé games for extensions of first-order logic form an essential tool for analysing the expressiveness of logics over finite models. An important class of such tools are the so called pebble games, which characterise equivalence in logics with finitely many variables. Such games have played an important role in a long-running story in finite model theory: the quest to find a logic that can capture polynomial time.

In this talk I give an overview of some standard pebble games and illustrate how those games can be used to establish inexpressibility results for the corresponding logics. I also introduce two new model-comparison games that are obtained by imposing linear-algebraic conditions on the moves in a pebble game. The first of these, called the *matrix-rank game*, characterises equivalence in the finite-variable fragments of matrix-rank logic, which was recently introduced as a candidate for capturing polynomial time on the class of all finite graphs. The second game, called the *invertible-map game*, yields a refinement of the equivalence defined by the matrix-rank game and we show that this game equivalence is polynomial-time decidable. As an application, this gives a family of polynomial-time approximations of graph isomorphism that is strictly stronger than the well-known Weisfeiler-Lehman method.

The results described in this talk are joint work with Anuj Dawar.

Arnold Beckmann, Benedikt Löwe (*eds.*). *Acts of the programme "Semantics and Syntax"*. Isaac Newton Institute for the Mathematical Sciences, January to July 2012.

Talk given at the SAS Seminar, 1 March 2012, 16:00–16:30.

My Current Interests in Computation

Rod Downey

Victoria University of Wellington, Wellington, New Zealand

E-mail: `Rod.Downey@msor.vuw.ac.nz`

In this lecture I have decided to give a brief account of some of the things I am currently interested in rather than a detailed lecture. The plan was to give an account that might attract others to interact with me. I spoke about four topics, listed in the followiung four sections.

1 Parameterized Complexity

Currently I am writing a book *Fundamentals of Parameterized Complexity* with Mike Fellows. This is an update of our 1999 book with Springer. There has been tremendous progress in this area, particularly in applications.

The idea behind this area is the following: A mathematical idealization is to identify "Feasible" with P (polynomial time). Parameterized complexity tries to map out P-FEASIBLE, and map a further boundary of intractability.

Parameterized complexity also allows for an extended "dialog" with the problem at hand. Others to use the hardness theory include the following in classical applications. For example, for the logically minded, (Alekhnovich and Razborov (AR01)). Neither resolution not tree-like resolution is automizable unless $W[P]$ is randomized FPT by a randomized algorithm with one-sided error. Also Frick and Grohe showed that towers of twos obtained from general tractability results with respect to model checking can't be gotten rid of unless $W[1] = $ FPT.

What parameters are we interested in ? Without even going into details, think of all the graphs you have given names to and each has a relevant parameter: planar, bounded genus, bounded cutwidth, pathwidth, treewidth, degree, interval, etc, etc. Also *nature* is kind in that for many practical problems the input (often designed by *us*) is nicely ordered.

Here are two basic examples:

VERTEX COVER
Input: A Graph G.
Parameter: A positive integer k.
Question: Does G have a size k vertex cover? (Vertices cover edges.)

---

and

Arnold Beckmann, Benedikt Löwe (*eds.*). *Acts of the programme "Semantics and Syntax"*. Isaac Newton Institute for the Mathematical Sciences, January to July 2012.

Talk given at the SAS Seminar, 1 March 2012, 16:00–16:30.

DOMINATING SET
Input: A Graph G.
Parameter: A positive integer k.
Question: Does G have a size k dominating set? (Vertices cover vertices.)

We now know that VERTEX COVER is solvable by an algorithm $\mathfrak{O}$ in time $f(k)|G|$, a behaviour we call *fixed parameter tractability*, (Specifically $1.2745^k k^2 + c|G|$, with c a small absolute constant independent of k.) Whereas the only known algorithm for DOMINATING SET is complete search of the possible k-subsets, which takes time $\Omega(|G|^k)$.

We say that a language L is *fixed parameter tractable* if there is a algorithm M, a constant C and a function f such that for all x, k,

$$(x, k) \in L \text{ iff } M(x) = 1 \text{ and}$$

$$\text{the running time of } M(x) \text{ is} f(k)|x|^C.$$

Vertex Cover has been implemented and shown to be practical for a class of problems arizing from computational biology for k up to about 7000 and n large, see for example [1].

In the lecture I will speak about the many positive techniques which have been developed to establish parameterized tractability:

- *Elementary ones* include Kernelization, Bounded search trees, Struction, Crown Reductions, IP Relaxation, Lenstra's IP bounded Variable, Iterative Compression.

- *Colour Coding and Greedy Localization.*

- *Graph Structure Theory* includes width metrics: treewidth, cutwidth d-inductive graphs etc. *Logical metatheorems* include Courcelle's Theorem, Excluded Minor theorems, Bidimensionality.

I will also look at reductions and intractability: There is a natural basic hardness class: $W[1]$.

SHORT NONDETERMINISTIC TURING MACHINE ACCEPTANCE
Instance: A nondeterministic Turing Machine M and a positive integer k.
Parameter: k.
Question: Does M have a computation path accepting the empty string in at most k steps?

Recent work has shown that if SHORT NTM is FPT then n-variable 3SAT is in DTIME($2^{o(n)}$) Given two parameterized languages $L, \widehat{L} \subseteq \Sigma^* \times \Sigma^*$, say $L \leq_{\text{FPT}} \widehat{L}$ iff there are (computable) $f, x \mapsto x', k \mapsto k'$ and a constant c, such that for all x,

$$(x, k) \in L \text{ iff } (x', k') \in \widehat{L},$$

in time $f(k)|x|^c$. Analog of Cook's Theorem: (Downey, Fellows, Cai, Chen) WEIGHTED 3SAT $\equiv_{\text{FPT}}$ SHORT NTM ACCEPTANCE. where:

WEIGHTED 3SAT

Input: A 3 CNF formula φ

Parameter: k

Question: Does φ has a satisfying assignment of Hamming weigth k, meaning exactly k literals made true?

Think about the usual poly reduction from SAT to 3SAT. It takes a clause of size p, and turns it into many clauses of size 3. *But* the weight control goes awry. A weight 4 assignment could go to anything. We don't think WEIGHTED CNF SAT $\leq_{\text{FPT}}$ WEIGHTED 3 SAT. This gives rise to a heirarchy:

$$W[1] \subseteq W[2] \subseteq W[3] \dots W[SAT] \subseteq W[P] \subseteq XP.$$

XP is quite important, it is the languages which are in DTIME($n^f(k)$) with various levels of uniformity, depending on the choice of reductions. There is a lot we don't understand. This methodology has been applied in many areas of human knowledge, and pretty well anywhere classical complexity goes, this goes but with a more refined eye. I will also indicate how the methodology is used for classical lower bounds.

2   Algorithms in nature

One of my own research agendas has been to understand why algorithms work better (or worse) than we expect. This is where *parameterized complexity* came from. (Exploiting the fact that almost all data from "real life" has parameters bounded in some way. This can yield a lot of good algorithmics.) One aspect of this came from *group theory* through the work of Schupp, Myasnakov, and others on "generic case complexity."

Again, Classical complexity, P, NP etc seems often the wrong model for actual behaviour of problems. New method suggested by Kapovich, Miasnikov, Schupp and Shpilrain in 2003. This is called generic computability, where we have a partial algorithm Φ which, if it halts it must be correct, and needs to halt on a set of Borel density 1. For example, generically decidable (in linear time) problems are the word problem for 1-relator groups with ≥ 3 generators similarly (no bound for Magnus' solution), plus iso-morphism problem; and braid groups, and automorphism problems for free groups etc. Boone's group also has a genrically decidable word problem and it is unknown if there is a one without a generically solvable word problem. (See also Gilman, Miasnikov and Osin for the strong case) There are lots of questions: (i) Understand this better. (ii) What about other structures. (iii) Generic case model theory and coarse model theory. (iv) How does this relate to classical complexity, etc.

3 Algorithmic Randomness

We have heard talks about how to use computation theory to understand randomness via things like effective null sets, effective betting. Recall α is ML-random iff α is not $\bigcap_n U_n$ where U_n is a c.e. open set of measure $\leq 2^{-n}$. Also recall A is K-trivial iff $K(A \upharpoonright n) \leq^K (n)$ all n iff $K^A =^+ K$. I have been looking at exact pairs for K-trivials, and integer valued randomness, especially with Barmpalias and with Nies.

For example, with Barmpalias, I classified the c.e. Turing degrees con-taining Ingeger valued randoms as the aray noncomputables. Randomness can be defined via (effective) martingales played on $2^{<\omega}$ and has $f(\sigma) = \frac{f(\sigma 0) = f(\sigma 1)}{2}$. (Fairness) α is ML-random iff no left c.e. martingale succeeds on it meaning that $\limsup_n f(\alpha \upharpoonright n) \to \infty$. α is *integer valued random* iff no integer valued martingale succeeds. (Think of a "real" casino.) Also I think we and Andre Nies can prove that the K-trivials have an exact pair (a reasonably longstanding technical question) With Barmpalias, I have also studied reals with $K(\alpha \upharpoonright n) \geq^+ K(\alpha \upharpoonright f(n))$ for each computable order f. (*weakly K-resolute*) We have shown that such c.e. sets can be Turing com-plete, not all c.e. degrees have them, and there is a non-K-trivial completely K-resolute degree. am Also talking with Ted Slaman's student Ian Herbert about mutual information for reals, akin to symmetry of information a 'la Levin.

4 Speculative, physics

There are obvious things like Brownian motion. The Asarin-Fouché-Kjos-Hanssen-Nerode approach is to look (as usual) at the space of continuous $f[0,1] \to \mathbb{R}$ with the uniform metric $d(f,g) = \sup |f(x) - g(x)|$ and Wiener measure. Then you can classify the notion of an individual random Brow-nain motion using Kolmogorov complexity. The question is what does this say about "real" Brownian motion? Classical physics treats space-time as a manifold. So most processes are pde's and presumably they are "com-putable" in the sense that if I closely approximate the input the same is true of the output. Thus in that context, the above would make some sense. As does algorithmic randomness.

There is a nice research programme and lots of interesting questions here. Can such a system generate randomness? or even incomputability (Pour-El, Richards)? According to my friendly physicist (Matt Visser) and most of my reading (e.g., Speakable and unspeakable in quantum physics, Bell's Theorem, the recent essay competition in FQXi), quantum phyics could be hard to reconcile with the manifold interpretation. At the heart of quantum physics at the Planck level, things seem highly non-continuous. When, for example, we observe spin, it (with some degree of randomness) chooses.

How can this be interpreted? There are at least four to six interpretations and one could speculate that algorithmic randomness might have a show at sheding light on this subject. It could be that at at some level *nothing* is computable yet (like looking at a TV from afar) it all looks smooth and computable. I am aware of no framework at all which can be used to computationally represent this, and it would seem a very interesting project to do this. I like it as I would need to learn some physics and could charm a physicist, maybe with logic. Also the work of Shannon→Lee Ruebel on GPAC if the world is a manifold.

5   Reverse mathematics

Looking at, e.g., FIP. Every infinite family has a maximal subfamily where every finite subset has nonempty finite intersection. As *Sets* this is equivalent to ACA_0 over RCA_0. With Diamondstone, Greenberg, Turetsky I have shown that as *families* the FIP (those that can compute solutions to all computable families) degrees below $0'$ are exactly the degrees bounding 1-generic ones. But there is a minimal one. Note Damir Dzharfarov has shown that the degrees are all hyperimmune. So the construction is a very complex full approximation one making a Δ_3^0 hyperimmune FIP degree.

6   Other things

I have been thinking about a lot of other things including truth table degree with Lempp, and computable structure theory with Lewis, Montalbán and others. You should ask me.

Bibliography

[1] M. A. Langston, A. D. Perkins, A. M. Saxton, J. A. Scharff, and B. H. Voy. Innovative computational methods for transcriptomic data analysis: A case study in the use of fpt for practical algorithm design and implementation. *The Computer Journal*, 51(1):26–38, 2008.

Beyond Inductive Definitions—Induction-recursion, Induction-induction, Coalgebras

Anton Setzer

Swansea University, Swansea, United Kingdom

E-mail: A.G.Setzer@swansea.ac.uk

Our proof theoretic programme, which is a form of a revised Hilbert's Programme, is to prove the consistency of proof theoretically strong theories via an ordinal analysis to predicatively justified extensions of Martin-Loef Type Type Theory. This gives rise to new data types, which can be used outside type theory as well. We will report on 3 extensions found this way: induction-recursion, induction-induction and weakly final coalgebras in dependent type theory.

Induction-recursion was originally introduced by Peter Dybjer in order to obtain a type theory which includes all possible extensions of type theory considered as acceptable at that time. We consider a closed formalisation by having one data type the elements of which are representatives of arbitrary inductive-recursive definitions. This data type has been applied to generic programming.

A (proof theoretic weak) variant of induction-recursion is called induction-induction, and has been investigated in collaboration with my PhD student Fredrik Forsberg. Variants of this concept occur frequently in mathematics, when one defines a set simultaneously with an order on it, and both are defined mutually inductively. An example are Conway's surreal numbers.

Finally we look at weakly final coalgebras in dependent type theory, where the role of elimination and and introduction rules are interchanged.

Arnold Beckmann, Benedikt Löwe (eds.). Acts of the programme "Semantics and Syntax". Isaac Newton Institute for the Mathematical Sciences, January to July 2012.

Talk given at the SAS Seminar, 1 March 2012, 17:00–17:30.

Fully Homomorphic Encryption

Nigel Smart

University of Bristol, Bristol, United Kingdom
E-mail: nigel@compsci.bristol.ac.uk

The talk describe the motivation behind, the latest research and the open problems in Fully Homomorphic Encryption (FHE). Taking cloud provided databases as its motivation the talk discussed what a FHE scheme is, i.e., an encryption algorithm $E(m)$ such that there are two operations $\oplus$ and $\otimes$ such that

$$E(m_1) \oplus E(m_2) = E(m_1 + m_2), \quad E(m_1) \otimes E(m_2) = E(m_1 \times m_2)$$

where $+$ and $\times$ denote the underlying operations on the message space (which is a ring).

The talk then went onto discuss the ring-LWE scheme introduced by Brakerski, Gentry and Vaikuntanathan. Issues such as key-switching and modulus-switching were briefly described. Since the underlying ring is a (the reduction of) the ring of integers of a Galois number field; one can apply Galois automorphisms of the message space. The ring-LWE scheme can support the homomorphic evaluation of such Galois automorphisms, as well as SIMD operations. This was used by Gentry, Halevi and Smart to show that BGV can be considered somewhat asymptotically "optimal" in the sense of the computational overhead of FHE, in addition Gentry, Halevi and Smart have also used the same techniques to actually implement FHE for relatively large circuits.

Arnold Beckmann, Benedikt Löwe (*eds.*). *Acts of the programme "Semantics and Syntax".* Isaac Newton Institute for the Mathematical Sciences, January to July 2012.

Talk given at the SAS Seminar, 6 March 2012, 16:00–16:30.

Bridging Formal Methods in Computer Science. Scientific Computing and Cognitive Science Modelling Tasks

Gregorio de Miguel Casado*

University of Zaragoza, Zaragoza, Spain
E-mail: gmiguel@unizar.es

The development of numerical methods for differential equations during the XIXth century was one of the most important motivations for the inception of computers, conceived as "programmable physical devices" capable of automating and increasing the speed of calculations and also of reusing abstractions (software) and resources (hardware). In this regard, the achievements done by Alan M. Turing and John von Neumann set up the basis for nowadays Theoretical Computer Science and Computer Architecture. Additionally, Alan M. Turing had a decisive contribution in the foundations of Artificial Intelligence, precisely due to the expectations raised by the possibility to embed artificial intelligent in computers [3]. Since then, it can be noticed that the development of Computer Science has brought about a high degree of specialization into independent fields of application which have grown their own objectives an knowledge.

In this talk, I present a global viewpoint of my research interests, which are focused in physical real world modelling issues using approaches based on the interdisciplinary application of formal methods. This is tackled by identifying similarities in both motivations and essential formalisms which allow for the alignment between paradigms from different Computer Science disciplines.

Firstly, the mathematical framework of my research in Scientific Computing (how does the world compute?) and Cognitive Science (how do we compute?) is presented. Some formal aspects about the design of hardware/software support for scientific computing tasks under the scope of Computable Analysis, Añlgebraic Specification of Processors and On-line Arithmetic are introduced. Secondly, some preliminary results of an ongoing research in Cognitive Science modelling tasks joint with Dr. M. Gonzalez Bedia (RETECOG) are presented.

Particularly, in our research, we wonder about how Turing would have shaped his ideas if he had lived today and knew other approaches such as the "embodied cognition" and the "enactive social cognition". These assume that recognizing other person is not a simulation process and that deducing

*Research supported by the Spanish Government MICINN Project TIN2011-27479-C04-01.

Arnold Beckmann, Benedikt Löwe (*eds.*). *Acts of the programme "Semantics and Syntax"*. Isaac Newton Institute for the Mathematical Sciences, January to July 2012.

Talk given at the SAS Seminar, 6 March 2012, 16:30–17:00.

the other's experience means is not always achieved through theoretical inference.

The first part shows how the role of interactive elements in social cognition can be considered so that to motivate a re-evaluation of the foundations and limits of the Turing test [7, 4, 1, 5]. A review of Turing's use of the notion of *time* in the interaction and concepts such as *interactive coupling* is addressed [2]. In the second part, these ideas are formalized under the scope of Computable Analysis. Rather than making an inference from what the other person does, we formalize the way to incorporate other people's actions in terms of their own goals/values within contextualized situations. In this regard, the notion of *intelligent project* is introduced [6] and then formalized using a computable function based using an embedding based on integrable functions [8]. It is obviously assumed that the human capacity to recognize other humans is rooted in strategies as the observation and reflection on others' actions. However, the objective of this research is to formalize the *coupling role* involved in a social process such as to provide a feasible application of it within Computer Science.

Bibliography

[1] M. Auvray, C. Lenay, and J. Stewart. Perceptual interactions in a minimalist virtual environment. *New Ideas in Psychology*, 27(1):32–47, Apr. 2009.

[2] R. Beer. Dynamical approaches to cognitive science. *Trends Cogn Sci*, 4(3):91–99, Mar. 2000.

[3] R. Epstein, G. Roberts, and G. Beber. *Parsing the Turing Test: Philosophical and Methodological Issues in the Quest for the Thinking Computer*. Springer Publishing Company, Incorporated, 1st edition, 2008.

[4] J. Hawkins and S. Blakeslee. *On intelligence*. Henry Holt and Company, 2005.

[5] A. Klin, W. Jones, R. Schultz, and F. Volkmar. The enactive mind, or from actions to cognition: lessons from autism. *Philosophical Transactions of the Royal Society of London. Series B: Biological Sciences*, 358(1430):345–360, Feb. 2003.

[6] J. Marina. *Teoría de la inteligencia creadora*. Compactos Anagrama. Anagrama, 2000.

[7] R. Pfeifer and F. Iida. Embodied artificial intelligence: Trends and challenges. In *Embodied Artificial Intelligence*, volume 2865 of *Lecture Notes in Computer Science*, pages 1–26, 2003.

[8] N. Zhong and K. Weihrauch. Computability theory of generalized functions. *J. ACM*, 50(4):469–505, July 2003.

Synthesis from Components

Moshe Y. Vardi

Rice University, Houston TX, United States of America
E-mail: vardi@cs.rice.edu

Synthesis is the automated construction of a system from its specification. In standard temporal-synthesis algorithms, it is assumed the system is constructed from scratch. This, of course, rarely happens in real life. In real life, almost every non-trivial system, either in hardware or in software, relies heavily on using libraries of reusable components. Furthermore, other contexts, such as web-service orchestration and choreography, can also be modeled as synthesis of a system from a library of components.

In this talk we describe and study the problem of compositional temporal synthesis, in which we synthesize systems from libraries of reusable components. We define two notions of composition: data-flow composition, which we show is undecidable, and control-flow composition, which we show is decidable. We then explore a variation of control-flow compositional synthesis, in which we construct reliable systems from libraries of unreliable components.

This is joint work with Yoad Lustig and Sumit Nain.

Arnold Beckmann, Benedikt Löwe (*eds.*). *Acts of the programme "Semantics and Syntax".*
Isaac Newton Institute for the Mathematical Sciences, January to July 2012.

Talk given at the SAS Seminar, 6 March 2012, 17:00–17:30.

On the Strongly Bounded Turing Degrees of the Computably Enumerable Sets

Klaus Ambos-Spies

Universität Heidelberg, Heidelberg, Germany

E-mail: ambos@math.uni-heidelberg.de

Recently two variants of strongly bounded Turing reductions (sbT-reductions for short) have been introduced. An identity bounded Turing reduction (ibT-reduction for short) is a Turing reduction where no oracle query is greater than the input while a computable Lipschitz reduction (cl-reduction for short) is a Turing reduction where the oracle queries on input x are bounded by $x + c$ for some constant c.

Though ibT-reductions occur quite frequently when dealing with computably enumerable (c.e.) sets (see, e.g., the permitting method or splitting theorems) a systematic study of the sbT-degrees was initiated only quite recently when these reducibilities started to play a role in the analysis of algorithmic randomness. The structures of the c.e. degrees induced by the sbT-reducibilities greatly differ from the degree structures induced by the classical reducibilities like Turing, weak-truth-table, truth-table or many-one reducibility. For instance, there are no complete c.e. sets under the sbT-reducibilities.

In our talk we will give a short summary of recent work in the sbT-degrees of the c.e. sets and give some hints at the proof techniques used in this area. In particular, we address two ongoing projects. The first project is devoted to the analysis of the structure of the sbT-degrees of simple sets. In the second project we analyze the structure of the c.e. ibT-degrees inside a single c.e. cl-degree and the the structure of the c.e. cl-degrees inside a single c.e. wtt-degree.

Arnold Beckmann, Benedikt Löwe (eds.). Acts of the programme "Semantics and Syntax". Isaac Newton Institute for the Mathematical Sciences, January to July 2012.

Talk given at the SAS Seminar, 8 March 2012, 16:00–16:30.

Hard Tautologies

Ján Pich

Charles University, Prague, Czech Republic

E-mail: janpich@yahoo.com

We present some known results about the unprovability of circuit lower bounds in various fragments of arithmetic. The unprovability is usually obtained by showing hardness of corresponding propositional formulas. Interestingely, the propositional formulas encoding circuit lower bounds seem to be good candidate hard tautologies for strong propositional proof systems like Frege or Extended Frege. However, it remains a big challenge to show that such systems do not admit short proofs of all tautologies. So far we have obtained the hardness results only for relatively weak proof systems, e.g., systems admitting feasible interpolation. In this presentation we will discuss feasible disjunction property and some related facts about intuitionistic logic that could help us to prove lower bounds for stronger systems.

Arnold Beckmann, Benedikt Löwe (eds.). Acts of the programme "Semantics and Syntax".
Isaac Newton Institute for the Mathematical Sciences, January to July 2012.

Talk given at the SAS Seminar, 8 March 2012, 16:30–17:00.

Two Visions from Turing: Universality and the Power of Constraining Resources

Jack H. Lutz

Iowa State University, Ames IA, United States of America

E-mail: lutz@cs.iastate.edu

This talk discusses two of my current research topics that are grounded in Turing's visions of computing. First, recent work with Doty, Patitz, Schweller, Summers, and Woods has established that Winfree's Tile Assembly Model of nanoscale self-assembly is *intrinsically* universal, which means that there is a single tile assembly system that can be initialized to directly, geometrically simulate any other. This raises the question of how far "beyond computation" Turing's universality phenomenon reaches.

The second vision discussed in this talk is the power of constraining resources. Naively, it would seem that imposing computability or complexity constraints on classical mathematical methods would at best weaken them. This is now known to be false. In 1966, Martin-Lof gave the first successful definition of the randomness of individual sequences by placing a computability constraint on Lebesgue measure. Over the past 20 years we have seen that complexity constraints on suitable formulations of Lebesgue measure, Baire category, and Hausdorff dimension enable us to analyze the measure, category, and dimension structures of computational complexity classes. And since 2000 we have seen that placing computability constraints on fractal dimensions sheds new, quantitative light on randomness and assigns useful dimensions to individual points in Euclidean space. In retrospect, the spirit of these developments was anticipated by Turing in his 1936 unpublished "A Note on Normal Numbers".

Arnold Beckmann, Benedikt Löwe (*eds.*). *Acts of the programme "Semantics and Syntax".* Isaac Newton Institute for the Mathematical Sciences, January to July 2012.

Talk given at the SAS Seminar, 13 March 2012, 16:00–16:30.

Computational Modeling of Emotions

Christian Becker-Asano

Albert-Ludwigs-Universität Freiburg, Freiburg, Germany
E-mail: christian@becker-asano.de

With the advance of virtual reality and social robotics computer scientists became increasingly interested in modeling inherently human, interpersonal states and processes. The quest of constructing machines that behave appropriately in direct human interaction affords to integrate social competence, which in turn includes a robot's ability to deal with such soft concepts as "emotions."

After a short motivation I give an overview of a selection of the many theories that emotion psychology has to offer. In particular, one possible distinction of three classes of emotions is being motivated, namely that of primary, secondary, and social emotions. These classes serve as basis for the introduction of "WASABI", a computational model of emotions, in which only the first two classes can be represented so far. Thus, in the end it is discussed, how dynamic epistemic logic might be used as basis for the additional integration of social emotions such as "embarrassment", "shame", or "guilt."

The ideas concerning the connection between dynamic epistemic logic and social emotions are joint work with Bernhard Nebel, Benedikt Löwe, Andreas Witzel, and Yanjing Wang.

Arnold Beckmann, Benedikt Löwe (eds.). *Acts of the programme "Semantics and Syntax".*
Isaac Newton Institute for the Mathematical Sciences, January to July 2012.

Talk given at the SAS Seminar, 13 March 2012, 16:30–17:00.

Limitwise Monotonicity Spectra and Uniformity

Iskander Kalimullin

Kazan Federal University, Kazan, Russia

E-mail: Iskander.Kalimullin@ksu.ru

An equivalent definition for limitwise monotonic sets is the following: a set $A \subseteq \omega$ is *limitwise monotonic* in a Turing degree $\mathbf{x}$ if and only if the family

$$\mathcal{LM}(A) = \{\omega \upharpoonright n : n \in A\}$$

is uniformly computably enumerable in the degree $\mathbf{x}$.

Now we say that a set A is *limitwise monotonically* reducible to a set B if for A is limitwise monotonic in every Turing degree $\mathbf{x}$ in which the set B is. Now we say also that a set A is *uniformly limitwise monotonically* if there is an effective procedure generating an enumeration of $\mathcal{LM}(A)$ given arbitrary enumeration of $\mathcal{LM}(B)$.

It is still unclear, are these two reducibilities coincide, and have these reducibilities an hyperarithmetical descriptions. It is only known that for families of finite sets the uniform and non-uniform reducibilities are not coincide.

Namely, we can take the Wehner's family

$$\mathcal{F}_1 = \{\{n\} \oplus F : F \text{ is finite } \& F \neq W_n\}$$

and the family

$$\mathcal{F}_2 = \{\{n\} \oplus F : F \text{ is finite } \& F \neq W_n^{X_n}\},$$

where $\{X_n\}_{n\in\omega}$ is a uniformly low sequence of non-computable sets such that $\deg(X_n) \cap \deg(X_m) = \mathbf{0}$ for $n \neq m$. Then every enumeration of the family $\mathcal{F}_2$ computes an enumeration of $\mathcal{F}_1$ but this computation is not uniform.

The answer to the problem for families $\mathcal{LM}(A)$ will allow understand relative complexity of the abelian p-groups in the form $\sum_{n\in A} \mathbb{Z}_{p^n}$.

Arnold Beckmann, Benedikt Löwe (eds.). *Acts of the programme "Semantics and Syntax".* Isaac Newton Institute for the Mathematical Sciences, January to July 2012.

Talk given at the SAS Seminar, 13 March 2012, 17:00–17:30.

Pattern Formation: The Inspiration of Alan Turing
14 – 16 March 2012

Bernold Fiedler[1], Benedikt Löwe[2,3] and Philip Maini[4]

[1]Freie Universität Berlin, Berlin, Germany
[2]University of Amsterdam, Amsterdam, The Netherlands
[3]Universität Hamburg, Hamburg, Germany
[4]University of Oxford, Oxford, United Kingdom
E-mail: fiedler@math.fu-berlin.de, b.loewe@uva.nl, maini@maths.ox.ac.uk

To celebrate the centenary of Alan Turing's birth and his seminal work in the mathematical modelling of biological pattern formation, this workshop aimed to show how mathematical modelling of pattern formation has led to (i) significant advances in the understanding of certain aspects of biology and chemistry, and (ii) new mathematical and computational challenges. It brought together researchers ranging from those who do experiments to demonstrate pattern formation, to those who develop mathematical and computational techniques to analyse proposed models. The common theme had been the emergence of pattern and form. The format consisted of a number of keynote lectures, given by experts in the field, and a series of shorter contributed talks.

The list of invited speakers consisted of Markus Bär (Physikalisch-Technische Bundesanstalt PTB), Markus Dahlem (Technische Universität Berlin), Patrick De Kepper (Centre national de la recherche scientifique), Irv Epstein (Brandeis University), Alan Garfinkel (University of California, Los Angeles), Shigeru Kondo (Nagoya University), Masayasu Mimura (Meiji University), Yasumasa Nishiura (Tohoku University), Hans Othmer (University of Minnesota), Kevin Painter (Heriot-Watt University), Arnd Scheel (University of Minnesota), Jonathan Sherratt (Heriot-Watt University), and Angela Stevens (Westfälische Wilhelms-Universitat Münster).

Arnold Beckmann, Benedikt Löwe (eds.). *Acts of the programme "Semantics and Syntax".* Isaac Newton Institute for the Mathematical Sciences, January to July 2012.

SAS Satellite Workshop "Pattern Formation: The inspiration of Alan Turing" (St. John's College, Oxford).

Far from Turing? Turing's Paradigm in Physiology

Alan Garfinkel

University of California, Los Angeles CA, United States of America

E-mail: agarfinkel@mednet.ucla.edu

Turing's original model was a linear instability in a 2-variable PDE, describing imaginary "morphogens" reacting and diffusing in a 2D domain. Since the discovery of physiological morphogens in the past few decades, even this simple model has had successful applications. The growing maturity of the applications has now led modelers to more complex scenarios. Developments have included the extension of the original model to include cell density variables, the inclusion of mechanical factors, the extension to 3D spatial domains, and the study of patterns, such as isolated spots, that occur far from the linear instability first studied by Turing. We will review examples of these new developments in the field of physiology and pathophysiology.

Arnold Beckmann, Benedikt Löwe (*eds.*). *Acts of the programme "Semantics and Syntax".* Isaac Newton Institute for the Mathematical Sciences, January to July 2012.

Talk given at the SAS Satellite Workshop "Pattern Formation: The inspiration of Alan Turing" (St. John's College, Oxford), 14 March 2012, 13:50–14:40.

Integrating Experiment and Theory to Elucidate the Chemical Basis of Hair and Feather Morphogenesis

Keven Painter

Heriot-Watt University, Edinburgh, United Kingdom

E-mail: painter@ma.hw.ac.uk

In his seminal 1952 paper, *The Chemical Basis of Morphogenesis*, Alan Turing lays down a milestone in the application of theoretical approaches to understand complex biological processes. The molecular revolution that has taken place during the six decades following this landmark publication has now placed this generation of theoreticians and biologists in an excellent position to rigorously test the theory and, encouragingly, a number of systems have emerged that appear to conform to some of Turing's fundamental ideas. In this talk I will describe how the integration between experiment and theory has been used to enhance understanding in a model system of embryonic patterning: the emergence of feathers and hair in the skins of birds and mammals.

Arnold Beckmann, Benedikt Löwe (*eds.*). *Acts of the programme "Semantics and Syntax".*
Isaac Newton Institute for the Mathematical Sciences, January to July 2012.

Talk given at the SAS Satellite Workshop "Pattern Formation: The inspiration of Alan Turing" (St. John's College, Oxford), 14 March 2012, 14:50–15:40.

Spiral-Wave Prediction in a Lattice of FitzHugh-Nagumo Oscillators

Miriam Grace, Marc-Thorsten Hütt

Jacobs University, Bremen, Germany

E-mail: m.grace@jacobs-university.de, m.huett@jacobs-university.de

In many biological systems, variability of the components can be expected to outrank statistical fluctuations in the shaping of self-organized patterns. The distribution of single-element properties should thus allow the prediction of features of such patterns. In a series of previous studies on established computational models of *Dictyostelium discoideum* pattern formation we demonstrated that the initial properties of potentially very few cells have a driving influence on the resulting asymptotic collective state of the colony [1,2]. One plausible biological mechanism for the generation of variability in cell properties and of spiral wave patterns is the concept of a 'developmental path', where cells gradually move on a trajectory through parameter space. Here we review the current state of knowledge of spiral-wave prediction in excitable systems and present a new one-dimensional developmental path based on the FitzHugh-Nagumo model, incorporating parameter drift and concomitant variability in the distribution of cells embarking on this path, which gives rise to stable spiral waves. Such a generic model of spiral wave predictability allows new insights into the relationship between biological variability and features of the resulting spatiotemporal pattern.

Bibliography

[1] Geberth, D. and Hütt, M.-Th. (2008) Predicting spiral wave patterns from cell properties in a model of biological self-organization. Phys. Rev. E 78, 031917.

[2] Geberth, D. and Hütt, M.-Th. (2009) Predicting the distribution of spiral waves from cell properties in a developmental-path model of Dictyostelium pattern formation. PLoS Comput. Biol 5, e1000422.

Arnold Beckmann, Benedikt Löwe (*eds.*). *Acts of the programme "Semantics and Syntax".* Isaac Newton Institute for the Mathematical Sciences, January to July 2012.

Talk given at the SAS Satellite Workshop "Pattern Formation: The inspiration of Alan Turing" (St. John's College, Oxford), 14 March 2012, 15:50–16:10.

Transport and Development in Fungal Networks

Luke Heaton[1], Nick Jones[2], Eduardo López[1], Philip Maini[1], Mark Fricker[1]

[1]University of Oxford, Oxford, United Kingdom
[2]Imperial College London, London, United Kingdom

E-mail: l.heaton1@physics.ox.ac.uk, nick.jones@imperial.ac.uk,
e.lopez1@physics.ox.ac.uk, philip.maini@maths.ox.ac.uk,
mark.fricker@plants.ox.ac.uk

Multi-cellular organisms have evolved sophisticated systems to supply individual cells with the resources necessary for survival. Plants circulate nutrients through the xylem and phloem, mammals have cardio-vascular systems, but how do fungi translocate materials? Cord-forming fungi form extensive networks that continuously adapt to their surroundings, but what is the developmental logic of such fungal networks, and how does fungal morphology enable efficient transport? In this talk I shall address these fundamental questions, and present the concept of growth-induced mass flows. The key idea is that aqueous fluids are incompressible, so as the fluid filled vessel expand, there must be movement of fluid from the sites of water uptake to the sites of growth. We have developed a model of delivery in growing fungal networks, and found good empirical agreement between our model and experimental data gathered using radio-labeled tracers. Our results lead us to suggest that in fora ging fungi, growth-induced mass flow is sufficient to account for long distance transport, if the system is well insulated. We conclude that active transport mechanisms may only be required at the very end of the transport pathway, near the growing tips.

Arnold Beckmann, Benedikt Löwe (eds.). Acts of the programme "Semantics and Syntax". Isaac Newton Institute for the Mathematical Sciences, January to July 2012.

Talk given at the SAS Satellite Workshop "Pattern Formation: The inspiration of Alan Turing" (St. John's College, Oxford), 14 March 2012, 16:10–16:30.

The Sensitivity of Turing's Pattern Formation Mechanism

Eamonn Gaffney[1], Sungrim Seirin Lee[2]

[1]University of Oxford, Oxford, United Kingdom
[2]RIKEN, Kobe, Japan
E-mail: `gaffney@maths.ox.ac.uk, seirin@cdb.riken.jp`

The prospect of long range signalling by diffusible morphogens initiating large scale pattern formation has been contemplated since the initial work of Turing in the 1950s and has been explored theoretically and experimentally in numerous developmental settings. However, Turing's pattern formation mechanism is notorious for its sensitivity to the details of the initial conditions suggesting that, in isolation, it cannot robustly generate pattern within noisy biological environments. Aspects of developmental self-organisation, in particular a growing domain, have been suggested as a mechanism for robustly inducing a sequential cascade of self-organisation, thus circumventing the difficulties of sensitivity. However the sensitivity question emerges once more for generalisations of Turing's model which include further biological aspects, for example, the inclusion of gene expression dynamics: this will be explored in detail.

Arnold Beckmann, Benedikt Löwe (*eds.*). *Acts of the programme "Semantics and Syntax".* Isaac Newton Institute for the Mathematical Sciences, January to July 2012.

Talk given at the SAS Satellite Workshop "Pattern Formation: The inspiration of Alan Turing" (St. John's College, Oxford), 14 March 2012, 16:30–16:50.

Turing's Instability Versus Cross-diffusion-driven Instability

Masayasu Mimura

Meiji University (Ikuta Campus), Kawasaki, Japan

E-mail: mimura@math.meiji.ac.jp

Turing' diffusion-driven instability has been observed in diverse complex and regularized spatio and/or temporal patterns in not only scientific but also engineering fields. Another instability on pattern formation, such ascross-diffusion-driven instability or chemotactic instability is discussed in ecological and biological systems. This talk was concerned with the relation between two types of instabilities above. As an application, self-organized aggregation of biological individuals with aggregation pheromones have been discussed.

Arnold Beckmann, Benedikt Löwe (eds.). Acts of the programme "Semantics and Syntax".
Isaac Newton Institute for the Mathematical Sciences, January to July 2012.

Talk given at the SAS Satellite Workshop "Pattern Formation: The inspiration of Alan Turing"
(St. John's College, Oxford), 14 March 2012, 17:10–18:00.

Patterns of Sources and Sinks in Oscillatory Systems

Jonathan Sherratt

Heriot-Watt University, Edinburgh, United Kingdom

E-mail: jas@ma.hw.ac.uk

In oscillatory systems, a fundamental spatiotemporal pattern is wave-trains, which are spatially periodic solutions moving with constant speed (also known as periodic travelling waves). In many numerical simulations, one observes finite bands of wavetrains, separated by sharp interfaces known as "sources" and "sinks". This talk is concerned with patterns of sources and sinks in the complex Ginzburg-Landau equation with zero linear dispersion; in this case the CGLE is a reaction-diffusion system. I will show that patterns with large source-sink separations occur in a discrete family, due to a constraint of phase-locking type on the distance between a source and its neighbouring sinks. I will then consider the changes in source-sink patterns in response to very slow increases in the coefficient of nonlinear dispersion. I will present numerical results showing a cascade of splittings of sources into sink-source-sink triplets, culminating in spatiotemporal chaos at a parameter value that matches the change in absolute stability of the underlying periodic travelling wave. In this case the gradual change in pattern form represents an ordered, structured transition from a periodic solution to spatiotemporal chaos. The presented work was done in collaboration with Matthew Smith (Microsoft Research, Cambridge) and Jens Rademacher (CWI, Amsterdam).

Arnold Beckmann, Benedikt Löwe (*eds.*). *Acts of the programme "Semantics and Syntax".*
Isaac Newton Institute for the Mathematical Sciences, January to July 2012.

Talk given at the SAS Satellite Workshop "Pattern Formation: The inspiration of Alan Turing" (St. John's College, Oxford), 14 March 2012, 18:10–19:00.

Experimental and Modeling Studies of Turing Patterns in Chemical Systems

Irving Epstein

Brandeis University, Waltham MA, United States of America

E-mail: epstein@brandeis.edu

This talk reviewed three decades of work on Turing patterns in our laboratory, from the discovery of pattern formation in the CIMA reaction to recent experiments on three-dimensional patterns using tomographic techniques. It discussed modeling efforts (including the Lengyel-Epstein model), approaches to designing systems that display Turing patterns, the effects of external perturbation, and the role of "structured media" (gels, microemulsions, surfaces).

Arnold Beckmann, Benedikt Löwe (eds.). Acts of the programme "Semantics and Syntax".
Isaac Newton Institute for the Mathematical Sciences, January to July 2012.

Talk given at the SAS Satellite Workshop "Pattern Formation: The inspiration of Alan Turing"
(St. John's College, Oxford), 15 March 2012, 09:30–10:20.

A Slow Pushed Front in a Lotka-Volterra Competition Model

Matt Holzer, Arnd Scheel

University of Minnesota, Minneapolis MN, United States of America

E-mail: mdholzer@math.umn.edu, scheel@math.umn.edu

We study the existence and stability of a traveling front in the Lotka-Volterra competition model when the rate of diffusion of one species is small. This front represents the invasion of an unstable homogeneous state by a stable one. It is noteworthy in two respects. First, we show that this front is the selected, or critical, front for this system. We utilize techniques from geometric singular perturbation theory and geometric desingularization. Second, we show that this front appears to be a pushed front in all ways except for the fact that it propagates slower than the linear spreading speed. We show that this is a result of the linear spreading speed arising as a simple pole of the resolvent instead of a branch pole. Using the pointwise Green's function, we show that this pole poses no a priori obstacle to stability of the nonlinear traveling front.

Arnold Beckmann, Benedikt Löwe (*eds.*). *Acts of the programme "Semantics and Syntax".* Isaac Newton Institute for the Mathematical Sciences, January to July 2012.

Talk given at the SAS Satellite Workshop "Pattern Formation: The inspiration of Alan Turing" (St. John's College, Oxford), 15 March 2012, 10:40–11:00.

Turing Patterns on Growing Surfaces

Chandrashekar Venkataraman

University of Warwick, Coventry, United Kingdom
E-mail: c.venkataraman@warwick.ac.uk

We investigate models for biological pattern formation via reaction diffusion systems posed on continuously evolving surfaces. The nonlinear reaction kinetics inherent in the models and the evolution of the spatial domain mean that analytical solutions are generally unavailable and numerical simulations are necessary. In the first part of the talk, we examine the feasibility of reaction-diffusion systems to model the process of parr mark pattern formation on the skin surface of the Amago trout. By simulating a reaction-diffusion system on growing surfaces of differing mean curvature, we show that the geometry of the surface, specifically the surface curvature, plays a central role in the patterns generated by a reaction-diffusion mechanism. We conclude that the curvilinear geometry that characterises fish skin should be taken into account in future modelling endeavours. In the second part of the talk, we investigate a model for cell motility and chemotaxis. Our model consists of a surface reaction-diffusion system that models cell polarisation coupled to a geometric evolution equation for the position of the cell membrane. We derive a numerical method based on surface finite elements for the approximation of the model and we present numerical results for the migration of two and three dimensional cells.

Arnold Beckmann, Benedikt Löwe (eds.). Acts of the programme "Semantics and Syntax".
Isaac Newton Institute for the Mathematical Sciences, January to July 2012.

Talk given at the SAS Satellite Workshop "Pattern Formation: The inspiration of Alan Turing" (St. John's College, Oxford), 15 March 2012, 11:00–11:20.

Influence of Cell-to-cell Variability on Spatial Pattern Formation

Christian Fleck[1], Bettina Greese[2], Martin Huelskamp[3]

[1]Albert-Ludwigs-Universität Freiburg, Freiburg, Germany
[2]Lund University, Lund, Sweden
[3]Universität zu Köln, Köln, Germany

E-mail: [1]christian.fleck@fdm.uni-freiburg.de, [2]bettina.greese@thep.lu.se,
[3]martin.huelskamp@uni-koeln.de

Many spatial patterns in biology arise through differentiation of selected cells within a tissue, which is regulated by a genetic network. This is specified by its structure, its parameterisation, and the noise on its components and reactions. The latter, in particular, is not well examined because it is rather difficult to trace. Using experimental data on trichomes, i.e., epidermal plant hairs, as an example, we examine the variability in pattern formation that is due to small differences among the cells involved in the patterning process. We employ suitable local mathematical measures based on the Voronoi diagram of the trichome positions to determine the noise level in of the pattern. Although trichome initiation is a highly regulated process we show that the experimentally observed trichome pattern is substantially disturbed by cell-to-cell variations. Using computer simulations we find that the rates concerning the availability of the protein complex which triggers trichome formation plays a significant role in noise-induced variations of the pattern. The focus on the effects of cell-to-cell variability yields further insights into pattern formation of trichomes. We expect that similar strategies can contribute to the understanding of other differentiation processes by elucidating the role of naturally occurring fluctuations in the concentration of cellular components or their properties.

Arnold Beckmann, Benedikt Löwe (eds.). Acts of the programme "Semantics and Syntax".
Isaac Newton Institute for the Mathematical Sciences, January to July 2012.

Talk given at the SAS Satellite Workshop "Pattern Formation: The inspiration of Alan Turing" (St. John's College, Oxford), 15 March 2012, 11:20–11:40.

Collision Dynamics in Dissipative Systems

Yasumasa Nishiura

Tohoku University, Sendai, Japan

E-mail: yasumasa@pp.iij4u.or.jp

Spatially localized dissipative structures are ubiquitous such as vortex, chemical blob, discharge patterns, granular patterns, and binary convective motion. When they are moving, it is unavoidable to observe various types of collisions. One of the main questions for the collision dynamics is that how we can describe the large deformation of each localized object at collision and predict its output. The strong collision usually causes topological changes such as merging into one body or splitting into several parts as well as annihilation. It is in general quite difficult to trace the details of the deformation unless it is a very weak interaction. We need a change in our way of thinking to solve this issue. So far we may stick too much to the deformation of each localized pattern and become shrouded in mystery. We try to characterize the hidden mechanism behind the deformation process instead. It may be instructive to think about the following metaphor: the droplet falling down the landscape with many valleys and ridges. The motion of droplets on such a rugged landscape is rather complicated; two droplets merge or split at the saddle points and they may sin k into the underground, i.e., annihilation. On the other hand, the profile of the landscape remains unchanged and in fact it controls the behaviors of droplets. It may be worth to describe the landscape itself rather than complex deformation, namely to find where is a ridge or a valley, and how they are combined to form a whole landscape. Such a change of viewpoint has been proposed recently claiming that the network of unstable patterns relevant to the collision process constitutes the backbone structure of the deformation process, namely the deformation is guided by the connecting orbits among the nodes of the network. Each node is typically an unstable ordered pattern such as steady state or time-periodic solution. This view point is quite useful not only for the problems mentioned above but also for more generalized collision problems, especially, the dynamics in heterogeneous media is one of the interesting applications, since the encounter with heterogeneity can be regarded as a collision. Similarly questions of adaptability to external environments in biological systems fall in the above framework when they are reformulated in an appropriate way. In summary a highly unstable and transient state arising in collision problems is an organizing center which produces various outputs in order to adjust the emerging environments.

Arnold Beckmann, Benedikt Löwe (eds.). Acts of the programme "Semantics and Syntax". Isaac Newton Institute for the Mathematical Sciences, January to July 2012.

Talk given at the SAS Satellite Workshop "Pattern Formation: The inspiration of Alan Turing" (St. John's College, Oxford), 15 March 2012, 12:00–12:50.

Localized Traveling Pulses in Migraine

Markus Dahlem

Technische Universität Berlin, Berlin, Germany

E-mail: dahlem@physik.tu-berlin.de

Cortical spreading depression (SD) is a massive but transient perturbation in the brain's ionic homoeostasis. It is the underlying cause of neurological symptoms during migraine. I present a mechanism by which localized SD pulse segments are formed as long-lasting but transient patterns in a subexcitable medium, in which the homogeneous steady state is a global attractor. Initial perturbed states can develop into distinct transient pulses caused by a ghost of a saddle-node bifurcation that leads to a slow passage through a bottle-neck. The location of the bottle-neck in phase space is associated with a characteristic form (shape, size) of the pulse segment that depends on the curvature of the medium, i.e., the human cortex. Similar patterns have been observed with fMRI and in patient's symptom reports. The emerging transient patterns and their classification according to size and duration offers a model-based analysis of phase-depended stimulation protocols for non-invasive neuromodulation devices, e.g., utilizing transcranial magnetic stimulation, to intelligently target migraine.

Arnold Beckmann, Benedikt Löwe (eds.). Acts of the programme "Semantics and Syntax".
Isaac Newton Institute for the Mathematical Sciences, January to July 2012.

Talk given at the SAS Satellite Workshop "Pattern Formation: The inspiration of Alan Turing"
(St. John's College, Oxford), 15 March 2012, 14:00–14:50.

Spatial Patterns for Reaction-diffusion Systems with Unilateral Conditions

Martin Vaeth

Freie Universität Berlin, Berlin, Germany

E-mail: vaeth@math.fu-berlin.de

It is well-known that Turing's effect can lead to stationary spatial pattern in reaction-diffusion systems of activator-inhibitor or substrate-depletion type. However, it is also known that this effect can occur only under certain assumptions about the diffusion speed. The aim of the talk is to discuss that conditions of unilateral type (obstacles) of various kind can lead to bifurcation of stationary spatial patterns even in a regime where classically no such phenomenon would occur.

Arnold Beckmann, Benedikt Löwe (eds.). Acts of the programme "Semantics and Syntax".
Isaac Newton Institute for the Mathematical Sciences, January to July 2012.

Talk given at the SAS Satellite Workshop "Pattern Formation: The inspiration of Alan Turing" (St. John's College, Oxford), 15 March 2012, 15:10–15:30.

A PDE Approach for the Dynamics of the Inflammatory Stage in Diabetic Wound Healing

Marta Pellicer

Universitat de Girona, Girona, Catalonia (Spain)

E-mail: martap@ima.udg.edu

Wound healing is an extremely complicated process and still not fully understood, moreover when diabetis mellitus is present. The inflammatory phase, the first one of this process, is where there exists a major difference between diabetic and nondiabetic wound healing. Here, we present a work in progress related with the modeling and analysis of the dynamics of some of the main agents involved in this first phase. We propose a reaction-diffusion system as a model for these dynamics. This model aims at generalizing the previous existing approach of Sherratt and Waugh, where an ODE system (only taking into account the time variable) is proposed as a simplified model for this situation. After obtaining this PDE approach, the well-posedness of the problem will be stated (both in a mathematical and a biological sense) and we will present some results related with the equilibria of the system. Finally, we will show some numerical simulations to illustrate the previous results. This is a joint work with Neus Consul (Universitat Politecnica de Catalunya) and Sergio M. Oliva (Universidade de Sao Paulo).

Arnold Beckmann, Benedikt Löwe (eds.). Acts of the programme "Semantics and Syntax". Isaac Newton Institute for the Mathematical Sciences, January to July 2012.

Talk given at the SAS Satellite Workshop "Pattern Formation: The inspiration of Alan Turing" (St. John's College, Oxford), 15 March 2012, 15:30–15:50.

Self-organisation of Cell Asymmetry: Turing's Inspiration is Alive in a Single Cell

Sungrim Seirin Lee, Tatsuo Shibata

RIKEN, Kobe, Japan
E-mail: seirin@cdb.riken.jp, tatsuoshibata@cdb.riken.jp

The development of multicellular organisms starts from a single fertilized egg but it finally involves the specification of diverse cell types. Such diversity is created via an asymmetric cell division, which is crucial to determine a distinct fate of the daughter cells and the most fundamental body plan for constructing a complex body system. The experimental investigation of the molecular levels proposes that differentially segregated protein or RNA determinants in the inside of a cell play a key role in the asymmetric cell divisions processes. The localization of specific proteins during an asymmetric cell division process is commonly observed in many model organisms, though related specific proteins or each step is observed in a slightly different way. Nonetheless, the schematic mechanism of the cell asymmetry division is still remained elusive. Moreover, the mechanism by which related proteins or RNA determinants can be localised to a specific region in a micro scale of small single cell is fully remained as a mystery. Thus to understand the mechanism by integrating the individual information of the molecular level is highly required. In this presentation, we present a mathematical model describing the asymmetric division process of *C. elegans* embryo cell. In particular, we explore the cortical flow effect on the localisation of membrane posterior PAR proteins and discuss the robustness of patterning length and timing arising in the establishment phase of the cell division. Finally, we show that how Turing's spirit is alive in a single cell.

Arnold Beckmann, Benedikt Löwe (*eds.*). *Acts of the programme "Semantics and Syntax".*
Isaac Newton Institute for the Mathematical Sciences, January to July 2012.

Talk given at the SAS Satellite Workshop "Pattern Formation: The inspiration of Alan Turing" (St. John's College, Oxford), 15 March 2012, 15:50–16:10.

Stochastic Reaction and Diffusion on Growing Domains: Understanding the Breakdown of Robust Pattern Formation

Thomas Woolley, Ruth Baker, Eamonn Gaffney, Philip Maini

University of Oxford, Oxford, United Kingdom

E-mail: woolley@maths.ox.ac.uk, ruth.baker@maths.ox.ac.uk,
eamonn.gaffney@maths.ox.ac.uk, philip.maini@maths.ox.ac.uk

All biological patterns, from population densities to animal coat markings, can be thought of as heterogeneous spatio-temporal distributions of mobile agents. Many mathematical models have been proposed to account for the emergence of this complexity, but, in general, they have consisted of deterministic systems of differential equations, which do not take into account the stochastic nature of population interactions. One particular, pertinent, criticism of these deterministic systems, is that the exhibited patterns can often be highly sensitive to changes in initial conditions, domain geometry, parameter values, etc. Due to this sensitivity, we seek to understand the effects of stochasticity and growth on paradigm biological patterning models. We extend spatial Fourier analysis and growing domain mapping techniques to encompass stochastic Turing systems. Through this we find that the stochastic systems are able to realise much richer dynamics than their deterministic counter parts, in that patterns are able to exist outside the standard Turing parameter range. Further, it is seen that the inherent stochasticity in the reactions appears to be more important than the noise generated by growth, when considering which wave modes are excited. Finally, although growth is able to generate robust pattern sequences in the deterministic case, we see that stochastic effects destroy this mechanism of pattern doubling. However, through Fourier analysis we are able to suggest a reason behind this lack of robustness and identify possible mechanisms by which to reclaim it.

Arnold Beckmann, Benedikt Löwe (eds.). Acts of the programme "Semantics and Syntax".
Isaac Newton Institute for the Mathematical Sciences, January to July 2012.

Talk given at the SAS Satellite Workshop "Pattern Formation: The inspiration of Alan Turing" (St. John's College, Oxford), 15 March 2012, 16:10–16:30.

Turing Pattern Formation without Diffusion

Shigeyuki Kondo

Nagoya University, Nagoya, Japan
E-mail: shigerukondo@gmail.com

The reaction-diffusion mechanism, presented by Alan Turing more than 60 years ago, is currently the most popular theoretical model explaining the biological pattern formation including the skin pattern. This theory suggested an unexpected possibility that the skin pattern is a kind of stationary wave (Turing pattern or reaction-diffusion pattern) made by the combination of reaction and diffusion. At first, biologists were quite skeptical to this unusual idea. However, the accumulated simulation studies have proved that this mechanism can not only produce various 2D skin patterns very similar to the real ones, but also predict dynamic pattern change of skin pattern on the growing fish. Now the Turing's theory is accepted as a hopeful hypothesis, and experimental verification of it is awaited. Using the pigmentation pattern of zebrafish as the experimental system, our group in Osaka University has been studying the molecular basis of Turing pattern formation. We have identified the genes related to the pigmentation, and visualized the interactions among the pigment cells. With these experimental data, it is possible to answer the crucial question, "How is the Turing pattern formed in the real organism?" The pigmentation pattern of zebrafish is mainly made by the mutual interactions between the two types of pigment cells, melanophores and xanthophores. All of the interactions are transferred at the tip of the dendrites of pigment cells. In spite of the expectation of many theoretical biologists, there is no diffusion of the chemicals involved. However, we also found that the lengths of the dendrites are different among the interactions, which makes it possible to generate the conditions of Turing pattern formation, "local positive feedback and long range negative feedback". Therefore, we think it is appropriate to call the identified mechanism as a Turing mechanism although it does not contain any diffusion.

Arnold Beckmann, Benedikt Löwe (*eds.*). *Acts of the programme "Semantics and Syntax"*.
Isaac Newton Institute for the Mathematical Sciences, January to July 2012.

Talk given at the SAS Satellite Workshop "Pattern Formation: The inspiration of Alan Turing" (St. John's College, Oxford), 15 March 2012, 16:50–17:40.

Pattern Formation in Active Fluids

Frank Jülicher

Max-Planck-Institute for the Physics of Complex Systems, Dresden, Germany

E-mail: julicher@pks.mpg.de

Biological matter is inherently dynamic and exhibits active properties. A key example is the force generation by molecular motors in the cell cytoskeleton. Such active processes give rise to the generation of active mechanical stresses and spontaneous flows in gel-like cytoskeletal networks. Active material behaviors play a key role for the dynamics of cellular processes such as cell locomotion and cell division. We will discuss intracellular flow patterns that are created by active processes in the cell cortex. By combining theory with quantitative experiments we show that observed flow patterns result from profiles of active stress generation in the system. We will also consider the situation where active stress is regulated by a diffusing molecular species. In this case, spatial concentration patterns are generated by the interplay of stress regulation and self-generated flow fields.

Arnold Beckmann, Benedikt Löwe (eds.). Acts of the programme "Semantics and Syntax". Isaac Newton Institute for the Mathematical Sciences, January to July 2012.

Talk given at the SAS Satellite Workshop "Pattern Formation: The inspiration of Alan Turing" (St. John's College, Oxford), 15 March 2012, 17:50–18:40.

Turing- and Non-Turing Type Pattern in Interacting Cell Systems

Angela Stevens

Westfälische Wilhelms-Universität Münster, Münster, Germany

E-mail: stevens@mis.mpg.de

Examples for pattern formation in interacting cell sytems are discussed, which result from direct cell-cell interaction and cellular motion. The analysis of the respective mathematical models—systems of partial differential equations of hyperbolic type and integro-differential equations—is partly done on the linearized level and partly done for suitable approximations. The long-time behavior of these models is discussed and the resulting patterns are set into context with experimental findings.

Arnold Beckmann, Benedikt Löwe (*eds.*). *Acts of the programme "Semantics and Syntax"*.
Isaac Newton Institute for the Mathematical Sciences, January to July 2012.

Talk given at the SAS Satellite Workshop "Pattern Formation: The inspiration of Alan Turing" (St. John's College, Oxford), 16 March 2012, 09:30–10:20.

Linear Stability Analysis of Turing Patterns on Arbitrary Manifolds

James Walsh, Christopher Angstmann, Paul Curmi

University of New South Wales, Sydney, Australia

E-mail: james.walsh@unsw.edu.au, c.angstmann@unsw.edu.au,
p.curmi@unsw.edu.au

Alan Turing's mathematical model for pattern formation, based on linear instabilities in reaction-diffusion systems, has been widely applied in chemistry, biology and physics. Most of the modelling applications have been implemented on flat two dimensional domains, even though many of the patterns under investigation, including the celebrated application to animal coat patterns, occur on non-Euclidean two dimensional manifolds. In this work we have described an extension of Turing instability analysis to arbitrary manifolds. Our approach is simple to implement and it readily enables exploration of the effect of the geometry on Turing pattern formation in reaction-diffusion systems on arbitrarily shaped and sized domains.

Arnold Beckmann, Benedikt Löwe (eds.). Acts of the programme "Semantics and Syntax".
Isaac Newton Institute for the Mathematical Sciences, January to July 2012.

Talk given at the SAS Satellite Workshop "Pattern Formation: The inspiration of Alan Turing" (St. John's College, Oxford), 16 March 2012, 10:40–11:00.

Pattern Formation During Growth Development: Models, Numerics and Applications

Anotida Madzvamuse

University of Sussex, Brighton, United Kingdom

E-mail: a.madzvamuse@sussex.ac.uk

Mathematical modelling, numerical analysis and simulations of spatial patterning during growth development in developmental biology and biomedicine is an emerging young research area with significant potential of elucidating mechanisms for pattern formation on real biological evolving skin surfaces. Since the seminal work of Turing in 1952 which showed that a system of reacting and diffusing chemical morphogens could evolve from an initially uniform spatial distribution to concentration profiles that vary spatially—a spatial pattern—many models have been proposed on stationary domains exploiting the generalised patterning principle of short-range activation, long-range inhibition elucidated by Meinhardt of which the Turing model is an example. Turing's hypothesis was that one or more of the morphogens played the role of a signaling chemical, such that cell fate is determined by levels of morphogen concentration. However, our recent results show that in the presence of domain growth, short-range inhibition, long-range activation as well as activator-activator mechanisms have the potential of giving rise to the formation of patterns only during growth development of the organism. These results offer us a unique opportunity to study non-standard mechanisms, either experimentally or hypothetically, for pattern formation on evolving surfaces, a largely unchartered research area. This talk discussed modelling, numerical analysis, computations and applications of the models for pattern formation during growth.

Arnold Beckmann, Benedikt Löwe (eds.). Acts of the programme "Semantics and Syntax".
Isaac Newton Institute for the Mathematical Sciences, January to July 2012.

Talk given at the SAS Satellite Workshop "Pattern Formation: The inspiration of Alan Turing" (St. John's College, Oxford), 16 March 2012, 11:00–11:20.

The Influence of Non-standard Boundary Conditions on the Generation of Spatial Patterns

Milan Kučera[1], Filip Jaros[2], Tomáš Vejchodský[1]

[1]Academy of Sciences of the Czech Republic, Prague, Czech Republic
[2]Charles University, Prague, Czech Republic

E-mail: kucera@math.cas.cz, jaros.filip@centrum.cz, vejchod@math.cas.cz

The influence of certain unilateral boundary or interior conditions to spatial Turing's patterns described by reaction-diffusion systems will be discussed. The conditions considered can model sources reflecting concentration in their neighbourhood in the following way. If the concentration exceeds a given threshold then the source is inactive, when the concentration is about to decrease below the threshold then the source either prevents it or at least decelerates the decrease by producing a morphogen (or ligand) and supplementing it into an extracellular space. Some interesting consequences follow. For instance, spatial patterns can arise in general for an arbitrary ratio of diffusion speeds, e.g., for fast diffusion of activator and slow diffusion of inhibitor (the opposite situation than in Turing's original idea), and can arise also for arbitrarily small domains. Simple numerical simulations using a model proposed for a description of pigmentation in animals (in particular felids) promise to describe patterns with spots and, moreover, with a darker strip along the spine, which are observed among some felids. The unilateral conditions can be described mathematically by variational inequalities or inclusions.

Arnold Beckmann, Benedikt Löwe (eds.). Acts of the programme "Semantics and Syntax". Isaac Newton Institute for the Mathematical Sciences, January to July 2012.

Talk given at the SAS Satellite Workshop "Pattern Formation: The inspiration of Alan Turing" (St. John's College, Oxford), 16 March 2012, 11:20–11:40.

Pattern Formation in Multiscale Systems: Homogenization and Beyond

Markus Bär

Physikalisch-Technische Bundesanstalt Berlin, Berlin, Germany
E-mail: markus.baer@ptb.de

Various relevant pattern formation applications are observed in intrinsically heterogeneous reaction-diffusion systems. We derive a simple homogenization scheme and demonstrate that the resulting effective equations are sufficient to qualitatively reproduce the rich pattern dynamics of wave and Turing structures in the BZ-AOT microemulsion system. Furthermore, we validate this effective medium theory by simulations of wave propagation in discrete heterogeneous bistable and excitable media. We find that the approach fails if the heterogeneous medium is near a percolation threshold. For a simple discrete heterogeneous model of cardiac tissue, complex fractionated dynamics and reentrant dynamics appears in such a situation. This is joint work with Sergio Alonso, Raymond Kapral and Karin John.

Arnold Beckmann, Benedikt Löwe (*eds.*). *Acts of the programme "Semantics and Syntax".*
Isaac Newton Institute for the Mathematical Sciences, January to July 2012.

Talk given at the SAS Satellite Workshop "Pattern Formation: The inspiration of Alan Turing" (St. John's College, Oxford), 16 March 2012, 12:00-12:50.

Wavenumber Selection in Closed Reaction-diffusion Systems

Arnd Scheel

University of Minnesota, Minneapolis MN, United States of America

E-mail: scheel@math.umn.edu

Motivated by the plethora of patterns observed in precipitation experiments starting with Liesegang's 1896 study, we investigate pattern formation in the wake of fronts in closed reaction-diffusion systems. We will briefly describe some models and the relation to phase separation models such as the Cahn-Hilliard equation and the Phase-Field System. We will then present results that characterize patterns formed in the wake of fronts.

Arnold Beckmann, Benedikt Löwe (eds.). Acts of the programme "Semantics and Syntax".
Isaac Newton Institute for the Mathematical Sciences, January to July 2012.

Talk given at the SAS Satellite Workshop "Pattern Formation: The inspiration of Alan Turing" (St. John's College, Oxford), 16 March 2012, 14:00–14:50.

Epileptic Seizure Dynamics as a Selforganised Spatio-temporal Pattern

Gerold Baier

The University of Manchester, Manchester, United Kingdom
E-mail: gerold.baier@manchester.ac.uk

Since their original conception as manifestations of electric brain activity by J. Hughlings Jackson, epileptic seizures have been considered an example of a pathology that is best described by a complex spatio-temporal pattern. Nevertheless, their understanding in terms of nonlinear dynamics is still surprisingly limited. In particular, the transition into and out of seizure dynamics is widely regarded to be due to specific parameter changes into and out of a region of periodic solutions, although these changes have never been pinned down to actual physiological observables. Here we present a modelling framework for spatio-temporal epileptic dynamics in humans which builds on the notion of neural mass excitability of a generic cortical circuit. We justify the components of the model by comparison to experimental (animal) and clinical (human) data and study potential mechanisms underlying generalised and partial seizures. We find that, in addition to the dynamics provided by periodic attractors, spatio-temporal epileptic rhythms could also be explained by intermittency (spontaneous switching), and complex rhythmic transients following perturbations. We discuss these concepts using different clinical seizure types. Finally, we use the model framework to propose practical stimulation protocols to test for the presence of regions of abnormality ("epileptic foci") in the human brain.

The research presented in this talk is joint work with Marc Goodfellow, Peter Taylor, Yuijang Wang and Dan Garry.

Bibliography

[1] M. Goodfellow, K. Schindler, and G. Baier. Intermittent spike–wave dynamics in a heterogeneous, spatially extended neural mass model. *NeuroImage*, 55(3):920–932, 2011.

[2] M. Goodfellow, K. Schindler, and G. Baier. Self-organised transients in a neural mass model of epileptogenic tissue dynamics. *NeuroImage*, 59(3):2644–2660, 2012.

[3] P. Taylor and G. Baier. A spatially extended model for macroscopic spike-wave discharges. *J. Comput. Neurosci.*, 31:679–684, 2011.

Arnold Beckmann, Benedikt Löwe (*eds.*). *Acts of the programme "Semantics and Syntax".*
Isaac Newton Institute for the Mathematical Sciences, January to July 2012.

Talk given at the SAS Satellite Workshop "Pattern Formation: The inspiration of Alan Turing" (St. John's College, Oxford), 16 March 2012, 15:10–15:30.

Spatial Pattern Formation in Phytoplankton Dynamics in 1-D and 2-D System

Swati Khare, R. Singh Baghel, J. Dhar, R. Jain

Hindustan College of Science and Technology, Farah, India
E-mail: swati9482@gmail.com

In this paper, we propose a mathematical model of infected phytoplankton dynamics with spatial movement. The reaction diffusion models in both one and two dimension space coordinates are studied. The proposed model is an extension of temporal model available [6] in spatiotemporal domain. It is observed that the reaction diffusion system exhibits spatiotemporal chaos in phytoplankton dynamics. The importantance of the spatially extension are established in this paper, as they display a wide spectrum of ecologically relevant behavior, including chaos. The stability of the system is studied with respect to disease contact rate and the growth fraction of infected phytoplankton indirectly rejoins the susceptible phytoplankton population. The results of numerical experiments in one dimension and two dimensions in space as well as time series in temporal models are presented using MATLAB simulation. Moreover, the stability of the corresponding temporal model is studied analytically . Finally, the comparisons of the three types of numerical experimentation are discussed in conclusion.

Arnold Beckmann, Benedikt Löwe (eds.). Acts of the programme "Semantics and Syntax".
Isaac Newton Institute for the Mathematical Sciences, January to July 2012.

Talk given at the SAS Satellite Workshop "Pattern Formation: The inspiration of Alan Turing" (St. John's College, Oxford), 16 March 2012, 15:30–15:50.

Spiral Wave Initiation in the Reaction-diffusion-mechanics Models

Louis Weise

Utrecht University, Utrecht, The Netherlands

E-mail: L.D.Weise@uu.nl

We introduce a discrete reaction-diffusion-mechanics (dRDM) model to study the effects of deformation on reaction-diffusion (RD) processes. The dRDM framework employs a FitzHugh-Nagumo type RD model coupled to a mass-lattice model, that undergoes finite deformations. The dRDM model describes a material whose elastic properties are described by a generalized Hooke's law for finite deformations (Seth material). Numerically, the dRDM approach combines a finite difference approach for the RD equations with a Verlet integration scheme for the equations of the mass-lattice system. Using this framework we study and find new mechanisms of spiral wave initiation in the contracting excitable medium in homogeneous and heterogeneous cases. In particular, we show that deformation alters the "classical," and forms a new vulnerable zone at longer coupling intervals. This mechanically caused vulnerable zone results in a new mechanism of spiral wave initiation, where unidirectional conduction block and rotation directions of the consequently initiated spiral waves are opposite compared to the mechanism of spiral wave initiation due to the "classical vulnerable zone." We also study and classify mechanisms of spiral wave initiation in excitable tissue with heterogeneity in passive and in active mechanical properties.

Arnold Beckmann, Benedikt Löwe (*eds.*). *Acts of the programme "Semantics and Syntax".*
Isaac Newton Institute for the Mathematical Sciences, January to July 2012.

Talk given at the SAS Satellite Workshop "Pattern Formation: The inspiration of Alan Turing" (St. John's College, Oxford), 16 March 2012, 15:50–16:10.

Chemotaxis and Morphogen Dynamics in Biological Tissues

Bakhtier Vasiev[1], Nigel Harrison[1], Ruth Diez del Corral[2], Cornelius Weijer[3]

[1]University of Liverpool, Liverpool, United Kingdom
[2]Instituto Cajal, Consejo Superior de Investigaciones Científicas, Madrid, Spain
[3]University of Dundee, Dundee, United Kingdom

E-mail: bnvasiev@liv.ac.uk, n.c.harrison@liv.ac.uk, r.diez@cajal.csic.es, c.j.weijer@dundee.ac.uk

In developmental biology patterns formed by morphogens are often affected by movement of cells producing the morphogens. The mutual effects of cell movement and dynamics of concentration patterns are enhanced when the movement is due to chemotactic response to the morphogens. Here we present a set of cell movement patterns with associated patterns in concentration fields of chemotactic agents obtained analytically in continuous model and numerically in individual-cell based model. We have found that group of cells can push itself to move, provided that it produces a chemical which acts as a chemorepellent to its constituent cells. Also the group of cells can be pulled to move by the chemoattractor produced by the surrounding cells in a tissue. Many other chemotactic scenarios are in play when the group of cells is inhomogeneous, i.e., when only part of cells is reacting chemotactically to the morphogen produced by the other part or in the surrounding tissue. We demonstrate the se scenarios on the models of primitive streak extension and regression in the chick embryo.

Arnold Beckmann, Benedikt Löwe (eds.). Acts of the programme "Semantics and Syntax". Isaac Newton Institute for the Mathematical Sciences, January to July 2012.

Talk given at the SAS Satellite Workshop "Pattern Formation: The inspiration of Alan Turing" (St. John's College, Oxford), 16 March 2012, 16:10–16:30.

The Design of Turing Patterns in Solution Chemistry

Patrick De Kepper[1], István Szalai[2], Daniel Cuiñas[3], Judit Horváth[1]

[1]Centre National de la Recherche Scientifique, Paris, France
[2]Eötvös Loránd University, Budapest, Hungary
[3]University of Santiago de Compostella, Santiago de Compostela, Spain

E-mail: dekepper@crpp-bordeaux.cnrs.fr, pisti@chem.elte.hu, horvath@crpp-bordeaux.cnrs.fr

Twenty-two years ago, the first experimental observation of the stationary symmetry breaking reaction-diffusion patterns, predicted by Alan Turing, was made. It boosted theoretical and experimental studies in this field. Though a considerable variety of patterns had been found after that first observation, the number of isothermal reactions producing such patterns was limited to only two for fifteen years. Recently, we proposed an effective method for producing stationary and non-stationary symmetry breaking patterns in open spatial reactors. In the last three years, stationary reaction-diffusion patterns have been found in four new reactions. Among these, two are for the first time not based on oxihalogen chemistry. We shall briefly present this design method and give an overview of experimental contributions in the field.

Arnold Beckmann, Benedikt Löwe (eds.). Acts of the programme "Semantics and Syntax".
Isaac Newton Institute for the Mathematical Sciences, January to July 2012.

Talk given at the SAS Satellite Workshop "Pattern Formation: The inspiration of Alan Turing" (St. John's College, Oxford), 16 March 2012, 16:50–17:40.

The Effect of the Signaling Scheme on the Robustness of Pattern Formation in Development

Hans Othmer

University of Minnesota, Minneapolis MN, United States of America

E-mail: othmer@math.umn.edu

Pattern formation in development is a complex process that involves spatially-distributed signals called morphogens that influence gene expression and thus the phenotypic identity of cells. Usually different cell types are spatially segregated, and the boundary between them may be determined by a threshold value of some state variable. The question arises as to how sensitive the location of such a boundary is to variations in properties, such as parameter values, that characterize the system. In this talk we discuss recent work on both deterministic and stochastic reaction-diffusion models of pattern formation with a view toward understanding how the signaling scheme used for patterning affects the variability of boundary determination between cell types in a developing tissue.

Arnold Beckmann, Benedikt Löwe (eds.). Acts of the programme "Semantics and Syntax".
Isaac Newton Institute for the Mathematical Sciences, January to July 2012.

Talk given at the SAS Satellite Workshop "Pattern Formation: The inspiration of Alan Turing" (St. John's College, Oxford), 16 March 2012, 17:50–18:40.

Proof Complexity Generators

Jan Krajíček

Charles University, Prague, Czech Republic

E-mail: krajicek@karlin.mff.cuni.cz

The talk outlined some ideas underlying an attempt to derive that NP is not closed under complementation from a computational hardness hypothesis.

Arnold Beckmann, Benedikt Löwe (eds.). *Acts of the programme "Semantics and Syntax".*
Isaac Newton Institute for the Mathematical Sciences, January to July 2012.

Talk given at the SAS Seminar, 20 March 2012, 16:00–16:30.

Definable Relations in the Turing Degree Structures

Marat M. Arslanov

Kazan Federal University, Kazan, Russia

E-mail: Marat.Arslanov@ksu.ru

In this talk I briefly discuss problems of definability in n-c.e. degree structures. The main open problem in the area is the definability of the various levels of the n-c.e. degree hierarchy, both relatively and within wider local structures; more specifically, questions related to the definability of the relations of 'computably enumerable' and 'computably enumerable in'.

Definability of classes of degrees in $\mathcal{E}_n$

Let $\mathcal{E}_n, 1 \leq n < \omega$, be the class of all n-c.e. sets. $\bar{\mathcal{E}}_n, 1 \leq n < \omega$, denotes the class of all co-n-c.e. sets. $\mathcal{E}_\infty = \{\bigcup_{1 \leq n < \omega} \mathcal{E}_n; \cup, \cap, \omega, \varnothing\}$. $\mathcal{E} = \mathcal{E}_1$ denotes the set of all c.e. sets. We denote $\bar{\mathcal{E}}^* = \mathcal{E}/_{=^*}$ (similarly for all others), where $A =^* B$ iff $(A - B \cup (B - A)$ finite. Let $\{V_{n,e}\}_{e \in \omega}$ denotes an effective enumeration of all n-c. e. sets, $n \geq 2$.

A set of Turing degrees $\mathcal{C}$ is definable in $\mathcal{E}_\infty$ (in $\mathcal{E}_n$ for some $n \geq 1$) if there is a definable in $\mathcal{E}_\infty$ (in $\mathcal{E}_n$) class of sets $S \subset \mathcal{E}_\infty$ such that $\mathcal{C} = \{\deg B \mid B \in S\}$.

For each $n > 0$, let $H_n = \{\mathbf{a} \text{ c.e.} \mid \mathbf{a}^{(n)} = \mathbf{0}^{(n+1)}\}$, $L_n = \{\mathbf{a} \text{ c.e.} \mid \mathbf{a}^{(n)} = \mathbf{0}^{(n)}\}$.

Theorem. *In $\mathcal{E} = \mathcal{E}_1$,*

a) *all classes $H_m, m \geq 1$, are definable (Martin ($m = 1$), Cholak-Harrington ($m > 1$)). and*

b) *all classes $\bar{H}_m, m \geq 1$, are non definable (Harrington-Soare, Cholak-Downey-Stob).*

Theorem. *In $\mathcal{E}$,*

a) *all classes $L_n, n \geq 1$, are not definable (Harrington-Soare, Cholak-Downey-Stob); and*

b) *all classes $\bar{L}_n, n > 1$, are definable (Lachlan,Shoenfield ($n = 2$), Cholak-Harrington ($n \geq 2$));*

c) *$\bar{L}_1$ not definable (R.Epstein).*

In case of n-c.e. sets ($n > 1$), the class of all computable sets is definable in each $\mathcal{E}_\alpha, 1 \leq \alpha \leq \omega$ by formula

$$\varphi(A) \quad := \quad A = \omega \vee \exists Z(\bar{A} \cap Z \neq \varnothing \,\&\, \bar{A} \cap \bar{Z} \neq \varnothing) \,\&$$
$$(\forall X \exists Y_0, Y_1(X = Y_0 \sqcup Y_1 \,\&\, Y_0 = X \cap A \,\&\, Y_1 = X \cap \bar{A}))$$

Arnold Beckmann, Benedikt Löwe (eds.). *Acts of the programme "Semantics and Syntax".* Isaac Newton Institute for the Mathematical Sciences, January to July 2012.

Talk given at the SAS Seminar, 20 March 2012, 16:30–17:00.

Theorem (Lempp, Nies). *The class $\mathcal{E}$ of c.e. sets is definable in $\mathcal{E}_2$.*

Corollary. *The c.e. degrees are definable in $\mathcal{E}_2$.*

Theorem. *The set of all high c.e. degrees H_1 is definable in each $\mathcal{E}_{2n}, 1 \le n < \omega$.*

For each $n > 1$ there exists a definable in $\mathcal{E}_{n+1}$ set of n-c.e. degrees $\mathcal{C}$ such that $\mathcal{C}$ contains all high n-c.e. degrees.

Definability in the degree structures

Let $\mathcal{D}$, $\mathcal{D}(\le \mathbf{0}')$ and $\mathcal{D}_n, 1 \le n < \omega$, be the partial ordered structures of all Turing degrees, all Turing degrees $\le \mathbf{0}'$, and all n-c.e. degrees, accordingly. $\mathcal{R} = \mathcal{D}_1$ denotes the set of c.e. degrees.

A set of Turing degrees $\mathcal{C}$ is definable in a structure $\mathcal{D}_n$, if there is a formula $\varphi(x)$ in its language $\mathcal{L} = \{\le\}$ such that $\mathcal{D}_n \models \varphi(\mathbf{a})$ iff $a \in \mathcal{C}$.

In the case of c.e. degrees, classes H_n and L_n (except possibly L_1) are definable (Nies, Shore and Slaman).

The formula $\varphi(x) = (\exists \mathbf{y} > \mathbf{x})(\forall \mathbf{z} \le \mathbf{y})(\mathbf{z} \le \mathbf{x} \vee \mathbf{x} \le \mathbf{z})$ defines in $\mathcal{D}_2$ an infinite set of c.e. degrees. (Arslanov, Kalimullin, Lempp)

Theorem. *a) (Yamaleev) For any properly d-c.e. degree and for any nontrivial splitting of $\mathbf{d} = \mathbf{d}_0 \cup \mathbf{d}_1$ into d-c.e. degrees $\mathbf{d}_0$ and $\mathbf{d}_1$, for an $i \le 1$ any d-c.e. degree $\mathbf{u}_i$, $\mathbf{d}_i < \mathbf{u}_i \le \mathbf{d}$, is splittable in d-c.e. degrees avoiding the upper cone of $\mathbf{d}_i$.*

b) There is a c.e. degree $\mathbf{c} > \mathbf{0}$ and a nontrivial splitting of $\mathbf{c} = \mathbf{c}_0 \cup \mathbf{c}_1$ into d-c.e. degrees $\mathbf{c}_0$ and $\mathbf{c}_1$ such that for each $i \le 1$ there is a d-c.e. degree $\mathbf{d}_i, \mathbf{c}_i < \mathbf{d}_i < \mathbf{c}$, which is not splittable into d-c.e. degrees avoiding the upper cone of $\mathbf{c}_i$.

Let $\mathcal{C}$ denote the (definable) class of c.e. degrees which have the property *b)* of this theorem.

Conjecture (Low Density Conjecture). *The class $\mathcal{C}$ dense in the low c.e. degrees: $(\forall \text{ low c.e. } \mathbf{a} < \mathbf{b})(\exists \mathbf{c} \in \mathcal{C})(\mathbf{a} < \mathbf{c} < \mathbf{b})$?*

Low density + Low splitting $\rightarrow$ definability of c.e. degrees in $\mathcal{D}_2$): For any given c.e. degree $\mathbf{a} > \mathbf{0}$, first split $\mathbf{a}$ into two low c.e. degrees $\mathbf{a}_0$ and $\mathbf{b}_0$: $\mathbf{a} = \mathbf{a}_0 \cup \mathbf{b}_0$, then find low c.e. degrees $\mathbf{a}_1, \mathbf{a} > \mathbf{a}_1 > \mathbf{a}_0$ and $\mathbf{b}_1, \mathbf{a} > \mathbf{b}_1 > \mathbf{b}_0$, after that, using low density theorem find $\mathcal{C}$-degrees $\mathbf{c}_0$ and $\mathbf{c}_1$ such that $\mathbf{a}_0 < \mathbf{c}_0 < \mathbf{a}_1$ and $\mathbf{b}_0 < \mathbf{c}_1 < \mathbf{b}_1$. We have $\mathbf{a} = \mathbf{c}_0 \cup \mathbf{c}_1$.

Theorem. *Let $\mathbf{a} > \mathbf{0}$ be a high c.e. degree ($\mathbf{a}' = \mathbf{0}''$). Then there exists a c.e. degree $\mathbf{c} \le \mathbf{a}$ and a nontrivial splitting of $\mathbf{c}$ into d-c.e. degrees $\mathbf{c}_0$ and $\mathbf{c}_1$ such that for each $i \le 1$ there exists a d-c.e. degree $\mathbf{d}_i, \mathbf{c}_i < \mathbf{d}_i < \mathbf{c}$, which is not splittable into d-c.e. degrees avoiding the upper cone of $\mathbf{c}_i$.*

Open Question. *Can we change in this theorem the condition* $\mathbf{a}' = \mathbf{0}''$ *(*$\mathbf{a}$ *is a high degree) by the condition* $\mathbf{a}' = \mathbf{0}'$ *(*$\mathbf{a}$ *is a low degree)?*

Theorem. *Let* $\mathbf{a} > \mathbf{0}$ *be a low n-c.e. degree for some* $n \geq 1$. *Then the set of n-c. e. degrees* $\{\mathbf{b} \mid \mathbf{b} \leq \mathbf{a}\}$ *is definable from parameters in* $\mathcal{D}(\leq \mathbf{0}')$.

Open Question.   • *Which other natural sets of n-c.e. degrees are definable (from parameters) in the* Δ_2^0*-degrees.*
  • *Is the set of all n-c.e. degrees for some* $n > 1$ *definable from parameters in the* Δ_2^0*-degrees?*
  • *Is the set of all c.e. degrees definable from parameters in the n-c.e. degrees for some /each* $n > 1$*?*

Infinite Chess: The Mate-in-n Problem Is Decidable, and the Omega One of Chess

Joel David Hamkins

City University of New York, New York NY, United States of America

E-mail: jhamkins@gc.cuny.edu

Infinite chess is chess played on an infinite edgeless chessboard. The familiar chess pieces move about according to their usual chess rules, and each player strives to place the opposing king into checkmate. The mate-in-n problem of infinite chess is the problem of determining whether a designated player can force a win from a given finite position in at most n moves. A naive formulation of this problem leads to assertions of high arithmetic complexity with $2n$ alternating quantifiers—there is a move for white, such that for every black reply, there is a countermove for white, and so on. In such a formulation, the problem does not appear to be decidable; and one cannot expect to search an infinitely branching game tree even to finite depth.

Nevertheless, in joint work with Dan Brumleve and Philipp Schlicht [1], confirming a conjecture of myself and C. D. A. Evans, we establish that the mate-in-n problem of infinite chess is computably decidable, uniformly in the position and in n. Furthermore, there is a computable strategy for optimal play from such mate-in-n positions. The proof proceeds by showing that the mate-in-n problem is expressible in what we call the first-order structure of chess, which we prove (in the relevant fragment) is an automatic structure, whose theory is therefore decidable. Unfortunately, this resolution of the mate-in-n problem does not appear to settle the decidability of the more general winning-position problem, the problem of determining whether a designated player has a winning strategy from a given position, since a position may admit a winning strategy without any bound on the number of moves required. This issue is connected with transfinite game values in infinite chess, and the exact value of the omega one of chess ω_1^{chess} is not known. The talk also discussed recent joint work with C. D. A. Evans and W. Hugh Woodin showing that the omega one of infinite positions in three-dimensional infinite chess is true ω_1: every countable ordinal is realized as the game value of such a position.

See http://jdh.hamkins.org/infinite-chess-cambridge-2012/ for discussion forum and relevant links.

Arnold Beckmann, Benedikt Löwe (eds.). Acts of the programme "Semantics and Syntax".
Isaac Newton Institute for the Mathematical Sciences, January to July 2012.

Talk given at the SAS Seminar, 22 March 2012, 16:00–16:30.

Bibliography

[1] D. Brumleve, J. D. Hamkins, and P. Schlicht. The mate-in-n problem of infinite chess is decidable. In S. B. Cooper, A. Dawar, and B. Löwe, editors, *How the World Computes*, volume 7318 of *Lecture Notes in Computer Science*, pages 78–88. Springer Berlin Heidelberg, 2012.

Mathematics and the Turing Renaissance

Robert I. Soare

The University of Chicago, Chicago IL, United States of America

E-mail: soare@cs.uchicago.edu

David Hilbert greatly influenced the foundations of mathematics from 1900 to 1930. First, Hilbert wanted a finite consistency proof for mathematics, beginning with arithmetic. Second, he proposed the *Entscheidungsproblem* (decision problem), which was to find an algorithm to decide whether a given statement in the language of mathematics is valid. In 1931 Kurt Gödel dramatically refuted the first program.

Turing and Alonzo Church (Turing's subsequent thesis adviser at Princeton) worked independently on the *Entscheidungsproblem*. Their approach was: (1) to find a precise mathematical definition for the computable functions; and (2) to demonstrate that every informally computable function was captured by the formal definition. Gödel doubted that this was even possible because "the notion of a finite computation is not defined, but serves as a heuristic principle." In 1934 and 1935 Church proposed two different solutions, but Gödel rejected both, even though the second was based on Gödel's own definition in 1934 of a recursive function. In contrast, Gödel immediately accepted Turing's 1936 analysis and wrote, "That this really is the correct definition of mechanical computability was established beyond any doubt by Turing."

By 1937, the three definitions of computable functions had been proved mathematically equivalent. In retrospect, Church got it right and got it first. Why should Church not get the credit? The problem, however, was not simply a mathematical one. Turing demonstrated extraordinary creative insight into the nature of computability. Like Michelangelo, Turing saw the figure in the marble more clearly than anyone else. Why Turing and not Church? The reply is, "Why Michelangelo and not Donatello?" This lecture will include slides of Renaissance art and a careful comparison to make this point.

The author maintains a website on the topic of the lecture.

Arnold Beckmann, Benedikt Löwe (*eds.*). *Acts of the programme "Semantics and Syntax".* Isaac Newton Institute for the Mathematical Sciences, January to July 2012.

Talk given at the SAS Seminar, 22 March 2012, 16:30–17:00.

Logical Approaches to Barriers in Complexity II
26 – 30 March 2012

Arnold Beckmann[1] and Anuj Dawar[2]

[1]Swansea University, Swansea, United Kingdom, and [2]Cambridge University, Cambridge, United Kingdom

E-mail: a.beckmann@swansea.ac.uk and Anuj.Dawar@cl.cam.ac.uk

Computational complexity theory has its origin in logic. The fundamental goal of this area is to understand the limits of efficient computation (that is understanding the class of problems which can be solved quickly and with restricted resources) and the sources of intractability (that is what takes some problems inherently beyond the reach of such efficient solutions). The most famous open problem in the area is the P = NP problem, listed among the seven Clay Millennium Prize problems. Logic provides a multifarious toolbox of techniques to analyse questions like this, some of which promise to provide deep insights in the nature and limits of efficient computation.

In our workshop, we focused on logical descriptions of complexity, i.e., descriptive complexity, propositional proof complexity and bounded arithmetic. Despite considerable progress by research communities in each of these areas, the main open problems remain. In finite model theory the major open problem is whether there is a logic capturing on all structures the complexity class P of polynomial time decidable languages. In bounded arithmetic the major open problem is to prove strong independence results that would separate its levels. In propositional proof complexity the major open problem is to prove strong lower bounds for expressive propositional proof systems.

The workshop brought together leading researchers covering all research areas within the scope of the workshop. We especially focused on work that had drawn on methods from the different areas which appealed to the whole community.

Tutorials were given by Samuel R. Buss (University of California, San Diego) and Stephan Kreutzer (Technische Universität Berlin).

The list of invited speakers consisted of Albert Atserias (Universitat Politècnica de Catalunya), Yijia Chen (Shanghai Jiao Tong University), Stefan Dantchev (Durham University), Arnaud Durand (Université Denis-Diderot Paris 7), Bjarki Holm (University of Cambridge), Juha Kontinen (University of Helsinki), Jan Krajíček (Charles University in Prague),

Arnold Beckmann, Benedikt Löwe (eds.). Acts of the programme "Semantics and Syntax".
Isaac Newton Institute for the Mathematical Sciences, January to July 2012.

SAS Workshop "Logical Approaches to Barriers in Complexity II".

Phuong The Nguyen (University of Montreal), Rahul Santhanam (The University of Edinburgh), Nicole Schweikardt (Goethe University) and Neil Thapen (Academy of Sciences of the Czech Republic).

(Picture courtesy of The Isaac Newton Institute)

In addition to the abstracts in this booklet, slides of some of the talks can be found at

http://www.newton.ac.uk/programmes/SAS/sasw01.html

Complexity of Computations and Proofs and Pseudo-finite Structures

Jan Krajíček

Charles University, Prague, Czech Republic

E-mail: krajicek@karlin.mff.cuni.cz

Problems to establish lower bounds for circuit size or for lengths of propositional proofs can be formulated as problems to construct expansions of pseudo-finite structures. This talk explains this relation, gives a few examples, and discusses some recent work aimed at proof complexity.

Arnold Beckmann, Benedikt Löwe (*eds.*). *Acts of the programme "Semantics and Syntax"*. Isaac Newton Institute for the Mathematical Sciences, January to July 2012.

Talk given at the SAS Workshop "Logical Approaches to Barriers in Complexity II", 26 March 2012, 9:30–10:30.

Proof Complexity of Paris-Harrington Tautologies

Nicola Galesi

Università degli Studi di Roma La Sapienza, Rome, Italy

E-mail: galesi@di.uniroma1.it

We study the proof complexity of Paris-Harrington's Large Ramsey Theorem for bicolorings of graphs. We prove a conditional lower bound in Resolution and a upper bound in bounded-depth Frege. The lower bound is conditional on a (very reasonable) hardness assumption for a weak (quasi-polynomial) Pigeonhole principle in Res(2). We show that under such assumption, there is no refutation of the Paris-Harrington formulas of size quasi-polynomial in the number of propositional variables. The proof technique for the lower bound extends the idea of using a combinatorial principle to blow-up a counterexample for another combinatorial principle beyond the threshold of inconsistency. A strong link with the proof complexity of an unbalanced Ramsey principle for triangles is established. This is obtained by adapting some constructions due to Erdős and Mills.

Arnold Beckmann, Benedikt Löwe (*eds.*). *Acts of the programme "Semantics and Syntax".*
Isaac Newton Institute for the Mathematical Sciences, January to July 2012.

Talk given at the SAS Workshop "Logical Approaches to Barriers in Complexity II",
26 March 2012, 11:00–11:30.

Logical Methods in the Complexity Analysis of Graph Algorithms

Stephan Kreutzer

Technische Universität Berlin, Berlin, Germany

E-mail: stephan.kreutzer@tu-berlin.de

A classical observation in complexity theory is that many common algorithmic problems on graphs are hard to solve. Consequently, much work has gone into studying restricted classes of admissible inputs on which tractability results can be retained. A particular rich source of structural properties which guarantee the existence of efficient algorithms for many problems on graphs come from structural graph theory, especially algorithmic graph minor theory. It has been found that most generally hard problems become tractable on graph classes of bounded tree-width and many remain tractable on planar graphs or graph classes excluding a fixed minor.

Besides many specific results giving algorithms for individual problems, of particular interest are results that establish tractability of a large class of problems on specific classes of instances. These results come in various flavours. In this tutorial we will focus on results that take a descriptive approach, i.e., results that use a logic to describe algorithmic problems and then establish general tractability results for all problems definable in that logic on specific classes of inputs. These results are usually referred to as algorithmic meta-theorems.

In some sense the first theorem of this form is Courcelle's famous result that all monadic second-order definable problems are solvable in linear time on all classes of structures of bounded tree-width. Subsequently many further theorems of this form and many tools for obtaining such results have been developed.

In this tutorial we will present the main methods and results obtained in this area. In the first part, the focus will be on logical tools that can be used to obtain algorithmic meta-theorems. In the second part of the tutorial we will focus on methods to establish corresponding lower bounds, i.e., intractability results for particular logics on classes of graphs that do not have any of the nice properties that make algorithmic meta-theorems possible. In particular, we will present a reasonably tight lower bound for Courcelle's theorem mentioned above.

Arnold Beckmann, Benedikt Löwe (eds.). Acts of the programme "Semantics and Syntax". Isaac Newton Institute for the Mathematical Sciences, January to July 2012.

Talk given at the SAS Workshop "Logical Approaches to Barriers in Complexity II", 26 March 2012, 11:30–12:30, and 27 March 2012, 11:30–12:30,.

Parameterised Proof Complexity

Stefan Dantchev

Durham University, Durham, United Kingdom

E-mail: s.s.dantchev@durham.ac.uk

I will start by introducing the basic notion of a parameterised proof as defined by Martin, Szeider and myself back in 2007, and will discuss a complexity gap theorem theorem for generic parameterisation of tree-like resolution. I will then move onto results that have been obtained since them by various researchers, including parameterised lower bounds for the pigeon-hole principle in resolution and for the maximum clique in random graphs in tree-like resolution. I will conclude with some new results due to Martin and myself on parameterised proofs for W[1] as well as with some open problems.

Arnold Beckmann, Benedikt Löwe (eds.). Acts of the programme "Semantics and Syntax".
Isaac Newton Institute for the Mathematical Sciences, January to July 2012.

Talk given at the SAS Workshop "Logical Approaches to Barriers in Complexity II",
26 March 2012, 14:00–15:00.

Parameterized Complexity of DPLL Search Procedures

Olaf Beyersdorff

Università degli Studi di Roma La Sapienza, Rome, Italy

E-mail: beyersdorff@thi.uni-hannover.de

We study the performance of DPLL algorithms on parameterized problems. In particular, we investigate how difficult it is to decide whether small solutions exist for satisfiability and other combinatorial problems. For this purpose we develop a Prover-Delayer game which models the running time of DPLL procedures and we establish an information-theoretic method to obtain lower bounds to the running time of parameterized DPLL procedures. We illustrate this technique by showing lower bounds to the parameterized pigeonhole principle and to the ordering principle. As our main application we study the DPLL procedure for the problem of deciding whether a graph has a small clique. We show that proving the absence of a k-clique requires $n^{\Omega(k)}$ steps for a non-trivial distribution of graphs close to the critical threshold. For the restricted case of tree-like Parameterized Resolution, this result answers a question asked in [1] of understanding the Resolution complexity of this family of formulas.

Bibliography

[1] O. Beyersdorff, N. Galesi, M. Lauria, and A. Razborov. Parameterized bounded-depth Frege is not optimal. In *Automata, languages and programming. Part I*, volume 6755 of *Lecture Notes in Comput. Sci.*, pages 630–641. Springer, Heidelberg, 2011.

Arnold Beckmann, Benedikt Löwe (*eds.*). *Acts of the programme "Semantics and Syntax"*. Isaac Newton Institute for the Mathematical Sciences, January to July 2012.

Talk given at the SAS Workshop "Logical Approaches to Barriers in Complexity II", 26 March 2012, 15:00–15:30.

Model Checking for Modal Intuitionistic Dependence Logic

Fan Yang

University of Helsinki, Helsinki, Finland

E-mail: `fan.yang@helsinki.fi`

In this paper we consider the complexity of model checking for modal intuitionistic dependence logic (MIDL). MIDL is a natural variant of first-order dependence logic (D), which was introduced by Väänänen [5], as a new approach to independence-friendly logic [3]. Sentences of D have exactly the same expressive power as sentences of existential second-order logic [5, 2, 7]. The compositional semantics of D is team semantics, originally developed by Hodges [4] for independence-friendly logic. Abramsky and Väänänen [1] studied Hodges' construction in a more general context and introduced BID-logic, which extends dependence and includes intuitionistic implication, Boolean disjunction, as well as linear implication. It was shown that the intuitionistic fragment of BID-logic, called intuitionistic dependence logic, has exactly the same expressive power as the full second-order logic, on the level of sentences [8]. The modal version of D, modal dependence logic (MDL) was defined by Väänänen [6]. A natural variant of MDL is modal intuitionistic dependence logic, where the intuitionistic implication and Boolean disjunction are added into the setting. In this paper we show that the model checking problem for MIDL in general is PSPACE-complete. Furthermore, we consider fragments of MIDL built by restricting the operators allowed in the logic. It turns out that apart from known NP-complete as well as tractable fragments there also are some coNP-complete fragments, e.g., propositional intuitionistic dependence logic.

Bibliography

[1] S. Abramsky and J. Väänänen. From IF to BI. *Synthese*, 167(2):207–230, 2009.

[2] H. Enderton. Finite partially-ordered quantifiers. *Zeitschrift fur Mathematische Logik und Grundlagen der Mathematik*, (16):393–397, 1970.

[3] J. Hintikka and G. Sandu. Informational independence as a semantical phenomenon. In R. H. J. E. Fenstad, I. T. Frolov, editor, *Logic, Methodology and Philosophy of Science*, pages 571–589. Amsterdam: Elsevier, 1989.

Arnold Beckmann, Benedikt Löwe (*eds.*). *Acts of the programme "Semantics and Syntax"*. Isaac Newton Institute for the Mathematical Sciences, January to July 2012.

Talk given at the SAS Workshop "Logical Approaches to Barriers in Complexity II", 26 March 2012, 16:00–16:30.

[4] W. Hodges. Compositional semantics for a language of imperfect information. *Logic Journal of the IGPL*, 5:539–563, 1997.

[5] J. Väänänen. *Dependence Logic: A New Approach to Independence Friendly Logic*. Cambridge: Cambridge University Press, 2007.

[6] J. Väänänen. Modal dependence logic. In K. R. Apt and R. van Rooij, editors, *New Perspectives on Games and Interaction*, volume 4 of *Texts in Logic and Games*, pages 237–254. Amsterdam University Press, 2008.

[7] W. Walkoe. Finite partially-ordered quantification. *Journal of Symbolic Logic*, (35):535–555, 1970.

[8] F. Yang. Expressing second-order sentences in intuitionistic dependence logic. *Studia Logica Special Issue on Dependence and Independence in Logic*, to appear.

Complexity Results for Dependence Logic

Juha Kontinen

University of Helsinki, Helsinki, Finland

E-mail: juha.kontinen@helsinki.fi

Dependence Logic, introduced by Jouko Väänänen in 2007, is a new logic incorporating the concept of dependence into first-order logic. The expressive power of dependence logic coincides with that of existential second-order logic, and the complexity class NP over finite structures. In the past few years, dependence logic has grown into a new framework in which various notions of dependence and independence can be formalized. We review recent results regarding the expressive power and complexity of certain fragments and extensions of dependence logic.

Arnold Beckmann, Benedikt Löwe (eds.). Acts of the programme "Semantics and Syntax".
Isaac Newton Institute for the Mathematical Sciences, January to July 2012.

Talk given at the SAS Workshop "Logical Approaches to Barriers in Complexity II",
26 March 2012, 17:00–17:30.

Indistinguishability in Counting Logics and the Complexity of Semi-Algebraic Proofs

Albert Atserias

Universitat Politècnica de Catalunya, Barcelona, Spain

E-mail: atserias@lsi.upc.edu

The recent connection between the concept of indistinguishability by the properties expressible in a certain formal language and a relaxation of structural isomorphism through linear programming brings the areas of descriptive complexity and propositional proof complexity a little bit closer together. In this talk I will overview this connection making emphasis on the questions it has answered, but also on the many new exciting questions that it raises.

Arnold Beckmann, Benedikt Löwe (eds.). Acts of the programme "Semantics and Syntax". Isaac Newton Institute for the Mathematical Sciences, January to July 2012.

Talk given at the SAS Workshop "Logical Approaches to Barriers in Complexity II", 27 March 2012, 9:00–10:00.

The Hierarchy of Equivalence Relations on the Natural Numbers under Computable Reducibility

Joel David Hamkins

City University of New York, New York NY, United States of America

E-mail: jhamkins@gc.cuny.edu

Many of the naturally arising equivalence relations in mathematics, such as isomorphism relations on various types of countable structures, turn out to be equivalence relations on a standard Borel space, and these relations form an intensely studied hierarchy under Borel reducibility. The topic of this talk is to introduce and explore the computable analogue of this robust theory, by studying the corresponding hierarchy of equivalence relations on the natural numbers under computable reducibility. Specifically, one relation E is computably reducible to another, F, if there is a unary computable function f such that $x \mathrel{E} y$ if and only if $f(x) \mathrel{F} f(y)$. This gives rise to a very different hierarchy than the Turing degrees on such relations, since it is connected with the difficulty of the corresponding classification problems, rather than with the difficulty of computing the relations themselves. The theory is well suited for an analysis of equivalence relations on classes of c.e. structures, a rich context with many natural examples, such as the isomorphism relation on c.e. graphs or on computably presented groups. An abundance of open questions remain, and the subject is an attractive mix of methods from mathematical logic, computability, set theory, particularly descriptive set theory, and the rest of mathematics, subjects in which many of the equivalence relations arise. This is joint work with Sam Coskey and Russell Miller.

Arnold Beckmann, Benedikt Löwe (eds.). Acts of the programme "Semantics and Syntax". Isaac Newton Institute for the Mathematical Sciences, January to July 2012.

Talk given at the SAS Workshop "Logical Approaches to Barriers in Complexity II", 27 March 2012, 10:00–10:30.

Ordinal Strength of Logic-enriched Type Theories

Robin Adams

Royal Holloway, University of London, Egham, United Kingdom

E-mail: robin@cs.rhul.ac.uk

Type theories are formal languages that can be read as either a programming language or a system of logic, via the propositions-as-types or proofs-as-programs paradigm. Their syntax and metatheory is quite different in character to that of "orthodox logics" (the familiar first-order logics, second-order logics, etc). So far, it has been difficult to relate type theories to the more orthodox systems of first-order logic, second-order logic, etc. Logic-enriched type theories (LTTs) may help with this problem. An LTT is a hybrid system consisting of a type theory (for defining mathematical objects) and a separate logical component (for reasoning about those objects). It is often possible to translate between a type theory and an orthodox logic using an LTT as an intermediate system, when finding a direct translation would be very difficult. In this talk, I shall summarise the work so far on the proof theory of type theories, including Anton Setzer's work on ordinal strength. I shall show how LTTs allow results about type theories to be applied to orthodox logics, and vice versa. This will include a recently discovered, elementary proof of the conservativity of ACA_0 over PA. I conclude by giving two new results: type-theoretic analogues of the classic results that P corresponds to first-order least fixed point logic, and NP to second-order existential logic.

Arnold Beckmann, Benedikt Löwe (eds.). Acts of the programme "Semantics and Syntax". Isaac Newton Institute for the Mathematical Sciences, January to July 2012.

Talk given at the SAS Workshop "Logical Approaches to Barriers in Complexity II", 27 March 2012, 11:00–11:30.

The Complexity of Enumeration and Counting for Acyclic Conjunctive Queries

Arnaud Durand

Université Denis-Diderot Paris 7, Paris, France
E-mail: durand@logique.jussieu.fr

Enumerating all the solutions of a problem or counting the number of these solutions are two related algorithmic tasks. Complexity measures, however, are of a different nature. For enumeration problem, for example, one of the main notion is that of delay between generated solutions. A problem is considered as tractable if one can enumerate the solutions one by one without repetition with a "reasonable" delay (e.g., polynomial, linear or constant time) between two solutions.

In this talk, we will make a tour on the complexity of enumeration and (weighted) counting for acyclic conjunctive queries (ACQ), a well-known tractable fragment (for decision) of conjunctive queries.

We first show that there is a dichotomy for enumeration and, up to some reasonable complexity assumption, such queries are either enumerable with a linear or with a "constant" delay. Hence, in all cases, enumeration is tractable.

For weighted counting, the situation is more complex. The unweighted quantifier free version of this problem is known to be tractable (for combined complexity), but it is also known that introducing even a single quantified variable makes it #P-hard. By introducing some polynomial representation of queries, we first show that weighted counting for quantifier-free ACQ is still tractable and that even minimalistic extensions of the problem lead to hard cases. We then introduce a new parameter for quantified queries that permits to isolate large island of tractability. We show that, up to a standard assumption from parameterized complexity, this parameter fully characterizes tractable subclasses for counting weighted solutions of ACQ queries. This completely determine the tractability frontier for weighted counting in this case.

Arnold Beckmann, Benedikt Löwe (*eds.*). *Acts of the programme "Semantics and Syntax"*. Isaac Newton Institute for the Mathematical Sciences, January to July 2012.

Talk given at the SAS Workshop "Logical Approaches to Barriers in Complexity II", 27 March 2012, 14:00–15:00.

Bounded Degree and Planar Spectra

Eryk Kopczynski

Uniwersytet Warszawski, Warsaw, Poland

E-mail: erykk@mimuw.edu.pl

There are many problems in finite model theory about which we know a lot in the unrestricted classes, but which are still not thoroughly researched in the case where we restrict the class of considered models (for example, in terms of properties of their Gaifman graphs). In this talk we consider the problem of spectra of formulae. A set of integers S is a spectrum of φ if $n \in S$ iff φ has a model of size n. It is well known that S is a spectrum of some formula iff the problem of deciding whether $n \in S$ is in NP when n is given in unary (equivalently, in NE when n is given in binary). Restricting the class of models we can get, for example, bounded degree spectra (S is a bounded degree spectrum of φ iff φ has a bounded degree model of size n), weak planar spectra (S is a bounded degree spectrum of φ iff φ has a planar model of size n), and forced planar spectra (S is a spectrum of φ which admits only planar models). We provide the complexity theoretic characterizations for these cases, similar to the one above. In case of bounded degree spectra, there is a very small (polylogarythmic) gap between our lower and upper bound. In case of weak planar spectra the gap is polynomial. We also provide a weaker complexity theoretic characterization of forced planar spectra.

Arnold Beckmann, Benedikt Löwe (eds.). Acts of the programme "Semantics and Syntax".
Isaac Newton Institute for the Mathematical Sciences, January to July 2012.

Talk given at the SAS Workshop "Logical Approaches to Barriers in Complexity II",
27 March 2012, 15:00–15:30.

SAT Solving: Present and Future

Oliver Kullmann

Swansea University, Swansea, United Kingdom

E-mail: o.kullmann@swansea.ac.uk

SAT solving experienced exciting developments, especially in the last ten years. It seems fair to say that certain areas of industry, like EDA (Electronic Design Automation) would not be able perform at the current level without "SAT technology." In the first part of my talk I will give some short overview on this development. Then, in the second part, I want to discuss directions for the future.

Arnold Beckmann, Benedikt Löwe (eds.). Acts of the programme "Semantics and Syntax".
Isaac Newton Institute for the Mathematical Sciences, January to July 2012.

Talk given at the SAS Workshop "Logical Approaches to Barriers in Complexity II",
27 March 2012, 16:00–16:30.

Phase Transitions and Computational Complexity

Moshe Y. Vardi

Rice University, Houston TX, United States of America

E-mail: vardi@cs.rice.edu

In the past 20 years there has been extensive research exploring the relationship between the statistical behavior of random combinatorial problems and their computational complexity. A specific focus of this research has been on random 3-SAT, a paradigmatic NP-complete problem. An underlying assumption of this line of research has been that there is a fundamental connection between the satisfiability phase transition observed in random 3-SAT and and the average-case complexity of random 3-SAT. The common belief, for example, has been that hard random 3-SAT instances are located at the phase-transition region.

In this talk we offer a skeptical look at this line of research and question its basic assumption. We demonstrate that there is no evidence for a fundamental connection between statistical behavior and intrinsic computational complexity. Rather, there seems to be a connection between statistical behavior and the performance of specific algorithms. This connection, however, is quite complicated and defies unifying explanation.

Arnold Beckmann, Benedikt Löwe (eds.). *Acts of the programme "Semantics and Syntax".*
Isaac Newton Institute for the Mathematical Sciences, January to July 2012.

Talk given at the SAS Workshop "Logical Approaches to Barriers in Complexity II",
27 March 2012, 16:30–17:00.

Lower Bounds for Frege from Lower Bounds for Constant-depth Frege

Rahul Santhanam

The University of Edinburgh, Edinburgh, United Kingdom

E-mail: rsanthan@inf.ed.ac.uk

I will discuss a recent result proved with Yuval Filmus and Toni Pitassi: exponential size lower bounds for constant-depth Frege imply superpolynomial size lower bounds for Frege. The proof is constructive in that it shows how to simulate polynomial size Frege proofs for any sequence of tautologies with sub-exponential size proofs in constant-depth Frege. The simulation is tight for tree-like proofs. I will also mention consequences of the result for weak automatizability of constant-depth Frege.

Arnold Beckmann, Benedikt Löwe (*eds.*). *Acts of the programme "Semantics and Syntax".*
Isaac Newton Institute for the Mathematical Sciences, January to July 2012.

Talk given at the SAS Workshop "Logical Approaches to Barriers in Complexity II",
28 March 2012, 9:00–10:00.

Separations in a Hierarchy of Propositional Proof Systems Related to Clause Learning

Jan Johannsen

Ludwig-Maximilians-Universität München, München, Germany

E-mail: Jan.Johannsen@ifi.lmu.de

Resolution trees with lemmas (RTL) are a resolution-based propositional proof system that is related to the DLL algorithm with clause learning, with its fragments $RTL(k)$ being related to clause learning algorithms where the width of learned clauses is bounded by k.

For every k up to $O(\log n)$, an exponential separation between the proof systems $RTL(k)$ and $RTL(k+1)$ is shown, indicating that a minimal increase in the width of learned clauses can lead to an exponential speed-up for clause learning algorithms.

Arnold Beckmann, Benedikt Löwe (eds.). Acts of the programme "Semantics and Syntax". Isaac Newton Institute for the Mathematical Sciences, January to July 2012.

Talk given at the SAS Workshop "Logical Approaches to Barriers in Complexity II", 28 March 2012, 10:00–10:30.

Towards a New Theory of Bounded Arithmetic for PSPACE Computations

Naohi Eguchi

Tohoku University, Tohoku, Japan

E-mail: eguchi@math.tohoku.ac.jp

I will present a second order extension of well-known first order theories of bounded arithmetic. The purpose of this work is to find a new proof-theoretic characterisation of the polynomial-space computable functions in terms of bounded arithmetic. This is joint work with Toshiyasu Arai (Chiba University, Japan) in progress.

Arnold Beckmann, Benedikt Löwe (eds.). Acts of the programme "Semantics and Syntax".
Isaac Newton Institute for the Mathematical Sciences, January to July 2012.

Talk given at the SAS Workshop "Logical Approaches to Barriers in Complexity II",
28 March 2012, 11:00–11:30.

NP Search Problems: Complexity, Provability and Reducibilities

Samuel R. Buss

University of California, San Diego, La Jolla, CA, United States of America

E-mail: sbuss@math.ucsd.edu

This is a survey talk about total NP search problems (TFNPs). The first part of the talk discusses the "classical" theory of TFNP's, including classes such as polynomial local search (PLS), parity principles such as PPAD, PPA, PPADS, and linear programming methods such as Nash and positive Linear Complementarity. The second part of the talk discusses total NP search problems that have arisen in bounded arithmetic, with an emphasis on the Game Induction principles, and the Local Improvement principles.

Arnold Beckmann, Benedikt Löwe (eds.). Acts of the programme "Semantics and Syntax".
Isaac Newton Institute for the Mathematical Sciences, January to July 2012.

Talk given at the SAS Workshop "Logical Approaches to Barriers in Complexity II",
28 March 2012, 11:30–12:30, and 29 March 2012, 11:30–12:30.

From Almost Optimal Algorithms to Logics for Complexity Classes via Listings and a Halting Problem

Yijia Chen

Shanghai Jiao Tong University, Shanghai, People's Republic of China

E-mail: yijia.chen@cs.sjtu.edu.cn

Let C denote one of the complexity classes "polynomial time," "log-space," or "nondeterministic logspace." We introduce a logic $L(C)_{inv}$ and show generalizations and variants of the equivalence ($L(C)_{inv}$ captures C if and only if there is an almost C-optimal algorithm in C for the set TAUT of tautologies of propositional logic.) These statements are also equivalent to the existence of a listing of subsets in C of TAUT by corresponding Turing machines and equivalent to the fact that a certain parameterized halting problem is in the parameterized complexity class XC_{uni}.

This is joint work with Jörg Flum.

Arnold Beckmann, Benedikt Löwe (*eds.*). *Acts of the programme "Semantics and Syntax".* Isaac Newton Institute for the Mathematical Sciences, January to July 2012.

Talk given at the SAS Workshop "Logical Approaches to Barriers in Complexity II", 29 March 2012, 9:00–10:00.

Space Complexity of Polynomial Calculus

Massimo Lauria

Academy of Sciences of the Czech Republic, Prague, Czech Republic

E-mail: lauria.massimo@gmail.com

During the last decade, an active line of research in proof complexity has been to study space complexity and time-space trade-offs for proofs. Besides being a natural complexity measure of intrinsic interest, space is also an important issue in SAT solving, and so research has mostly focused on weak systems that are used by SAT solvers.

There has been a relatively long sequence of papers on space in resolution and resolution-based proof systems, and it is probably fair to say that resolution is reasonably well understood from this point of view. For other natural candidates to study, however, such as polynomial calculus or cutting planes, very little has been known. We are not aware of any nontrivial space lower bounds for cutting planes, and for polynomial calculus the only lower bound has been for CNF formulas of unbounded width in [1], where the space lower bound is smaller than the initial width of the clauses in the formulas. Thus, in particular, it has been consistent with current knowledge that polynomial calculus could be able to refute any k-CNF formula in constant space.

In this paper, we prove several new results on space in polynomial calculus (PC), and in the extended proof system polynomial calculus resolution (PCR) studied in [1]:

1. We prove an $\Omega(n)$ space lower bound in PC for the canonical 3-CNF version of the pigeonhole principle formulas PHP_n^m with m pigeons and n holes, and show that this is tight.

2. For PCR, we prove an $\Omega(n)$ space lower bound for a bitwise encoding of the functional pigeonhole principle with m pigeons and n holes. These formulas have width $O(\log(n))$, and so this is an exponential improvement over [1] measured in the width of the formulas.

3. We then present another encoding of a version of the pigeonhole principle that has constant width, and prove an $\Omega(n)$ space lower bound in PCR for these formulas as well.

4. Finally, we prove that any k-CNF formula can be refuted in PC in simultaneous exponential size and linear space (which holds for resolution and thus for PCR, but was not obviously the case for PC). We also characterize a natural class of CNF formulas for which the space complexity in resolution and PCR does not change when the formula

Arnold Beckmann, Benedikt Löwe (eds.). Acts of the programme "Semantics and Syntax". Isaac Newton Institute for the Mathematical Sciences, January to July 2012.

Talk given at the SAS Workshop "Logical Approaches to Barriers in Complexity II", 29 March 2012, 10:00–10:30.

is transformed into a 3-CNF in the canonical way, something that we believe can be useful when proving PCR space lower bounds for other well-studied formula families in proof complexity.

The research presented in this talk is joint work with Yuval Filmus, Jakob Nordström, Neil Thapen, Noga Zewi.

Bibliography

[1] M. Alekhnovich, E. Ben-Sasson, A. A. Razborov, and A. Wigderson. Space complexity in propositional calculus. *SIAM J. Comput.*, 31(4):1184–1211, 2002.

Toda's Theorem in Bounded Arithmetic with Parity Quantifiers and Bounded Depth Proof Systems with Parity Gates

Leszek Kołodziejczyk

Uniwersytet Warszawski, Warsaw, Poland

E-mail: lak@mimuw.edu.pl

The "first part" of Toda's theorem states that every language in the polynomial hierarchy is probabilistically reducible to a language in $\oplus P$. The result also holds for the closure of the polynomial hierarchy under a parity quantifier. We use Jeřábek's framework for approximate counting to show that this part of Toda's theorem is provable in a relatively weak fragment of bounded arithmetic with a parity quantifier. We discuss the significance of the relativized version of this result for bounded depth propositional proof systems with parity gates.

The reseach presented here is joint work with Sam Buss and Konrad Zdanowski.

Arnold Beckmann, Benedikt Löwe (*eds.*). *Acts of the programme "Semantics and Syntax".* Isaac Newton Institute for the Mathematical Sciences, January to July 2012.

Talk given at the SAS Workshop "Logical Approaches to Barriers in Complexity II", 29 March 2012, 11:00–11:30.

Descriptive Complexity of Linear Algebra

Bjarki Holm

University of Cambridge, Cambridge, United Kingdom

E-mail: bjarki.holm@cl.cam.ac.uk

An important question that has motivated much work in finite model theory is that of finding a logical characterisation of polynomial-time computability. That is to say, to find a logic in which a class of finite structures is expressible if, and only if, membership in the class is decidable in deterministic polynomial time (PTIME).

Much of the research in this area has focused on the extension of inflationary fixed-point logic by counting terms (FPC). This logic has been shown to capture polynomial time on many natural classes of structures, including all classes of graphs with excluded minors. At the same time, it is also known that FPC is not expressive enough to capture polynomial time on the class of all finite graphs. Noting that the various examples of properties in polynomial-time that are not definable in FPC can be reduced to testing the solvability of systems of linear equations, Dawar et al. (2009) introduced the extension of fixed-point logic with operators for expressing matrix rank over finite fields (FPR). Fixed-point rank logic strictly extends the expressive power of FPC while still being contained in PTIME and it remains an open question whether there are polynomial-time properties that are not definable in this logic.

In this talk I give an overview of the main results in the logical study of linear algebra and present new developments in this area. After reviewing the background to this study, I define logics with rank operators and discuss some of the properties that can be expressed with such logics. In order to delimit the expressive power of FPR, I present variations of Ehrenfeucht-Fraïssé games that are suitable for proving non-definability in finite-variable rank logics. Using the rank games, I show that if we restrict to rank operators of arity two, then there are graph properties that can be defined by first-order logic with rank over $GF(p)$ that are not expressible by any sentence of fixed-point logic with rank over $GF(q)$, for all distinct primes p and q. Finally, I discuss how we can suitably restrict these rank games to get an algebraic game equivalence that can be decided in polynomial time on all classes of finite structures. As an application, this gives a family of polynomial-time approximations of graph isomorphism that is strictly stronger than the well-known Weisfeiler-Lehman method.

Arnold Beckmann, Benedikt Löwe (*eds.*). *Acts of the programme "Semantics and Syntax"*. Isaac Newton Institute for the Mathematical Sciences, January to July 2012.

Talk given at the SAS Workshop "Logical Approaches to Barriers in Complexity II", 29 March 2012, 14:00–15:00.

Definability of Linear Equation Systems over Groups and Rings

Wied Pakusa

RWTH Aachen University, Aachen, Germany

E-mail: pakusa@logic.rwth-aachen.de

One of the major open question in finite model theory is whether there is a logic for PTIME. As one promising candidate, fixed-point logic with counting, FPC, has been studied extensively, and indeed, FPC has been shown to capture PTIME on important classes of structures.

Although Cai, Fürer and Immerman ruled out FPC for the general case already in 1992, it was only in 2007 that Atserias, Bulatov and Dawar [1] found a class of natural problems explaining the major shortcoming of FPC. Specifically, they proved that the important problem of solving linear equation systems (SLES) over finite Abelian groups cannot be expressed in FPC; moreover, all other known queries separating FPC from PTIME turned out to be reducible to SLES via simple logical reductions. Hence, problems from algebra provide a new source of operators which have polynomial-time data complexity and which might be used to strictly extend the expressive power of FPC (cf. the notion of rank logics [2]).

Motivated by these insights, we study SLES over various classes of finite groups and rings from the viewpoint of logical (inter-)definability. All problems that we consider are decidable in polynomial time, but not expressible in FPC. Based on the structure theory of finite rings, we prove that on important classes of rings, SLES can be reduced to SLES over cyclic groups, which constitute the most basic class of tractable domains for SLES. Furthermore, we prove closure properties for classes of queries that reduce to SLES over fixed rings. As one application, these closure properties provide normal forms for logics extended with solvability operators.

The research presented in this talk is joint work with Anuj Dawar, Erich Grädel, Bjarki Holm and Eryk Kopczynski.

Bibliography

[1] Albert Atserias, Andrei A. Bulatov, and Anuj Dawar. Affine systems of equations and counting infinitary logic. *Theor. Comput. Sci.*, 2009.

[2] Anuj Dawar, Martin Grohe, Bjarki Holm, and Bastian Laubner. Logics with rank operators. In *LICS '09: Proceedings of the 2009 24th Annual IEEE Symposium on Logic In Computer Science*, 2009

Arnold Beckmann, Benedikt Löwe (*eds.*). Acts of the programme "Semantics and Syntax". Isaac Newton Institute for the Mathematical Sciences, January to July 2012.

Talk given at the SAS Workshop "Logical Approaches to Barriers in Complexity II", 29 March 2012, 15:00–15:30.

Proof Complexity of Circuit Lower Bounds

Ján Pich

Charles University, Prague, Czech Republic

E-mail: janpich@yahoo.com

Techniques that could resolve P vs. NP are considerably restricted by well-known barriers in computational complexity. There are several corresponding results in logic stating that certain fragments of arithmetic are not sufficiently strong to prove that P differs from NP or some similar conjectures. We investigate possible extensions of these barriers to stronger theories. Mainly, Razborov's conjecture about hardness of Nisan-Wigderson generators for Extended Frege systems and natural proofs in proof systems admitting feasible disjunction property pointed out by Rudich.

Arnold Beckmann, Benedikt Löwe (*eds.*). *Acts of the programme "Semantics and Syntax"*. Isaac Newton Institute for the Mathematical Sciences, January to July 2012.

Talk given at the SAS Workshop "Logical Approaches to Barriers in Complexity II", 29 March 2012, 16:00–16:30.

Developing Logical Theories for Several NP Search Classes

Phuong The Nguyen

Université de Montréal, Montreal QC, Canada

E-mail: pnguyen@cs.toronto.edu

We present finitely-axiomatizable two-sorted first-order theories associated with several NP search classes in the sense that search problems in a class are precisely those that are provable total in the associated theory. These theories are in the same vein as the family of theories associated with many subclasses of polytime, developed earlier by Nguyen and Cook. We consider proving several theorems in these new theories.

The research presented in this talk is joint work with Antonina Kolokolova.

Arnold Beckmann, Benedikt Löwe (eds.). *Acts of the programme "Semantics and Syntax".*
Isaac Newton Institute for the Mathematical Sciences, January to July 2012.

Talk given at the SAS Workshop "Logical Approaches to Barriers in Complexity II",
29 March 2012, 16:30–17:30.

Fragments of Approximate Counting

Neil Thapen

Academy of Sciences of the Czech Republic, Prague, Czech Republic
E-mail: thapen@math.cas.cz

We pose the question: are there any simple sentences, provable using bounded induction, that cannot already be proved using approximate counting of simple sets? More precisely, we study the long-standing open problem of giving $\forall \Sigma_1^b$ separations for fragments of bounded arithmetic in the relativized setting, but rather than considering the usual fragments defined by the amount of induction they allow, we study Jeřábek's theories for approximate counting and their subtheories. We prove separations for some of the subtheories, and also give new propositional translations, in terms of random resolution refutations, for the consequences of T_2^1 augmented with a certain weak pigeonhole principle.

The research presented in this talk is joint work with Sam Buss and Leszek Kołodziejczyk.

Arnold Beckmann, Benedikt Löwe (*eds.*). *Acts of the programme "Semantics and Syntax".*
Isaac Newton Institute for the Mathematical Sciences, January to July 2012.

Talk given at the SAS Workshop "Logical Approaches to Barriers in Complexity II",
30 March 2012, 9:00–10:00.

Root Finding in TC^0 and Open Induction

Emil Jeřábek

Academy of Sciences of the Czech Republic, Prague, Czech Republic

E-mail: jerabek@math.cas.cz

It is known that elementary arithmetic operations are computable in uniform TC^0, and some (multiplication, division) are even complete for this complexity class. The corresponding theory of bounded arithmetic, VTC^0, duly defines addition, multiplication, and ordering, and proves that integers form a discretely ordered ring under these operations. It is a natural question what other first-order properties of elementary arithmetic operations are provable in VTC^0. In particular, we are interested whether VTC^0 (or a theory of similar strength) can prove open induction in the basic language of arithmetic (Shepherdson's theory IOpen). This turns out equivalent to the problem whether there are TC^0 root-finding algorithms for constant-degree polynomials whose soundness is provable in VTC^0. In this talk, we will establish that such root-finding algorithms exist in the real (or rather, complex) world, and we will discuss the prospects of their formalization in bounded arithmetic.

Arnold Beckmann, Benedikt Löwe (*eds.*). *Acts of the programme "Semantics and Syntax"*. Isaac Newton Institute for the Mathematical Sciences, January to July 2012.

Talk given at the SAS Workshop "Logical Approaches to Barriers in Complexity II", 30 March 2012, 10:00–10:30.

Infinitary Methods in Finite Model Theory

Steven Lindell

Haverford College, Haverford PA, United States of America

E-mail: `slindell@haverford.edu`

The accepted wisdom is that standard techniques from classical model theory fail to apply in the finite. We attempt to dispel this notion by presenting new proofs of the Gaifman and Hanf locality theorems, as they appear in Libkin's textbook on finite model theory. In particular, using compactness over an expanded vocabulary, we obtain strikingly simple arguments that apply over both finite and infinite structures—all without the complexity of Ehrenfeucht-Fraïssé games normally used. Our techniques rely on internalizing most of the relevant mathematical features into the first-order theory itself. It remains to be seen whether these methods can be extended to proving order-invariant locality.

Arnold Beckmann, Benedikt Löwe (*eds.*). *Acts of the programme "Semantics and Syntax"*.
Isaac Newton Institute for the Mathematical Sciences, January to July 2012.

Talk given at the SAS Workshop "Logical Approaches to Barriers in Complexity II",
30 March 2012, 11:00–11:30.

Locality from Circuit Lower Bounds

Nicole Schweikardt

Goethe-Universität Frankfurt, Frankfurt, Germany

E-mail: schweika@informatik.uni-frankfurt.de

We study the locality of an extension of first-order logic that captures graph queries computable in AC^0, i.e., by families of polynomial-size constant-depth circuits. The extension considers first-order formulas over finite relational structures which may use arbitrary numerical predicates in such a way that their truth value is independent of the particular interpretation of the numerical predicates. We refer to such formulas as Arb-invariant FO. In this talk I will show how to use circuit lower bounds for proving that Arb-invariant FO queries are Gaifman-local in the following sense: They cannot distinguish between two tuples that have the same neighborhood up to distance $(\log n)^c$, where n represents the number of elements in the structure and c is a constant depending on the query.

Arnold Beckmann, Benedikt Löwe (*eds.*). *Acts of the programme "Semantics and Syntax".*
Isaac Newton Institute for the Mathematical Sciences, January to July 2012.

Talk given at the SAS Workshop "Logical Approaches to Barriers in Complexity II",
30 March 2012, 11:30–12:30.

Alan Turing: The Creative Power of Mathematics

Andrew Hodges

University of Oxford, Oxford, United Kingdom
E-mail: andrew.hodges@wadh.ox.ac.uk

Nowadays it is widely acknowledged that Turing's 1936 definition of computability, and his discovery of the concept of the universal machine, provided the foundation for the emergence of the digital computer in 1945. But Turing was not simply a logician. In this talk, I shall bring out how Turing's youthful 1936 work arose from a wide field of enquiry with mathematical, physical and philosophical elements. Then, that Turing's broad approach to mathematics and technology led him through the wartime cryptographic work into his own electronic computer plan of 1945. This extraordinary breadth of knowledge and application also created the setting for his later Artificial Intelligence plans and for his theory of biological growth.

Arnold Beckmann, Benedikt Löwe (*eds.*). *Acts of the programme "Semantics and Syntax".*
Isaac Newton Institute for the Mathematical Sciences, January to July 2012.

SAS Special Evening Lecture, 27 March 2012, 17:30–18:30.

The Complexity of Query Answering in Inconsistent Databases

Phokion G. Kolaitis

University of California at Santa Cruz and IBM Almaden Research Center, San Jose CA, United States of America

E-mail: kolaitis@cs.ucsc.edu

An inconsistent database is a database that fails to satisfy one or more integrity constraints that the data are hand are supposed to obey. Inconsistency in databases arises in a variety of applications, including data integration and data warehousing, where the task is to bring together data distributed over different sources that may obey mutually incompatible constraints. In practice, inconsistency is handled mainly via data cleaning, which means that the inconsistent database is transformed, through deletions or additions, to a consistent one that is then used for query answering or for warehousing purposes. This process, however, forces arbitrary choices to be made, because, in general, there is a multitude of ways in which an inconsistent databases can be transformed to a consistent one. The framework of database repairs, introduced by Arenas, Bertossi and Chomicki in 1999, provides a principled approach to managing inconsistency in databases. In particular, the consistent answers of a query on an inconsistent database provide sound semantics and the guarantee that the values obtained are those returned by the query on every repair of the given inconsistent database.

In this talk, we give an overview on recent results concerning the data complexity of the consistent answers of conjunctive queries for set-based repairs and with respect to classes of constraints that, in the past decade, have been extensively studied in the context of data exchange and data integration. We also present and discuss dichotomy conjectures, which, if established, will yield a complete classification of the complexity of consistent query answering for conjunctive queries.

This is based on joint work with Balder ten Cate, Gaëlle Fontaine, and Enela Pema.

Arnold Beckmann, Benedikt Löwe (eds.). Acts of the programme "Semantics and Syntax". Isaac Newton Institute for the Mathematical Sciences, January to July 2012.

Talk given at the SAS Seminar, 3 April 2012, 16:00–16:30.

Propositional Calculus and the Nature of Reality

Samson Abramsky

University of Oxford, Oxford, United Kingdom

E-mail: samson@comlab.ox.ac.uk

I discussed three topics of current interest which I hope to work on during my attendance at the SAS program.

1. Firstly, I discussed an approach to Bell inequalities in terms of logical consistency conditions, developed in recent joint work with Lucien Hardy. This gives a strikingly direct access to the challenging issues in quantum foundations, while also leading a number of new kinds of results.

2. Secondly, I discussed a novel approach to contextuality developed in recent work with Adam Brandenburger. This leads to a unified treatment of non-locality and contextuality in quantum mechanics, but also connects to a number of issues in computer science.

3. Finally, I discussed Robert Rosen's notion of metabolism-repair systems in biology, and the idea of 'closure under efficient causation'. I presented a recent analysis of these ideas by Mossio, Longo and Stewart in terms of the lambda-calculus. I pointed out that this analysis requires not only recursion, but reflexive types and self-application. This leads on to a number of interesting questions about reflexivity phenomena.

These topics lead on to a number of things I hope to work on while at the Newton Institute.

- One is a program to classify quantum states in terms of their non-locality and entanglement properties.

- Another is to delineate a sense in which quantum mechanics is 'fully abstract'.

- Intensional recursion (in the sense of Kleene's second recursion theorem), and connections to Rosen's (M,R)-systems.

- A paper connecting relational databases and Bell's theorem. This has now been written.

Arnold Beckmann, Benedikt Löwe (eds.). Acts of the programme "Semantics and Syntax".
Isaac Newton Institute for the Mathematical Sciences, January to July 2012.

Talk given at the SAS Seminar, 3 April 2012, 16:30–17:00.

Reasoning in Non-wellfounded Modal Logics

Dirk Pattinson

Imperial College London, London, United Kingdom

E-mail: dirk.pattinson@anu.edu.au

The *modal μ-calculus* extends the modal logic K with the capability to reason about *least* and *greatest* fixpoints. This is a huge step in expressivity: while fixpoint-free modal formulae only describe a world in terms of other worlds that are *finitely many* steps away, fixpoint formulae provide the capability to speak about ongoing behaviour.

Formulae of the modal μ-calculus can be thought of as infinite, but regular, trees where every sub-tree is marked as corresponding to a least or greatest fixpoint. Correspondingly, decision procedures for the μ-calculus are based on the construction of *regular tableaux*. The difficulty in this construction lies in the fact that not every closed, regular tableaux is in fact a witness of unsatisfiability: in addition, closed tableaux need to satisfy a trace requirement that can be checked using an ω-regular automata.

The aim of this talk is to understand the μ-calculus directly in terms of *non-wellfounded formulae*, i.e., formulae that are represented by not necessarily regular infinite trees. Without any markers that designate the type of fixpoint intended, we can read both the semantics and proof rules in an inductive (well-founded) and coinductive (non-wellfounded) manner. Our first result is that the (co-)inductive reading of the semantics is sound and complete with respect to the (co-)inductive understanding of the proof calculus. reading of the semantics is sound and complete with respect to the (co-)inductive understanding of the proof calculus. The main novelty is clearly the co-inductive reading of the proof calculus that construes proofs as *non-wellfounded* trees. The regular fragment of this language can be seen to correspond to the μ-calculus with only least (only greatest) fixpoint operators under the inductive (coinductive) reading. We discuss strategiesto recover both the semantics and the proof theory of the μ-calculus from this starting point.

Arnold Beckmann, Benedikt Löwe (*eds.*). *Acts of the programme "Semantics and Syntax".* Isaac Newton Institute for the Mathematical Sciences, January to July 2012.

Talk given at the SAS Seminar, 3 April 2012, 17:00–17:30.

Disjoint NP-pairs, Automatizability and Games

Pavel Pudlák

Academy of Sciences of the Czech Republic, Prague, Czech Republic
E-mail: pudlak@math.cas.cz

This is a report on work in progress done with Neil Thapen.

We study properties of two basic proof systems: resolution and a depth 2 Frege system. Resolution plays an important role both in practical applications of the propositional calculus and theoretical studies. The property of resolution that we are interested in is called *weak automatizability*. When stated specifically for resolution, it is the following problem.

Open Problem. *Does there exists an algorithm with the following properties? For a given set of clauses Γ and a number n, where n is at least the length of Γ, the algorithm outputs 0 or 1 in time polynomial in n so that*

1. *if the output is 0, Γ is not satisfiable, and*

2. *if the output is 1, Γ does not have a refutation of length at most n.*

This is closely related to the problem of proof-search in resolution, which is essentially the question whether it is possible to find a resolution proof if we know that a short proof exists. Alechnovich and Razborov proved that under a plausible hypothesis from parameterized complexity the proof search for resolution is hard. The weaker problem above is still open.

The second property in which we are interested is the feasible interpolation property. Roughly speaking, a proof system P has the feasible interpolation property if, given a proof of a disjunction $\varphi \vee \psi$ where φ and ψ have disjoint sets of variables, one can determine in polynomial time at least one of the formulas of the disjunction that is a tautology. It is well-known that resolution has this property, while bounded depth Frege proof systems do not, provided that some plausible conjectures are true. The result concerning bounded depth Frege proof systems only concerns depths larger than 2; for depth 2 it is still an open problem.

Atserias and Bonet proved that weakly automatizability of resolution is equivalent to depth 2 Frege systems having the feasible interpolation property. So these are just two version of one problem. We study this problem using the concept of disjoint **NP** pairs. Both versions of the problem can be stated as questions about polynomial separability of disjoint **NP** pairs.

Our result is a definition of a disjoint **NP** pair that is equivalent to the pairs associated with these problems. The pair is defined in terms of games

Arnold Beckmann, Benedikt Löwe (*eds.*). *Acts of the programme "Semantics and Syntax".* Isaac Newton Institute for the Mathematical Sciences, January to July 2012.

Talk given at the SAS Seminar, 5 April 2012, 16:00–16:30.

and thus avoids mentioning logical calculi. This may help to find polynomial reduction of this pair to others, or, vice versa, others to this pair.

Materialization of Universal Turing Machines

Rainer Glaschick

Heinz Nixdorf MuseumsForum, Paderborn, Germany

E-mail: `rainer@glaschick.de`

Alan Turing could read and speak German Language, and has probably read Hilbert's *Grundzüge der theoretische Logik* in German, where the *Entscheidungsproblem* was defined; so it is not really astonishing that this word was in the title of his epochal publication *On Computable Numbers, with an Application to the Entscheidungsproblem*. He was personally in Germany four times, but never could follow invitations of the University of Münster in Westphalia, Germany.

In Münster, the *Institut für mathematische Logik und Grundlagenforschung* was founded 1936 by Heinrich Scholz. They were the only foreign institute that recognized the importance of Turing's article and asked for a reprint. Moreover, Hans Hermes, who followed Heinrich Scholz as a director after the war, already 1937 published a first article (in German) with details about Turing's development, and after the war two other articles in 1952 and 1954. Hermes made the Turing Machine a central part of his book on Computability [1] that became for many years a standard in German university courses.

Gisbert Hasenjaeger also worked in Münster and had graduated from there. During the war, Hasenjaeger was the only person in the German military to hunt for weaknesses of the Enigma, and in a certain sense, unconsiously for both, the only counterpart for Alan Turing and the Bletchley park team. He did not find the vulnerabilities that Turing exploited in breaking the code, and later said: *Fortunately! Otherwise the war would have lasted even longer!*

Hasenjaeger tried very early to build extremely small and cheap models for Turing Machines. Started as a personaly curiositiy, it was his way to investigate a facet of a theory. He called it *materialization*, because the machines were *of no proper use*, he wrote 1987. As he could only make non-erasing tapes in his home workshop, the publication of Moore's UTM with 15 states and three binary tapes in 1953 was the first step towards his goal, because Moore's showed how to use non-erasable tapes, and mentionend that pyhsical realisation would be possible. After Wang 1957 published a new encoding of the state machine, which is like a programme, Hasenjaeger soon had built a machine, which was later called the *Old Wang*. The machine has 28 relays and can be functionally wired via a plugboard. This and other artefacts have been kept by the wifes of Hasenjaeger and Rödding and are now in the Heinz Nixdorf MuseumsForum for further study.

Arnold Beckmann, Benedikt Löwe (*eds.*). *Acts of the programme "Semantics and Syntax".* Isaac Newton Institute for the Mathematical Sciences, January to July 2012.

Talk given at the SAS Seminar, 16 April 2012, 14:00–15:00.

Probably some years later, he build a second machine with only 16 relays and a fixed behaviour. It is a Universal Turing Machine with only four states and three binary non-erasing tapes. As no documents on this machine were available, a complete reverse enginering had to be done to recover its functioning. The state table and more details are to appear in the book *Alan Turing: His Work and Impact*. This machine is currently shown here in the Isaac Newton Institute and will go back to the Heinz Nixdorf MuseumsForum in Paderborn, Germany, where it will stay and be shown in the Turing Exposition.

The problems with Turing tapes, even the non-erasable ones, lead to the desire to find more appropriate models. Dieter Rödding, who was also student in Münster and the last director of Scholz's institute, was fully engaged in the *materialization* efforts, although he *soon went into theoretical considerations* and studied tapes used as counters, which lead to register machines, and finally to the composition of automata.

No publication of Hasenjaeger for this remarkable machine has been found until now, only some hints in later cursory articles. He might have considered the solution not important enough, although the combination of only four states with two symbols was surely remarkable, even if the use of three tapes saves states in the state machine. Since Shannon's article, small Turing Machines have been studied, and many with more than one tape, but there has not yet been developed a clear comparison of machines with different numbers and kinds of tapes, expanding Shannon's state-symbol product.

I am very grateful that the SAS organizers invited Damien Woods, Turlogh Neary, Niall Murphy and me to study this in more detail, and the very preliminary numbers shown in the talk given were encouraging, but still need to be further evaluated.

Literaturverzeichnis

[1] H. Hermes. *Aufzählbarkeit, Entscheidbarkeit Berechenbarkeit: Einführung in die Theorie der rekursiven Funktionen*. Die Grundlehren der mathematischen Wissenschaften, Bd. 109. Springer-Verlag, Berlin, 1961.

Uniformity, Circuits and Non-deterministic Turing Machines

Niall Murphy

Universidad Politécnica de Madrid, Madrid, Spain
E-mail: niall.murphy@upm.es

In this seminar I present the latest results from joint work with Damien Woods on uniform families of Boolean circuits. There are two distinct notions of uniformity: The first is the most common and well understood, where each input length is mapped to a single circuit that computes on the finite set of inputs of that length. The second, called semi-uniformity, is where each input is mapped to a specific circuit for that input. The former notion is well-known and used in circuit complexity, while the latter notion is frequently found in literature on nature-inspired computation from the past 20 years or so.

For circuits using both AND, OR and NOT gates, these notions have the same computational power in the sense that the choice of either uniformity or semi-uniformity leads to characterisations of the same complexity classes. We have shown that if circuits with only AND gates and only OR gates are considered, these notions are distinct.

A more subtle problem has been to characterise the class of problems solved by uniform families of circuits with OR (or AND) gates only. We present our current best characterisations these circuit families using non-deterministic Turing machines that take unary input.

Arnold Beckmann, Benedikt Löwe (eds.). Acts of the programme "Semantics and Syntax".
Isaac Newton Institute for the Mathematical Sciences, January to July 2012.

Talk given at the SAS Seminar, 17 April 2012, 16:00–16:30.

The Computational Complexity of Small Universal Turing Machines

Damien Woods

California Institute of Technology, Pasadena CA, United States of America

E-mail: woods@caltech.edu

This seminar will discuss some of the simplest known computationally universal models of computation. These include universal Turing machines with very short programs and intuitively simple models such as Post tag systems and elementary cellular automata. Although they are universal and so can simulate any program, for many years these systems were thought to be exponentially slow. In joint work with Turlough Neary, we have shown that this is not the case and indeed that these machines are efficient polynomial-time simulators.

A small universal Turing machine constructed by Hasenjaeger in the 1960s out of relays and other parts is currently on display at the INI. Hasenjaeger's machine simulates a model of Hao Wang's, although Wang's proof introduces an exponential slow-down. In joint work with Rainer Glaschick, Turlough Neary and Niall Murphy, we have shown that the machines of both Wang and Hasenjaeger can be programmed so that they efficiently simulate Turing machines.

Arnold Beckmann, Benedikt Löwe (eds.). Acts of the programme "Semantics and Syntax".
Isaac Newton Institute for the Mathematical Sciences, January to July 2012.

Talk given at the SAS Seminar, 17 April 2012, 16:30–17:00.

The Program-size Complexity of Universal Turing Machines

Turlough Neary

University of Zürich and Eidgenössische Technische Hochschule Zürich, Zürich, Switzerland

E-mail: tneary@ini.phys.ethz.ch

We survey work on small universal Turing machines spanning from the early 1950s until the present. Following a brief overview of some historical milestones, we turn our attention to the single-tape model which continues to receive the most attention in the literature. We see that despite efforts from many authors, there remains a significant gap between the smallest standard single-tape universal machines and the lower bound inferred from the state-symbol pairs for which the halting problem has been proved decidable. We discuss approaches to exploring this gap in the form of semi-weakly and weakly universal machines for the single-tape model. Semi-weakly (weakly) universal machines have an infinitely repeated word on one side (both sides) of their initial input. Unsurprisingly, these generalisations give rise to universal machines with less states and symbols. However, often the lower bounds given for standard machines are not applicable to these models.

The discussion continues with a brief review of generalisations and restrictions of the model including machines with multiple tapes, multi-dimensional tapes, reversible machines, and machines that never write to their tape. Finally, we discuss the relationship between 2-counter machines, non-writing Turing machines with a single 2D tape and generalised Collatz functions (iterated piecewise affine maps in 1 dimension), in terms of their time efficiency.

This is joint work with Damien Woods.

Arnold Beckmann, Benedikt Löwe (*eds.*). *Acts of the programme "Semantics and Syntax".* Isaac Newton Institute for the Mathematical Sciences, January to July 2012.

Talk given at the SAS Seminar, 17 April 2012, 17:00–17:30.

Proof Complexity of Expander Graph Techniques

Antonina Kolokolova

Memorial University of Newfoundland, St. John's NL, Canada

E-mail: kol@cs.toronto.edu

In the recent years there were several major results in complexity theory that used the properties of expander graphs—a special type of graphs that are both sparse and well-connected. Ajtai, Komlos and Szemeredi used expanders to construct a monotone logarithmic depth sorting network, using constructions based on expanders allowed Reingold to give an algorithm for solving undirected reachability problem in LogSpace (an alternative, but also expander-based proof was given by Rozenman and Vadhan); Dinur used them to give a combinatorial proof of the PCP theorem.

This presents a natural question about the complexity (in bounded reverse mathematics sense) of proofs that use expander graphs. Even though some expander graph constructions are simple to describe, their analysis can be highly non-trivial, using deep results in mathematics and estimating algebraic properties of adjacency matrices of graphs rather than combinatorial expansion. Showing that expander graphs techniques have low proof complexity has additional implications in the proof complexity by recent work of Jeřábek.

In this talk we will discuss expander graphs, pose the question of formalizing the techniques based on expander graphs in theories of bounded arithmetic, and suggest some directions for achieving such a formalization.

Arnold Beckmann, Benedikt Löwe (eds.). Acts of the programme "Semantics and Syntax".
Isaac Newton Institute for the Mathematical Sciences, January to July 2012.

Talk given at the SAS Seminar, 1 May 2012, 16:00–16:30.

Cryptographic Theory for Practice's Sake

Kenny Paterson

Royal Holloway, University of London, Egham, United Kingdom
E-mail: kenny.paterson@rhul.ac.uk

In this talk, I'll discuss some recent developments in cryptographic theory that can be applied to protocols used in the real world. In particular, I'll look at recent developments in our understanding of the TLS and DTLS protocols, reflecting on how cryptographic theory helps us to study these protocols, but also on why it is that despite having good theory, implementations of these protocols can still turn out to be insecure. This talk is based on recent work of the speaker with Nadhem AlFardan, Thomas Ristenpart and Thomas Shrimpton.

Arnold Beckmann, Benedikt Löwe (*eds.*). *Acts of the programme "Semantics and Syntax"*. Isaac Newton Institute for the Mathematical Sciences, January to July 2012.

Talk given at the SAS Seminar, 1 May 2012, 16:30–17:00.

Yin and Yang of Computer Science: Algorithms versus Lower Bounds

Valentine Kabanets

Simon Fraser University, Burnaby BC, Canada

E-mail: kabanets@sfu.ca

Algorithms and lower bounds play complementary roles in computer science. Both contribute to better understanding of what is and is not efficiently computable, the fundamental question in computational complexity, but approach this question from the opposite sides.

In this talk, I will argue that there is deep connection between algorithms (for certain "general enough" computational problems) and lower bounds (for related problems). Such a connection has been discovered in a number of cases already, and was used to advance both the discovery of new algorithms and the proofs of new lower bounds. I will discuss a few such important examples, and suggest directions for further exploration of this intriguing connection.

Arnold Beckmann, Benedikt Löwe (eds.). Acts of the programme "Semantics and Syntax". Isaac Newton Institute for the Mathematical Sciences, January to July 2012.

Talk given at the SAS Seminar, 3 May 2012, 16:00–16:30.

Circularity, Paradoxes, and Proofs

Raja Natarajan

Tata Institute of Fundamental Research, Mumbai, India
E-mail: raja@tifr.res.in

There are deep connections between the formulations of various paradoxes and *reductio ad absurdum* proofs of various theorems in logic and foundations of mathematics. Of particular interest are the connections between the kinds of logical primitives and reasoning mechanisms that are invoked in paradoxes and in the proofs of theorems. A closer study of such connections leads to alternate proofs of several theorems, which can be carried out in leaner formalisms [1, 2, 3].

Bibliography

[1] Raja, N., A Negation-Free Proof of Cantor's Theorem, Notre Dame Journal of Formal Logic, 46 (2005) 231–233.

[2] Raja, N., Yet Another Proof of Cantor's Theorem, Dimensions of Logical Concepts, Coleção CLE, Vol. **54**, Campinas (2009) 209–217.

[3] Yanofsky, N.S.: A Universal Approach to Self-Referential Paradoxes, Incompleteness and Fixed Points, Bulletin of Symbolic Logic, 9 (2003) 362–386.

Arnold Beckmann, Benedikt Löwe (*eds.*). *Acts of the programme "Semantics and Syntax".*
Isaac Newton Institute for the Mathematical Sciences, January to July 2012.

Talk given at the SAS Seminar, 3 May 2012, 16:30–17:00.

Hyperarithmetical Categoricity and Abelian Groups

Alexander Melnikov

Nanyang Technological University, Singapore, People's Republic of China

E-mail: alexander.g.melnikov@gmail.com

We discuss some classical and recent results on effectively presentable abelian groups with an emphasis to categoricity relative to an oracle. These results include theorems from our recent joint paper with Rod Downey where we find an application of semi-low sets to computable abelian group theory. Goncharov asked if the categoricity hierarchy of computable torsion-free abelian groups is proper. We conjecture that the problem of Goncharov has a positive solution.

Arnold Beckmann, Benedikt Löwe (eds.). Acts of the programme "Semantics and Syntax".
Isaac Newton Institute for the Mathematical Sciences, January to July 2012.

Talk given at the SAS Seminar, 3 May 2012, 17:00–17:30.

Ajtai's Completeness Theorem for Nonstandard Finite Structures

Michal Garlik

Charles University, Prague, Czech Republic

E-mail: michal.garlik@gmail.com

Ajtai's generalization of the completeness theorem for nonstandard finite structures can be used to construct extensions of a nonstandard finite structure to models of a given theory. In this talk I will give a few examples to illustrate how these kinds of model extensions relate to problems in complexity theory. One of them is a model-theoretic argument showing that parity is not in AC_0. I will also sketch some steps of a different proof of the Ajtai's completeness theorem.

Arnold Beckmann, Benedikt Löwe (*eds.*). *Acts of the programme "Semantics and Syntax".*
Isaac Newton Institute for the Mathematical Sciences, January to July 2012.

Talk given at the SAS Seminar, 8 May 2012, 16:00–16:30.

Open Problems II: A Discussion Session

This open problem session was a continuation of the earlier one, cf. pp. 85–95.

1 Network Coding

The first set of open problems was presented by Søren Riis: Network coding is a field of information theory and coding theory and is a method of attaining maximum information flow in a communication network. A number of fundamental problems in Network coding can be restated as problems about circuits computing the identity function.

An important problem in network coding is the so-called multiple unicast problem. Here, we are given an acyclic graph with n source nodes and n sink nodes as well as a finite alphabet A. Each source node is associated to a sink node, and the task of the communication network is to send messages assigned to the source nodes to the corresponding sink nodes. The following two Network Coding problems are fundamentally important:

Problem 1 (cf. [1]). *Is the following desition problem decidable? Given a directed acyclic network N, decide if it is solvable over some finite alphabet.*

Problem 2 (cf. [2]). *Can a multiple-unicast network have coding capacity different from the coding capacity of its reverse.*

These problems can be restated in terms of circuits. Problem 1) is equivalent to the following

Problem 3. *Is it decidable if a given acyclic graph N, with n input nodes and n output nodes, for some finite alphabet A, can compute (when viewed as a circuit over A) the identity function $f\colon A^n \to A^n$?*

[7, Theorem 5] can be restated in terms of circuits:

Theorem 4 ([7]). *There exists an acyclic graph N with n input and n output nodes such that:*

1. *By a suitable choice of boolean gates N computes the identity function*
2. *The reversed graph N' (where all edge directions of N have been reversed) cannot be turned into a boolean circuit which compute the identity function.*

We may ask if this phenomenon can be amplified. Expressed informally, is it possible to construct graphs N, which in one direction can compute the identity function, but in the reverse direction fails "miserably" in being able to this. There are many variants of this problem. A special case of Problem 2 can be stated as the following

Arnold Beckmann, Benedikt Löwe (eds.). Acts of the programme "Semantics and Syntax".
Isaac Newton Institute for the Mathematical Sciences, January to July 2012.

Talk given at the SAS Seminar, 8 May 2012, 16:30–17:30.

Problem 5. *Is there an acyclic graph N (with n input and n output nodes) such that:*

1. *N that can be converted to a boolean circuit that computes the identity function*
2. *The reversed graph N' cannot compute the identity function even if the capacity of each node is doubled (i.e. such that each computational node is allowed to take 4 values).*

2   Is p-randomness Closed Under Base-change?

This open problem was presented by Elvira Mayordomo: Martin-Löf randomness is closed under base-change. This means that for instance given a Martin-Löf-random binary sequence if we interpret it as the binary representation of (the non integer part of) a real number and then translate it into a different base the resulting sequence is also Martin-Löf random.

PSPACE-randomness (defined by Lutz using polynomial-space computable martingales) is closed under base-change. FS-randomness (defined using finite-state computable martingales) is equivalent to normality, and therefore base-dependent (since there are normal numbers that are not absolutely normal).

What happens with p-randomness (defined by Lutz using polynomial-time computable martingales)? Is it closed under base-change? The answer is true for p-dimension but usual techniques fail for p-randomness, and more sophisticated techniques (such as those by Fenner 2011) work for functions with better behavior than base-change.

This question was solved in 2011 by Silveira in an unpublished Master's thesis [10]. We encourage the author of this thesis to have this result published.

3   Feasible Disjunction Properties

The following open problem was presented by Jan Krajíček: Let PC be one of the usual logical calculi for propositional logic. If A and B are two propositional formulas in disjoint sets of variables and PC proves their disjunction, then at least one of them is a tautology and hence provable in PC. The question is if one can establish this statement with a non-trivial lengths-of-proof upper bound. For example, does there exists a constant $c \geq 1$ such that whenever a disjunction $A \vee B$ of formulas in disjoint sets of variables has a PC-proof of size m, one of A or B must have a PC-proof of size at most $c \cdot m$?

4 Three Problems

In connection to the randomness questions presented by Elvira Mayordomo in §2, Rod Downey presented a few more: In the following, we refer to members of $\{0,1\}^* = 2^{<\omega}$ as *strings*, and infinite binary sequences (members of 2^ω, Cantor space) as *reals*. The set 2^ω is endowed with the tree topology, which has as basic clopen sets

$$[\sigma] := \{X \in 2^\omega : \sigma \prec X\},$$

where $\sigma \in 2^{<\omega}$. The *uniform* or *Lebesgue measure* on 2^ω is induced by giving each basic open set $[\sigma]$ measure $\mu([\sigma]) := 2^{-|\sigma|}$. The most common kind of randomness is the following.

Definition 6 (Martin-Löf [5]).   1. A *Martin-Löf test* is given by a sequence $\{U_n\}_{n\in\omega}$ of uniformly Σ_1^0 classes such that $\mu(U_n) \leq 2^{-n}$ for all n.

2. A class $C \subset 2^\omega$ is *Martin-Löf null* if there is a Martin-Löf test $\{U_n\}_{n\in\omega}$ such that $C \subseteq \bigcap_n U_n$.

3. A set $A \in 2^\omega$ is *Martin-Löf random* if $\{A\}$ is not Martin-Löf null.

The idea is that no random real should have statistically rare effective properties. Another notion of randomness is based on (super-) martingales.

Definition 7 (Levy [4]). A function $d : 2^{<\omega} \to \mathbb{R}^{\geq 0}$ is a *martingale*[1] if for all σ,

$$d(\sigma) = \frac{d(\sigma 0) + d(\sigma 1)}{2}.$$

d is a *supermartingale* if for all σ,

$$d(\sigma) \geq \frac{d(\sigma 0) + d(\sigma 1)}{2}.$$

A (super)martingale d *succeeds* on a set A if $\limsup_n d(A \upharpoonright n) = \infty$. The collection of all sets on which d succeeds is called the *success set* of d, and is denoted by $S[d]$.

The idea is that a martingale $d(\sigma)$ represents the capital that we have after betting on the bits of σ while following a particular betting strategy ($d(\lambda)$ being our starting capital). The *martingale condition* $d(\sigma) = \frac{d(\sigma 0)+d(\sigma 1)}{2}$ is a fairness condition, ensuring that the expected value of our capital after a

---

[1]A more complex notion of martingale is used in probability theory. We will discuss this notion, and the connection between it and ours, in [3], where it is discussed how computable martingale processes can be used to characterize 1-random reals.

bet is equal to our capital before the bet. Ville [11] proved that the success sets of (super)martingales correspond precisely to the sets of measure 0.

Now again we will need a notion of effective betting strategy. We will say that the martingale is computable if d is a computable function (with range $\mathbb{Q}$, without loss of generality), and we will say that d is c.e. iff d is given by an effective approximation $d(\sigma) = \lim_s d_s(\sigma)$ where $d_{s+1}(\sigma) \geq d_s(\sigma)$. This means that we are allowed to bet more as we become more confident of the fact that σ is the more likely outcome in the betting, as time goes on.

Theorem 8 (Schnorr [8, 9]). *A set is 1-random iff no c.e. (super)martingale succeeds on it.*

It seems strange that to define randomness we use c.e. martingales and not computable ones. The first question is: "Can we use some kind of computable randomness to define 1-randomness?". The suggested method to do this is to use a computable *but nonmonotonic* notion of randomness, where we have a betting strategy which bets on bits one at a time, but instead of being increasing can bet in some arbitrary order, and may not bet on all bits. The order is determined by what has happened so far. This gives a notion called *Kolmogorov-Loveland* (or nonmonotonic) randomness and the following question has been open for quite a while.

Question 9 (Muchnik, Semenov, and Uspensky [6]). *Is every nonmonotonically random sequence 1-random?*

A discussion of known results can be found in the monograph by Downey and Hirschfeldt.

The second and third questions actually stem from the proof where we show that there is a translation of Martin-Löf tests into c.e. supermartingales. There, we start with a uniformly c.e. sequence $R_0, R_1, \ldots$ of prefix-free generators for a Martin-Löf test. We build a c.e. supermartingale d that bets evenly on $\sigma 0$ and $\sigma 1$ until it finds that, say, $\sigma 0 \in R_n$, at which point it starts to favor $\sigma 0$, to an extent determined by n. If later d finds that $\sigma 1 \in R_m$, then what it does is determined by the relationship between m and n. If $m < n$ then d still favors $\sigma 0$, though to a lesser extent than before. If $m = n$ then d again bets evenly on $\sigma 0$ and $\sigma 1$. If $m > n$ then d switches allegiance and favors $\sigma 1$. This can happen several times, as we find more R_i to which $\sigma 0$ or $\sigma 1$ belong.

The computable enumerability of d is essential in the above. A computable supermartingale (which we have seen we may assume is rational-valued without loss of generality) has to decide which side to favor, if any, immediately. Hitchcock has asked whether an intermediate notion, where we allow our supermartingale to be c.e. but do not allow it to switch allegiances in the way described above, is still powerful enough to capture

1-randomness. The purest version of this question was suggested by Kaster-mans. A *Kastergale* is a pair consisting of a partial computable function $g : 2^{<\omega} \to \{0, 1\}$ and a c.e. supermartingale d such that $g(\sigma) \downarrow = i$ iff $\exists s \, (d_s(\sigma i) > d_s(\sigma(1-i)))$ iff $d(\sigma i) > d(\sigma(1-i))$. A set is *Kastermans random* if no Kastergale succeeds on it. A *Hitchgale* is the same as a Kastergale, except that in addition the proportion $\frac{d_s(\tau j)}{d_s(\tau)}$ (where we regard $\frac{0}{0}$ as being 0) is a Σ_1^0 function, so that if we ever decide to bet some percentage of our capital on τj, then we are committed to betting at least that percentage from that point on, even if our total capital on τ increases later. A set is *Hitchcock random* if no Hitchgale succeeds on it. It is unknown if these notions differ from 1-randomness and the import is that *is any bias allowed in the definition of 1-randomness?*

Bibliography

[1] R. Dougherty, C. Freiling, and K. Zeger. Linear network codes and systems of polynomial equations. *IEEE Trans. Inform. Theory*, 54(5):2303–2316, 2008.

[2] R. Dougherty and K. Zeger. Nonreversibility and equivalent constructions of multiple-unicast networks. *Information Theory, IEEE Transactions on*, 52(11):5067–5077, Nov. 2006.

[3] R. G. Downey and D. R. Hirschfeldt. *Algorithmic randomness and complexity*. Theory and Applications of Computability. Springer, New York, 2010.

[4] P. Lévy. *Théorie de l'Addition des Variables Aléatoires*. Gauthier-Villars, 1937.

[5] P. Martin-Löf. The definition of random sequences. *Information and Control*, 9:602–619, 1966.

[6] A. A. Muchnik, A. L. Semenov, and V. A. Uspensky. Mathematical metaphysics of randomness. *Theoret. Comput. Sci.*, 207(2):263–317, 1998.

[7] S. Riis. Reversible and irreversible information networks. *IEEE Trans. Inform. Theory*, 53(11):4339–4349, 2007.

[8] C.-P. Schnorr. A unified approach to the definition of random sequences. *Math. Systems Theory*, 5:246–258, 1971.

[9] C.-P. Schnorr. *Zufälligkeit und Wahrscheinlichkeit. Eine algorithmische Begründung der Wahrscheinlichkeitstheorie.* Lecture Notes in Mathematics, Vol. 218. Springer-Verlag, Berlin, 1971.

[10] J. G. Silveira. Invariancia por cambio de base de la aleatoriedad computable y la aleatoriedad con recursos acotados. Master's thesis, Univ. Buenos Aires, 2011.

[11] J. Ville. *Étude Critique de la Notion de Collectif.* Gauthier-Villars, 1939.

Valiant's Shift Problem: A Reduction to a Problem about Graph Guessing Games

Søren Riis

Queen Mary, University of London, London, United Kingdom
E-mail: soren.riis@eecs.qmul.ac.uk

The talk surveyed a number of results that were partly developed during the author's visit at the Newton Institute. We show that Valiant's Shift problem/conjecture, which has been open for more than 30 years, naturally reduce to questions about guessing games. In the talk, a new perspective is provided on information bottlenecks in Boolean Circuits/Communication Networks.

Arnold Beckmann, Benedikt Löwe (eds.). Acts of the programme "Semantics and Syntax". Isaac Newton Institute for the Mathematical Sciences, January to July 2012.

Talk given at the SAS Seminar, 9 May 2012, 14:00–15:00.

Consistency, Physics and Coinduction

Anton Setzer

Swansea University, Swansea, United Kingdom
E-mail: a.g.setzer@swan.ac.uk

In the first part of this talk we discuss the consistency problem of mathematics. Although we have very well verified mathematical proofs of Π_1-statements such as Fermat's last theorem, we cannot, because of Gödel's 2nd incompleteness theorem, exclude the existence of a counterexample with absolute certainty—a counterexample would, unless there was a mistake in the proof, prove the inconsistency of the mathematical framework used. This uncertainty has similarities with physics, where we cannot exclude that nature does not follow the laws of physics as determined up to now. All it would imply is that the laws of physics need to be adjusted. Whereas physicists openly admit this as a possibility, in mathematics this fact is not discussed very openly.

We discuss how physics and mathematics are in a similar situation. In mathematics we have no criterion to check with absolute certainty that mathematics is consistent. In physics we cannot conduct an experiment which determines any law of physics with absolute certainty. All we can do is to carry out experiments to test whether nature follows in one particular instance the laws of physics formulated by physicists. In fact we know that the laws of physics are incomplete, and therefore not fully correct, and could see a change of the laws of physics during the historical evolving of physics. Changes of the laws of physics did not affect most calculations made before, because these were thoroughly checked by experiments. The changes had to be made only in extreme cases (high speed, small distances). In the same way, we know by reverse mathematics that most mathematical theorems can be proved in relatively weak theories, and therefore would not be affected by a potential inconsistency which probably would make use of proof theoretically very strong principles. In both mathematics and physics we can carry out tests for the axiom systems used. In physics these tests are done by experiments and as well theoretical investigations. In mathematics this is done by looking for counter examples to theorems which have been proved, and by applying the full range of meta mathematical investigations, especially by proof theoretic analysis, normalisation proofs and the formation of constructive foundations of mathematics.

As the laws of physics are empirical, so are Π_1-theorems (phrasing it like this is due to an informal comment by Peter Aczel). As one tries in physics to determine the laws of physics and draw conclusions from them, in logic one tries to determine the laws of the infinite, and derive conclusions

Arnold Beckmann, Benedikt Löwe (eds.). *Acts of the programme "Semantics and Syntax".*
Isaac Newton Institute for the Mathematical Sciences, January to July 2012.

Talk given at the SAS Seminar, 10 May 2012, 16:00–16:30.

from those laws. We can obtain a high degree of certainty, but no absolute certainty, and still can have trust in the theorems derived.

In the second part we investigate informal reasoning about coinductive statements. Although one could use the definition of an inductive data type such as the set of natural numbers to reason about it, mathematicians have derived the principle of induction, and are used to apply it informally by referring to the induction hypothesis in appropriate places. In the same way one can derive from the principle of coinductive data types, which are greatest fixed points, a coinduction principle. This principle allows to carry out proofs by using the coinduction hypothesis in appropriate places. One can argue informally using the coinduction principle, and has as in case of induction to be careful when to use the coinduction hypothesis. We will carry out some example proofs, especially a proof of bisimulation, to demonstrate how to argue informally coinductively. We will see that with some experience such proofs can be more intuitive than standard coinductive arguments.

Syntax and Semantics—Another Look, Especially for Dependent Type Theories

Peter Aczel

The University of Manchester, Manchester, United Kingdom

E-mail: petera@cs.man.ac.uk

The aim of my talk was to explain my motivation for getting the following result.

Theorem. *Each Generalised Type Setup (GTS) can be viewed as a Full Comprehension category (FCC) without abstracting away the free variables of the GTS.*

There was no time to give the technical details of the notions of a GTS and FCC or present a proof of the result.

My notion of a GTS abstracts away from some of the details of the traditional concrete syntax of a (dependent) type theory, such as the use of explicit bound variables, definitional equality and the inductive generation of types and terms using the symbols of a signature. But it does keep the use of the traditionally explicit free variables in types and terms and explicit substitution maps using variable assignments for the free variables that may occur in types and terms. The representation of a concrete syntax as a GTS is a trivial matter and does not require any quotient construction.

The category theorists' usual approach to the abstract syntax of a type theory uses a quotient construction that does abstract away from both the traditional free variables as well as the bound ones so as to obtain a suitable abstract notion. In the categorical logic literature there have been a large number of such suitable abstract notions that have been introduced largely to represent a possible semantics for type dependency; e.g., contextual categories, categories with attributes, categories with families, etc. Perhaps the most general and most flexible such notion is the notion of an FCC, introduced by Bart Jacobs in his book, Categorical Logic and Type Theory. Fortunately, as the theorem states, each GTS, and hence each concretely presented type theory can be viewed as an FCC.

Arnold Beckmann, Benedikt Löwe (*eds.*). *Acts of the programme "Semantics and Syntax".* Isaac Newton Institute for the Mathematical Sciences, January to July 2012.

Talk given at the SAS Seminar, 10 May 2012, 16:30–17:00.

Effective Fractal Dimension in Computational Complexity and Algorithmic Information Theory

Elvira Mayordomo

Universidad de Zaragoza, Zaragoza, Spain

E-mail: elvira@unizar.es

In my talk I present effective dimension, its applications to Computational Complexity and Algorithmic Information Theory, and a list of open problems that include those I am working on during this stay.

The effectivization of Hausdorff dimension is based on Lutz characterization of 2000 that is based on the concept of gale, a generalization of martingale. I will review this characterization since it simplifies Hausdorff original definition (by uniformizing the different covers needed in Hausdorff measure) and in order to introduce effective dimension.

Effective dimension for abundance proofs is used in Computational Complexity as a probabilistic method and for new hypothesis and insights. I will illustrate with an example each of these uses and then present open questions on the p-dimension of NP, on BPP and on the p-dimension of P/poly.

Arnold Beckmann, Benedikt Löwe (eds.). Acts of the programme "Semantics and Syntax". Isaac Newton Institute for the Mathematical Sciences, January to July 2012.

Talk given at the SAS Seminar, 10 May 2012, 17:00–17:30.

Elementary Real Analysis

Robert Lubarsky

Florida Atlantic University, Boca Raton FL, United States of America
E-mail: Robert.Lubarsky@alum.mit.edu

The elementary functions are a subclass of the computable functions, characterized by being closed under exponentiation, bounded primitive recursion (i.e. bounded by an elementary function), and composition. A predicate is said to be elementary if its characteristic function is elementary. As an example of what's essentially different about this class compared with the computable functions is that it allows for a non-trivial notion of an honest function. A function is said to be honest if it is monotonically non-decreasing, dominates the exponential function, and, most crucially, has an elementary graph. This means that on an input x you may not be able to compute the value $f(x)$ elementarily, but given a possible output y it is elementary to decide whether $y = f(x)$ or not. As usual, there is a notion of relative computability, which induces a partial pre-order on the honest functions. What gives this subject much of its flavor is the Growth Theorem: for honest functions f and g, f is elementarily reducible to g iff f is pointwise dominated by a finite iteration of g. So the information-theoretic notion of oracle computation comes down to a rate-of-growth question. As one should expect, when you mod out by the induced equivalence relation you get a notion of degree, which carries the induced partial order. This p.o. is somewhat understood—it's a lattice, it carries a natural jump operator—but much is still open. (Most of this work has been done by Lars Kristiansen, Jan-Christoph Schlage-Puchta, and Andreas Weiermann.)

Just as computable functions bring with them the notion of a computable real number, so do the elementary functions challenge us to come up with a notion of an elementary real number. There seem though to be many possibilities as to what this might mean. We say that a real r is strongly Dedekind if there is a 0-1 valued elementary function f such that, for all rational numbers q, if $f(q) = 0$ then $q \leq r$ and if $f(q) = 1$ then $q \geq r$; membership Dedekind if $f(p, q) = 0$ iff $p < r < q$; located Dedekind if either $f(p, q) = p$ and $p < r$ or $f(p, q) = q$ and $q > r$; Cauchy if the sequence $f(n)$ is a Cauchy sequence with modulus of convergence 2^{-n} and limit r; honest Cauchy if f as above is honest; and interval Dedekind if f enumerates all rational intervals (p, q) with $p < r < q$. Clearly one of the first things to do is to determine all implications among these properties. Andreas Weiermann has asked which of these notions yields a real closed field; this is of course another basic question to address.

Arnold Beckmann, Benedikt Löwe (eds.). Acts of the programme "Semantics and Syntax".
Isaac Newton Institute for the Mathematical Sciences, January to July 2012.

Talk given at the SAS Seminar, 15 May 2012, 16:00–16:30.

Consistency Statements in Bounded Arithmetic

Arnold Beckmann

Swansea University, Swansea, United Kingdom

E-mail: a.beckmann@swansea.ac.uk

The aim of my talk is to point out the subtle differences between two similar looking but very different results involving consistency statements in bounded arithmetic, and draw some natural open problems I am interested in from these observations. Bounded arithmetic theories are connected to computational complexity classes of functions [2]. The question whether the hierarchy of bounded arithmetic theories S_2^i is strict or not is connected to a similar question about levels of the polynomial time hierarchy of functions [3, 6].

The first result I want to mention is due to Buss and Ignjatović [4]. Consider the equational theory PV^- based on Cobham's characterization of polynomial time computable functions by limited recursion on notation [5]; axioms are recursive definitions of function symbols plus some finite set of further axioms; formulas are build from equality $=$ and inequality $\leq$ using Boolean connectives; lines in proofs are sequents of formulas; and rules in proofs are given by equational reasoning (i.e., equality being irreflexive, symmetric and transitive, and compatible with function symbols) plus rules for propositional connectives (like the propositional part of Gentzen's LK). In particular, PV^- does not contain any form of induction. Let $\mathrm{Con}(PV^-)$ be the statement that in this formalism one cannot derive a contradiction of the form $0 = 1$.

Theorem 1 (Buss and Ignjatović [4]). S_2^1 *does not prove* $\mathrm{Con}(PV^-)$.

On the other hand, a very similar looking consistency statement is provable in S_2^1. Let F be some set of recursively defined functions. Let $\mathrm{Eqt}(F)$ be the equational theory based on the recursive definition of function symbols in F (no other axioms are allowed); formulas and lines in proofs are equations; and rules in proofs are given by equational reasoning.

Theorem 2 (Beckmann [1]). S_2^1 *proves* $\mathrm{Con}(\mathrm{Eqt}(F))$.

In particular, let $\mathrm{Eqt}(\mathrm{purePV}^-)$ be the equational theory in the latter sense based on the function symbols of PV^-. Then

Corollary 3. S_2^1 *proves* $\mathrm{Con}(\mathrm{Eqt}(\mathrm{purePV}^-))$.

The difference between Theorem 1 and Corollary 3 is that PV^- uses further axioms besides the recursive definition of function symbols, and that

Arnold Beckmann, Benedikt Löwe (*eds.*). *Acts of the programme "Semantics and Syntax".*
Isaac Newton Institute for the Mathematical Sciences, January to July 2012.

Talk given at the SAS Seminar, 15 May 2012, 16:30–17:00.

PV^- is formulated in the more liberal sequent calculus setting. As Buss and Ignjatović [4] pointed out the sequent calculus setting can be turned into the pure equational setting via a suitable arithmetization of language.

The open problems which naturally occur at this point is to make such an arithmetization precise. In particular, the task would be to identify the additional axioms needed to carry out the arithmetization. The result would be an explicit finite set of axioms which distinguishes provability from unprovability of such consistency statements in bounded arithmetic. This should then be the starting point for further investigations of these axioms, in order to find out which of them cause the transition from consistency being provable to being unprovable.

Bibliography

[1] A. Beckmann. Proving consistency of equational theories in bounded arithmetic. *J. Symbolic Logic*, 67:279–296, 2002.

[2] S. R. Buss. *Bounded Arithmetic*. Bibliopolis, 1986. Revision of 1985 Princeton University Ph.D. thesis.

[3] S. R. Buss. Relating the bounded arithmetic and the polynomial time hierarchies. *Annals of Pure and Applied Logic*, 75:67–77, 1995.

[4] S. R. Buss and A. Ignjatović. Unprovability of consistency statements in fragments of bounded arithmetic. *Ann. Pure Appl. Logic*, 74(3):221–244, 1995.

[5] A. Cobham. The intrinsic computational difficulty of functions. In Y. Bar-Hillel, editor, *Logic, Methodology and Philosophy of Science, Proceedings of the Second International Congress, held in Jerusalem, 1964*, Amsterdam, 1965. North-Holland.

[6] D. Zambella. Notes on polynomially bounded arithmetic. *Journal of Symbolic Logic*, 61:942–966, 1996.

A Complexity Class Based on Comparator Circuits

Stephen A. Cook

University of Toronto, Toronto ON, Canada

E-mail: sacook@cs.toronto.edu

This talk is partly based on the CSL 2011 paper [3]. We omit the logical theory developed in that paper and add new results enhancing and simplifying the complexity-theoretic aspects.

Comparator circuits were originally introduced for sorting numbers [2], but here we consider them as a restricted form of Boolean circuits. We visualize a comparator circuit as m horizontal wires with input bits at the left end, comparator gates placed sequentially between pairs of wires, and output bits at the right end. Each comparator gate is a vertical bar connecting two of the wires. If the gate connects wires x and y then one end (say x) is labelled with a dot and converts the x-wire to $x \wedge y$ and the other end (say y) is labelled with an arrow and converts the y-wire to $x \vee y$.

The *Comparator Circuit Value Problem* (CCV) is: Given a comparator circuit with specified Boolean inputs, determine the output value of a designated wire. The complexity class CC was originally defined to be the set of problems log-space many-one reducible to CCV, and several problems were proved complete for the class, including the stable marriage problem and finding the lexicographical first maximal matching in a bipartite graph. Also

$$\mathrm{NL} \subseteq \mathrm{CC} \subseteq \mathrm{P}$$

where NL is nondeterministic log space. The main references here are [5, 4].

We redefine CC to be as above except we change the reducibility from log-space many-one to AC^0 many-one. We prove that the two definitions are equivalent, and the complete problems mentioned above remain complete under the new reducibility. The equivalence follows from our introduction of an AC^0-uniform family $\mathrm{UNIV}(m, n)$ of universal comparator circuits where $\mathrm{UNIV}(m, n)$ can simulate an arbitrary comparator circuit with at most m wires and n comparator gates. As further consequences of these universal circuits we show

- The function class associated with CC is closed under composition.

- CC is closed under AC^0-Turing reductions.

- CC can be characterized in terms of uniform cirucit families of comparator circuits, analgous to other circuit-based complexity classes such as $\mathrm{AC}^0, \mathrm{NC}^1, \mathrm{TC}^1, \ldots$.

Arnold Beckmann, Benedikt Löwe (*eds.*). *Acts of the programme "Semantics and Syntax".*
Isaac Newton Institute for the Mathematical Sciences, January to July 2012.

Talk given at the SAS Seminar, 17 May 2012, 16:00–16:30.

We conjecture that the complexity classes CC and NC are incomparable. In an effort to make this more plausible we introduce the relativized complexity class $CC(f)$ where f is a family $\{f_k\}_{k \in \mathbb{N}}$, and

$$f_k : \{0,1\}^k \to \{0,1\}^k$$

Comparator circuits computing a problem in $CC(f)$ are allowed to have oracle f_k-gates for various k. We use a result in [1] to prove

$$CC(f) \not\subseteq NC(f)$$

We are working on proving

$$NC(f) \not\subseteq CC(f)$$

The intuition for this direction comes from the following easy result.

Lemma For each comparator circuit C (with no oracle gates) and for each bit setting of inputs $x_1, \ldots, x_m$ and for each $i \in [m]$, if input x_i is flipped (i.e., replaced by $\neg x_i$) then there is a unique 'flip-path' in C from the input x_i to some output such that each wire segment on the path is flipped (and no other wire segment is flipped).

In general NC circuits satisfy no such result since their gates are allowed multiple fanout.

In summary, the (little-known) class CC is the only known subclass of P satisfying

- is robust (closed under AC^0-Turing reductions)

- has interesting complete problems (stable marriage etc.)

- seems to be incomparable with NC

The research presented in this talk is joint work with Dai Tri Man Lê, Yuval Filmus, and Yuli Ye.

Bibliography

[1] K. Aehlig, S. Cook, and P. Nguyen. Relativizing small complexity classes and their theories. In *Computer science logic, 21st International Workshop, CSL 2007, 16th Annual Conference of the EACSL, Lausanne, Switzerland, September 11-15, 2007, Proceedings*, volume 4646 of *Lecture Notes in Comput. Sci.*, pages 374–388. Springer, Berlin, 2007.

[2] K. E. Batcher. Sorting networks and their applications. In *Proceedings of the April 30–May 2, 1968, spring joint computer conference*, AFIPS '68 (Spring), pages 307–314, New York, NY, USA, 1968. ACM.

[3] D. T. M. Lê, S. A. Cook, and Y. Ye. A formal theory for the complexity class associated with the stable marriage problem. In *Computer Science Logic 2011*, volume 12 of *LIPIcs. Leibniz Int. Proc. Inform.*, pages 381–395. Schloss Dagstuhl. Leibniz-Zent. Inform., Wadern, 2011.

[4] E. W. Mayr and A. Subramanian. The complexity of circuit value and network stability, 1992.

[5] A. Subramanian. *The computational complexity of the circuit value and network stability problems*. PhD thesis, Dept. of Computer Science, Stanford University, 1990.

Algebra-valued Models of Set Theories

Sourav Tarafder

University of Calcutta, Kolkata, India
E-mail: souravt07@yahoo.com

The link between algebraic properties and axioms of set theory.
It is well known that if $\mathbb{B}$ is a complete Boolean algebra then the so-called
Boolean-valued model $V^{(\mathbb{B})}$ is a model of ZFC. A complete Heyting algebra
$\mathbb{H}$ makes the so-called *Heyting-valued model* $V^{(\mathbb{H})}$ a model of *Intuitionistic
Zermelo-Fraenkel set theory*, IZF. It can be proved that the Law of Excluded
Middle LEM holds in $V^{(\mathbb{H})}$ iff $\mathbb{H}$ is a Boolean algebra:

- If $\mathbb{H}$ is a Boolean algebra, then LEM is true in $V^{(\mathbb{H})}$.

- If LEM holds in $V^{(\mathbb{H})}$ then for any formula ψ, we get $\psi \vee \neg\psi$ is true
  in $V^{(\mathbb{H})}$. For any element a of this Heyting algebra, the formula $\psi :=$
  $(\varnothing \in \{\langle \varnothing, a \rangle\})$ is such that $[\![\psi]\!] = a$. Hence it can be proved that
  for any element a of this Heyting algebra $a \vee a^* = 1$, where a^* is
  the complement of a. So, LEM holds in $V^{(\mathbb{H})}$ implies that $\mathbb{H}$ satisfies
  $a \vee a^* = 1$ for any element a of $\mathbb{H}$. Hence $\mathbb{H}$ is a Boolean algebra.

From the above result it follows that for a Heyting algebra $\mathbb{H}$, the following
are equivalent:

(i) $\mathbb{H}$ is a Boolean algebra, and

(ii) the Axiom of Choice is valid in $V^{(\mathbb{H})}$.

Proof. It is known that Axiom of Choice implies the Law of Excluded Middle. Now if $V^{(\mathbb{H})}$ is a model of the Axiom of Choice then $V^{(\mathbb{H})}$ is also a
model of LEM. Therefore from the above result, $\mathbb{H}$ is a Boolean algebra.
Hence we can conclude that for a Heyting algebra $\mathbb{H}$ with some a in $\mathbb{H}$ such
that $a \vee a^* \neq 1$, the Axiom of Choice cannot be true in $V^{(\mathbb{H})}$.   Q.E.D.

This result is an example linking algebraic properties of an algebra $\mathbb{H}$ to
set theoretic axioms valid in the model $V^{(\mathbb{H})}$. In the following, we shall aim
at similar results for other axioms of set theory.

Generalizing the Boolean-valued construction. The Boolean-valued
construction can easily be generalized for arbitrary algebras $\mathbb{A}$ of the same
signature. In the spirit of the result proved in the first section, for each
axiom A of set theory, we can now ask which algebraic properties of A will
make sure that A is valid in $V^{(\mathbb{A})}$. We aim at a collection of basic algebraic
axioms that are sufficient to prove all of the ZFC axioms. We shall call an
algebra that satisfies these algebraic axioms a *Basic algebra*.

Arnold Beckmann, Benedikt Löwe (*eds.*). *Acts of the programme "Semantics and Syntax".*
Isaac Newton Institute for the Mathematical Sciences, January to July 2012.

Talk given at the SAS Seminar, 17 May 2012, 16:30–17:00.

A model of paraconsistent set theory. In the case where $\mathbb{A}$ is a Boolean algebra or a Heyting algebra, the logic of $V^{(\mathbb{A})}$ reflects the logic of $\mathbb{A}$. We therefore expect that the same is true for our Basic algebras, and that a Basic algebra of a paraconsistent logic would give rise to a model of paraconsistent set theory.

Polylogarithmic Cuts in Models of Weak Arithmetic

Sebastian Müller[*]

Charles University, Prague, Czech Republic

E-mail: muller@karlin.mff.cuni.cz

In my talk, I intended to introduce a model-theoretic view onto some questions in Proof Complexity. To this end, I restated the definition of initial cuts M of models N of weak two-sorted Bounded Arithmetics in the language $\mathcal{L}_A^2$, as substructures of N such that

- $M_1 \subseteq N_1$, $M_2 \subseteq N_2$,

- $0^M = 0^N$, $1^M = 1^N$,

- M_1 is closed under $+^N, \cdot^N$ and downwards with respect to $\leq^N$,

- $M_2 = \{X \in N_2 \mid X \subseteq M_1\}$, and

- $\circ^M$ is the restriction of $\circ^N$ to M_1 and M_2 for all relation and function symbols $\circ \in \mathcal{L}_A^2$.

Such a cut is the *Polylogarithmic Cut* iff

$$x \in M_1 \Leftrightarrow \exists a \in N_1, k \in \mathbb{N} \; x \leq |a|^k.$$

Intuitively, such cuts are models of a stronger theory. This intuition is justified as the following can be proved

Theorem 1. *Let* $N \models \mathbf{V}^0$ *and* $M \subseteq N$ *be the polylogarithmic cut. Then* $M \models \mathbf{VNC}^1$.

From this result various results in Proof Complexity straightforwardly follow. For example the following recent simulation result by Filmus, Pitassi and Santhanam follows directly from Theorem 1 by a simple calculation and the application of the Reflection Principle for Frege.

Theorem 2 ([2]). *Every Frege system is sub exponentially simulated by* AC^0-*Frege systems.*

---

[*]Supported by the Marie Curie Initial Training Network in Mathematical Logic—MALOA—From MAthematical LOgic to Applications, PITN-GA-2009-238381

Arnold Beckmann, Benedikt Löwe (*eds.*). *Acts of the programme "Semantics and Syntax".* Isaac Newton Institute for the Mathematical Sciences, January to July 2012.

Talk given at the SAS Seminar, 17 May 2012, 17:00–17:30.

Also, from a recent result of Tzameret and me, we can straightforwardly conclude the following separation theorem between Resolution and AC^0-Frege. To this end first observe that by a result from Chvátal and Szemerédi [1] Resolution does not admit subexponential proofs of random 3CNF with a variable density below $n^{1.5-\varepsilon}$. The separation then follows from the following theorem, which is an easy corollary of the main result from [3] and Theorem 1.

Theorem 3. *For almost every random 3CNF A with n variables and $m = c \cdot n^{1.4}$ clauses, where c is a large constant, $\neg A$ has subexponentially bounded AC^0-Frege proofs.*

As possibilities for future research it might be interesting to consider other theories than $\mathbf{V}^0$ for the base model N. Namely, strengthening the theory to $\mathbf{VNC}^k$ would yield a sort of weak barrier results for the family of circuit classes NC^k, if the polylogarithmic cut of such a structure would be a model of $\mathbf{VNC}^{k+1}$.

If, on the other hand, one weakens the theory significantly, it would be very interesting to try and prove the correctness of some cryptographical protocols in the theory of the cut. This might lead to non-automatizability results for very weak proof systems.

Bibliography

[1] V. Chvátal and E. Szemerédi. Many hard examples for resolution. *J. Assoc. Comput. Mach.*, 35(4):759–768, 1988.

[2] Y. Filmus, T. Pitassi, and R. Santhanam. Exponential lower bounds for AC^0-Frege imply superpolynomial Frege lower bounds. In J. S. Luca Aceto, Monika Henzinger, editor, *Automata, Languages and Programming. Part I*, volume 6755 of *Lecture Notes in Comput. Sci.*, pages 618–629. Springer, Heidelberg, 2011.

[3] S. Müller and I. Tzameret. Short propositional refutations for dense random 3CNF formulas. Manuscript, 2011.

On the Computational Content of the Minimal-bad-sequence Argument

Monika Seisenberger

Swansea University, Swansea, United Kingdom

E-mail: m.seisenberger@swansea.ac.uk

The overall theme of our research can be summarised in one sentence as:

> Establish Program Extraction from Formal Proofs as a Competitive Method for Program Development and Verification.

The concrete agenda to achieve this is:

- Extend theory to cover a large range of proofs (e.g., inductive and coinductive definitions, classical reasoning and program extraction, A-translation and Dialectica interpretation)

- Demonstrate advantages over other methods for program development and verification.

- Demonstrate feasibility: (1) in larger applications (modularisation, fine-tuning), (2) also when classical principles are involved.

- Apply program extraction from proofs to new areas to extract new algorithms.

- Provide suitable tool support.

Tool support: We are using the interactive proof system Minlog, a first-order natural deduction system which has the partial continuous functionals as semantics, see e.g. [5], and http://www.minlog-system.de for the tool. Program extraction is available via Modified Realisability.

In the talk we will give two examples of program extraction from constructive proofs and then concentrate on program extraction from classical proofs, in particular the case when classical choice principle are involved.

The main case study discussed will be Higman's Lemma which has a nice proof due to Nash-Williams [4] using the so-called Minimal-Bad-Sequence argument.

Definition. Let $(Q, \leq)$ be a quasiorder (i.e., $\leq$ is reflexive and transitive). Then, $(Q, \leq)$ is a well quasiorder (wqo) if every infinite sequence in Q is 'good', i.e., $\forall (q_i)_{i < \omega} \exists i, j . i < j \wedge q_i \leq q_j$.

Arnold Beckmann, Benedikt Löwe (*eds.*). *Acts of the programme "Semantics and Syntax".* Isaac Newton Institute for the Mathematical Sciences, January to July 2012.

Talk given at the SAS Seminar, 2 May 2012, 16:00–16:30.

Definition. Let A^* be the set of finite sequences, also called words, with elements in a quasiorder $(A, \leq)$. A sequence $[a_1, \ldots, a_n]$ is embeddable $(\leq^*)$ in $[b_1, \ldots, b_m]$ if there is a strictly increasing map $f: \{1, \ldots, n\} \to \{1, \ldots, m\}$ such that $a_i \leq_A b_{f(i)}$ for all $i \in \{1, \ldots n\}$.

Higman's Lemma. If $(A, \leq)$ is a well quasiorder, then so is $(A^*, \leq^*)$.

Proof. That a bad sequence of words, i.e., a sequence that is not good, is impossible is an immediate consequence of the following two facts:

1. For every bad sequence $(\alpha_n)_{n \in \omega}$ of words there exists a bad sequence $(\alpha'_n)_{n \in \omega}$ which is lexicographically smaller, i.e., there is an index n_0, such that $\alpha'_i = \alpha_i$ for all $i < n_0$ and α'_{n_0} is a proper initial segment of α_{n_0}.

2. If there exists a bad sequence of words, then there also exists a minimal bad sequence of words (with respect to the above lexicographic ordering).

We only sketch 2 as this refers to the so-called minimal bad sequence argument. Assume there is a bad sequence of words. We define a minimal bad sequence of words by repeated non-constructive choices: if words $\alpha_0, \ldots, \alpha_{n-1}$ have already been chosen such that they begin a bad sequence, we choose a shortest word α_n such that $\alpha_0, \ldots, \alpha_{n-1}, \alpha_n$ begins bad sequence as well. Clearly, the resulting sequence $(\alpha_n)_{n \in \omega}$ is bad and lexicographically minimal.   Q.E.D.

We have formalised Higman's Lemma in the proof assistant Minlog, applied A-translation to automatically generate a constructive proof, and extracted a program. The (A-translated) principle of dependent choice has been realised using Modified Bar-Recursion (see e.g. [2, 6]). Its defining equation is

$$\Psi(Y, G, s) \stackrel{\tau}{=} Y(s \# \lambda k. G(k, s, \lambda x. \Psi(Y, G, s * x))).$$

where k has the type nat of natural numbers, s is a finite list of elements of type ρ, where ρ is an arbitrary type, $\#$ denotes concatenation of a finite list and an infinite list, and $*$ is used for concatenation of one element. The type τ is not allowed to contain any arrow types. To order to show termination of the functional Ψ, we need continuity of Y. Finally, any program making use of this functional needs to be evaluated in a lazy programming language.

A more direct program is expected if instead of realising DC we realise the (A-translated) Minimal-Bad-Sequence argument. This is possible as the Minimal-Bad-Sequence argument is logically equivalent to the Open Induction Principle [3]

$$\forall\alpha(\forall\beta <_{\mathsf{lex}} \alpha U(\beta) \to U(\alpha)) \ \to \ \forall\alpha U(\alpha)$$

where U ranges over open predicates on sequences, such as the property of being good. A realiser for this principle has been given by Berger [1]. For this approach we only need to show that A-translation preserves open induction.

The formalisation of this new approach and the analysis of the resulting program as well as the comparison with other programs extracted from Higman's Lemma should be carried out during the stay at the Isaac Newton Institute.

Bibliography

[1] U. Berger. A computational interpretation of open induction. In F. Titsworth, editor, *Proceedings of the Nineteenth Annual IEEE Symposium on Logic in Computer Science*, pages 326–334. IEEE Computer Society, 2004.

[2] U. Berger and P. Oliva. Modified bar recursion and classical dependent choice. In *Logic Colloquium '01*. Proceedings of the Annual European Summer Meeting of the Association for Symbolic Logic held in Vienna, August 6-11, 2001. Edited by Matthias Baaz, Sy-David Friedman and Jan Krajícek. Volume 20 of *Lect. Notes Log.*, pages 89–107. Assoc. Symbol. Logic, Urbana, IL; A K Peters, Ltd., Wellesley, MA, 2005.

[3] T. Coquand. Constructive topology and combinatorics. In J. Paul Myers Jr., Michael J. O'Donnell (Eds.): *Constructivity in computer science (San Antonio, TX, 1991)*, volume 613 of *Lecture Notes in Comput. Sci.*, pages 159–164. Springer, Berlin, 1992.

[4] C. St. J. A. Nash-Williams. On well–quasi–ordering finite trees. *Proceedings of the Cambridge Philosophical Society*, 59:833–835, 1963.

[5] H. Schwichtenberg and S. S. Wainer. *Proofs and computations*. Perspectives in Logic. Cambridge University Press, Cambridge, 2012.

[6] M. Seisenberger. Programs from proofs using classical dependent choice. *Annals of Pure and Applied Logic*, 153(1–3):97–110, 2008.

Coinduction in Computable Analysis

Ulrich Berger

Swansea University, Swansea, United Kingdom

E-mail: u.berger@swansea.ac.uk

Coinduction is a concept of increasing importance in mathematics and computer science, in particular in non-wellfounded set theory, process algebra and database theory. Probably the best-known example of a coinductive relation is bisimilarity of processes. In this talk I present applications of coinduction computable analysis in general and exact real number computation in particular.

Intuitively, coinduction is about deconstructing, or observing data, or describing how a process evolves. This is in contrast to induction, which is about constructing data. A real number, say π, is a typical candidate for coinduction. We cannot construct pi (completely and exactly), but we can make observations about it, by, for example, successively computing digits of π. Similarly, a computable continuous functions on the real numbers can be viewed as a coinductive process: we successively compute digits of the output while reading digits of the input. In fact, it turns out that the computation of a single correct output digit is an inductive process. Therefore, continuous real functions are described by a combination of induction and coinduction.

In the talk I will explain how the inductive/coinductive approach to continuous real functions leads to the automatic synthesis of provably correct programs for exact real numbers using a suitable realisability interpretation which allows to extract provably correct programs form constructive proofs.

The formal proofs from which programs are extracted are carried out in an extension of first-order logic by inductive and coinductive predicates viewed as least and greatest fixed points of monotone predicate operators. The mathematical objects themselves (real number, real functions, etc.) are introduced abstractly and axiomatically. Their computational aspects expressed solely by means of predicates in the formal system, and it is only the realisability interpretation which makes these aspects explicit. This is in contrast to constructive type theory where mathematical objects are constructed within the formal system, including their computational behaviour. I will argue that the abstract approach has advantages regarding usability and flexibility.

Arnold Beckmann, Benedikt Löwe (*eds.*). *Acts of the programme "Semantics and Syntax"*. Isaac Newton Institute for the Mathematical Sciences, January to July 2012.

Talk given at the SAS Seminar, 22 May 2012, 16:30–17:00.

Complexity of Exponential Integer Parts on Real Closed Exponential Fields

Karen Lange

Wellesley College, Wellesley MA, United States of America

E-mail: karen.lange@wellesley.edu

An *integer part* I for an ordered field R is a discrete ordered subring containing 1 such that for all $r \in R$ there exists a unique $i \in I$ with $i \leq r < i + 1$. Mourgues and Ressayre [1] showed that every real closed field R has an integer part by constructing a special embedding of R into a field $k\langle\langle G \rangle\rangle$ of generalized power series. Let k be the residue field of R, and let G be the value group of R. The field $k\langle\langle G \rangle\rangle$ consists of elements of the form $\Sigma_{g \in S} a_g g$ where $a_g \in k$ and the support of the power series $S \subseteq G$ is well ordered. Ressayre [2] showed that every real closed exponential field has an integer part I that is closed under 2^x for positive elements of I using the same approach as in [1]. However, he had to choose more carefully the value group G and the embedding of R into $k\langle\langle G \rangle\rangle$. We demonstrate that these alterations cause Ressayre's construction in the exponential case to be much more complex than Mourgues and Ressayre's original construction.

This is joint work with Paola D'Aquino, Julia Knight, and Salma Kuhlmann.

Bibliography

[1] M.-H. Mourgues and J. P. Ressayre. Every real closed field has an integer part. *J. Symbolic Logic*, 58(2):641–647, 1993.

[2] J.-P. Ressayre. Integer parts of real closed exponential fields (extended abstract). In *Arithmetic, proof theory, and computational complexity. Papers from the conference held in Prague, July 2-5, 1991*, volume 23 of *Oxford Logic Guides*, pages 278–288. Oxford Univ. Press, New York, 1993.

Arnold Beckmann, Benedikt Löwe (*eds.*). *Acts of the programme "Semantics and Syntax".* Isaac Newton Institute for the Mathematical Sciences, January to July 2012.

Talk given at the SAS Seminar, 22 May 2012, 17:00–17:30.

Uniform Distribution and Algorithmic Randomness

Jeremy Avigad

Carnegie Mellon University, Pittsburgh PA, United States of America

E-mail: avigad@cmu.edu

A seminal theorem due to Weyl states that if (a_n) is any sequence of distinct integers, then, for almost every $x \in \mathbb{R}$, the sequence $(a_n x)$ is uniformly distributed modulo one. In particular, for almost every x in the unit interval, the sequence $(a_n x)$ is uniformly distributed modulo one for every *computable* sequence (a_n) of distinct integers. Call such an x *UD random*. Here it is shown that every Schnorr-random real is UD random, but there are Kurtz-random reals that are not UD random. On the other hand, Weyl's theorem still holds relative to a particular effectively closed null set, so there are UD random reals that are not Kurtz random.

Arnold Beckmann, Benedikt Löwe (*eds.*). *Acts of the programme "Semantics and Syntax".*
Isaac Newton Institute for the Mathematical Sciences, January to July 2012.

Talk given at the SAS Seminar, 29 May 2012, 16:00–16:30.

Automrophisms of Models of Set Theory and NFU

Zachiri McKenzie

University of Cambridge, Cambridge, United Kingdom

E-mail: z.mckenzie@dpmms.cam.ac.uk

NFU is the subsystem of Quine's 'New Foundations' (NF) obtained by weakening the extensionality axiom to allow urelements first introduced by Ronald Jensen in [1]. Jensen demonstrated that a model of NFU can built from a model of a subsystem of ZFC that admits an automorphism. We will recall Jensen's construction and demonstrate that models of natural strong extensions of NFU can be built from models of subsystems of ZFC that admit automorphisms with certain 'nice' properties. Our particular focus will be on an extension of NFU obtained by adding $AxCount_\leq$ which is a natural weakening of Rosser's Axiom of Counting [2]. A model of NFU + $AxCount_\leq$ can be obtained from a model of a strong enough subsystem of ZFC that admits an automorphism which does not move any natural number down. We will indicate how a model admitting such an automorphism can be produced from a non-standard ω-model of a subsystem of ZFC. This result allows us to show that NFU plus Rosser's Axiom of Counting proves the consistency of NFU + $AxCount_\leq$. We will also discuss the axiom $AxCount_\geq$. We ask if NFU + $AxCount_\geq$ is equiconsistent with NFU?

Bibliography

[1] R. B. Jensen. On the consistency of a slight (?) modification of Quine's "New Foundations". *Synthese*, 19:250–263, 1968.

[2] J. B. Rosser. *Logic for mathematicians*. McGraw-Hill Book Company, Inc., New York-Toronto-London, 1953.

Arnold Beckmann, Benedikt Löwe (*eds.*). *Acts of the programme "Semantics and Syntax".* Isaac Newton Institute for the Mathematical Sciences, January to July 2012.

Talk given at the SAS Seminar, 29 May 2012, 16:30–17:00.

Bounds on Proof Size and Security Verification

R. Ramanujam

Institute of Mathematical Sciences, Chennai, India

E-mail: jam@imsc.res.in

In the formal analysis of security protocols, what the intruder infers from messages travelling on the network can be abstracted into checking whether a term is derivable in an inference system from a given finite set of terms (subject to some equations). This is often referred to as the Dolev-Yao theory, and this problem is typically in polynomial time, which can be established by showing a subterm property: every term occurring in a normal proof is a subterm of some term in the input.

When encryption is distributive over pairing (as we need, for instance, in blind signatures), we no longer have the subterm property as one can form nontrivial encryption sequences in which keys may repeat. We show that in such a system, we get proof of size exponential in the size of the input, and that the term derivability is, in fact DEXPTIME-complete. The upper bound uses the fact that the key sequences that may arise in a proof form a regular set and hence uses an automaton saturation technique.

The result is to be contrasted with distributive encryption in the presence of an abelian group operator where only a non-elementary upper bound is known.

Arnold Beckmann, Benedikt Löwe (*eds.*). *Acts of the programme "Semantics and Syntax"*. Isaac Newton Institute for the Mathematical Sciences, January to July 2012.

Talk given at the SAS Seminar, 31 May 2012, 16:00–16:30.

Definability via $\mathcal{K}$-pairs

Mariya I. Soskova

Sofia University, Sofia, Bulgaria
E-mail: msoskova@fmi.uni-sofia.bg

I will describe the advancements and future directions in a joint project with Ganchev which studies definability properties of the upper semilattice of the enumeration degrees. The main technique arises from the notion of a $\mathcal{K}$-pair. A pair of sets of natural numbers A and B are a $\mathcal{K}$-pair if there exists a c.e. set W, such that $A \times B \subseteq W$ and $\overline{A} \times \overline{B} \subseteq \overline{W}$. $\mathcal{K}$-pairs are defined and used by Kalimullin to show that the enumeration jump operator is first order definable. We give an alternative first order definition of the enumeration jump, as an illustration of the main technique and suggest that a similar method can still be used to attack the long-standing open problem of the definability of the total degrees, an isomorphic copy of the Turing degrees in the enumeration degrees.

Arnold Beckmann, Benedikt Löwe (eds.). Acts of the programme "Semantics and Syntax".
Isaac Newton Institute for the Mathematical Sciences, January to July 2012.

Talk given at the SAS Seminar, 31 May 2012, 16:30–17:00.

Searchable Sets and Ordinals in System T

Martin Escardo

The University of Birmingham, Birmingham, United Kingdom

E-mail: m.escardo@cs.bham.ac.uk

We consider subsets of the Cantor space with a T-definable selection function, without assuming continuity, and we call them T-searchable. Here T, or Gödel's system T, is the simply typed lambda calculus with base types for booleans and natural numbers, and higher-type primitive recursion. Any successor ordinal below epsilon zero, regarded as an ordered set, can be embedded in the lexicographic order of the Cantor space so that it is T-searchable, with selection function that finds smallest witnesses. We conclude with some questions we are investigating in joint work with Dag Normann, for example whether every T-searchable set must be countable with Cantor rank smaller than epsilon zero, and more generally what are precisely the T-searchable subsets of the Cantor space and the Baire space.

Arnold Beckmann, Benedikt Löwe (eds.). Acts of the programme "Semantics and Syntax".
Isaac Newton Institute for the Mathematical Sciences, January to July 2012.

Talk given at the SAS Seminar, 31 May 2012, 17:00–17:30.

The Complexity of Computable Categoricity

Andrew E. M. Lewis

University of Leeds, Leeds, United Kingdom
E-mail: aemlewis@aemlewis.co.uk

A computable structure is computably categorical if any computable structure isomorphic to it is computably isomorphic. It has been a long-standing question to establish how hard it is to decide whether a structure is computably categorical. Earlier this year, in joint work with Downey, Kach, Lempp, Montalban and Turetsky, we were able to answer this question: the index set is Π_1^1-complete. I shall give a short introduction to the area and then describe some aspects of the proof without going into many technical details.

Arnold Beckmann, Benedikt Löwe (eds.). Acts of the programme "Semantics and Syntax".
Isaac Newton Institute for the Mathematical Sciences, January to July 2012.

Talk given at the SAS Seminar, 7 June 2012, 16:00–16:30.

Conservative Extensions and the Jump of a Structure

Alexandra A. Soskova

Sofia University, Sofia, Bulgaria

E-mail: asoskova@fmi.uni-sofia.bg

The degree spectrum of an abstract structure is a measure of its complexity. We consider a relation between abstract structures $\mathfrak{A}$ and $\mathfrak{B}$, possibly with different signatures and $|\mathfrak{A}| \subseteq |\mathfrak{B}|$, called conservative extension. We give a characterization of this relation in terms of definability by computable Σ_n^c formulae on these structures. We show that this relation provides a finer complexity measure than the one given by degree spectra. As an application, we receive that the nth jump of a structure and its Marker's extension are conservative extensions of the original structure. We present a jump inversion theorem for abstract structures. We prove that for every natural numbers n and k and each complex enough structure $\mathfrak{A}$, there is a structure $\mathfrak{B}$, such that the definable by computable Σ_n^c formulae sets on $\mathfrak{A}$ are exactly the definable by computable Σ_k^c formulae on $\mathfrak{B}$.

The research presented in this talk is joint work with Ivan N. Soskov and Stefan V. Vatev.

Arnold Beckmann, Benedikt Löwe (*eds.*). *Acts of the programme "Semantics and Syntax".* Isaac Newton Institute for the Mathematical Sciences, January to July 2012.

Talk given at the SAS Seminar, 7 June 2012, 16:30–17:00.

The Incomputable
Kavli Royal Society International Centre, Chicheley Hall
12 – 15 June 2012

Mariya I. Soskova[1] and S. Barry Cooper[2]

[1]Sofia University, Sofia, Bulgaria
[2]University of Leeds, Leeds, United Kingdom
E-mail: msoskova@fmi.uni-sofia.bg, pmt6sbc@maths.leeds.ac.uk

The Incomputable was one of a series of special events, running throughout the Alan Turing Year, celebrating Turing's unique impact on mathematics, computing, computer science, informatics, morphogenesis, philosophy and the wider scientific world. It was held in association with the Turing Centenary Conference (CiE 2012) in Cambridge following it, running up to the June 23rd centenary of Turing's birth, and culminating with a birthday celebration at Turing's old college, King's College, Cambridge.

The Incomputable was unique in its focus on the mathematical theory of incomputability, and its relevance for the real world. This is a core aspect of Turing's scientific legacy—and this meeting for the first time reunites (in)computability theory and "big science" in a way not attempted since Turing's premature passing. In 2012, the annual Workshop on Computability Theory is being held in conjunction with The Incomputable.

Chicheley Hall is a truly extraordinary venue for the meeting, beautifully maintained by the Royal Society, and offering superb facilities for the talks, accommodation, and informal discussions. Set in a beautiful country landscape, it offers many comforts and opportunities for exciting and novel interactions.

The Incomputable, generously supported by the John Templeton Foundation, was a historic event, bringing the mathematical theory of incomputability centre-stage once again.

Invited Plenary Speakers. Samson Abramsky (University of Oxford), Hajnal Andréka (Hungarian Academy of Sciences at Budapest), Martin Davis (University of California at Berkeley / City University of New York), Fay Dowker (Imperial College London), Seth Lloyd (Massachusetts Institute of Technology), Philip Maini (University of Oxford), Yuri Matiyasevich (Russian Academy of Sciences at St. Petersburg), Cris Moore (Santa Fe Institute), István Németi (Hungarian Academy of Sciences at Budapest), Theodore A. Slaman (University of California at Berkeley), Robert I Soare (The University of Chicago), and Vlatko Vedral (University of Oxford).

Arnold Beckmann, Benedikt Löwe (*eds.*). *Acts of the programme "Semantics and Syntax"*. Isaac Newton Institute for the Mathematical Sciences, January to July 2012.

Talk given at the SAS Satellite Workshop "The Incomputable" (Chicheley Hall, Newport Pagnell).

Invited Special Session Speakers. Klaus Ambos-Spies (University of Heidelberg), Marat M. Arslanov (Kazan State University), Mark Bishop (Goldsmiths, University of London), Cristian Calude (The University of Auckland), Douglas Cenzer (University of Florida at Gainesville), Peter Cholak (University of Notre Dame), Bob Coecke (University of Oxford), José Félix Costa (Instituto Superior Técnico, Lisbon), Vincent Danos (The University of Edinburgh), Rod Downey (University of Wellington), Steven Ericsson-Zenith (Institute for Advanced Science and Engineering, Palo Alto), Luciano Floridi (University of Hertfordshire/University of Oxford), Sy Friedman (University of Vienna), Sergey Goncharov (University of Novosibirsk), Noam Greenberg (University of Wellington), Joel David Hamkins (City University of New York), Valentina Harizanov (University of Washington), Denis Hirschfeldt (The University of Chicago), Mark Hogarth (University of Cambridge), Elham Kashefi (The University of Edinburgh), Julia Knight (University of Notre Dame), Antonina Kolokolova (Memorial University of Newfoundland), Antonin Kučera (Charles University), Andrew Lewis (University of Leeds), Giuseppe Longo (École Normale Supérieure at Paris), Ursula Martin (Queen Mary, University of London), Antonio Montalban (The University of Chicago), André Nies (The University of Auckland), Mehrnoosh Sadrzadeh (University of Oxford), Richard A Shore (Cornell University), Aaron Sloman (The University of Birmingham), Andrea Sorbi (Universitá degli Studi di Siena), Ivan Soskov (Sofia University), Alexandra A. Soskova (Sofia University), Christof Teuscher (Portland State University), John Tucker (Swansea University), Kumaraswamy (Vela) Velupillai (University of Trento), Peter Wegner (Brown University), Philip Welch (University of Bristol), and Jiří Wiedermann (Academy of Sciences of the Czech Republic at Prague).

Scientific advisers. Cristian Calude (The University of Auckland), Rod Downey (University of Wellington), Luciano Floridi (University of Hertfordshire/University of Oxford), and Jiří Wiedermann (Academy of Sciences of the Czech Republic at Prague).

(Picture courtesy of Virginia Davis)

In addition to the the abstracts in this booklet, slides of some of the talks can be found at

http://www.mathcomp.leeds.ac.uk/turing2012/inc/

Turing Computability and Information Content

Robert I. Soare

The University of Chicago, Chicago IL, United States of America
E-mail: soare@uchicago.edu

Turing's most famous contribution is his definition [2] of an automatic machine (a-machine), now called a Turing machine. Less famous is Turing's very brief suggestion [3, §4] of an oracle machine (o-machine), a Turing machine which could consult an outside database which he called an "oracle." Post [1] took Turing's sketch and developed it into the theory of one set B being reducible to another set A which he named "Turing reducibility." The latter is the most important concept in computability because it encompasses plain computability, gives a model for accessing a data base which we do every time we go the internet, and it enables us to measure the information content of a mathematical structure. It allows us to measure the complexity of algebraic structures, unsolvable problems in mathematics, Kolmogorov complexity, and algorithmic complexity, objects in model theory, and many other structures in mathematics and computer science.

Bibliography

[1] E. L. Post. Recursively enumerable sets of positive integers and their decision problems. *Bull. Amer. Math. Soc.*, 50:284–316, 1944.

[2] A. M. Turing. On computable numbers, with an application to the Entscheidungsproblem. *Proc. London Math. Soc.*, S2-42(1):230, 1936.

[3] A. M. Turing. Systems of Logic Based on Ordinals. *Proc. London Math. Soc.*, s2-45(1):161–228, 1939.

Arnold Beckmann, Benedikt Löwe (*eds.*). *Acts of the programme "Semantics and Syntax"*. Isaac Newton Institute for the Mathematical Sciences, January to July 2012.

Talk given at the SAS Satellite Workshop "The Incomputable" (Kavli Royal Society International Centre, Chicheley Hall, Newport Pagnell), 12 June 2012, 09:00–10:00.

A Turing Test for Free Will

Seth Lloyd

Massachusetts Institute of Technology, Cambridge MA, United States of America
E-mail: slloyd@mit.edu

I show that the theory of computation implies that even when our decisions arise from a completely deterministic decision-making process, the outcomes of that process are intrinsically unpredictable, even to—especially to—ourselves. I argue that this intrinsic computational unpredictability of the decision making process is what give rise to our impression that we possess free will. Finally, I propose a "Turing test" for free will: a decision maker who passes this test will tend to believe that he, she, or it possesses free will, whether the world is deterministic or not.

Arnold Beckmann, Benedikt Löwe (*eds.*). *Acts of the programme "Semantics and Syntax"*. Isaac Newton Institute for the Mathematical Sciences, January to July 2012.

Talk given at the SAS Satellite Workshop "The Incomputable" (Kavli Royal Society International Centre, Chicheley Hall, Newport Pagnell), 12 June 2012, 10:00–11:00.

Generalised Transfinite Turing Machines and Strategies for Games

Philip Welch

University of Bristol, Bristol, United Kingdom

E-mail: p.welch@bristol.ac.uk

For levels of determinacy for two person perfect information games which are for open or Σ_2^0 games in the arithmetic hierarchy, strategies can be found related to certain classes of monotone inductive definitions. We try to expand this to the next level using generalised notions both of transfinite Turing machine and inductive definition.

Arnold Beckmann, Benedikt Löwe (eds.). Acts of the programme "Semantics and Syntax".
Isaac Newton Institute for the Mathematical Sciences, January to July 2012.

Talk given at the SAS Satellite Workshop "The Incomputable" (Kavli Royal Society International Centre, Chicheley Hall, Newport Pagnell), 12 June 2012, 11:30–12:00.

Categoricity Properties for Computable Algebraic Fields

Denis Hirschfeldt

The University of Chicago, Chicago IL, United States of America

E-mail: drh@math.uchicago.edu

I will examine issues related to the computable dimension of algebraic fields, including results that show that this class of structures sits at the border between classes with good structure theorems from the point of view of computable structure theory and classes that permit "pathological" examples, such as structures of finite computable dimension greater than one.

This is joint work with Ken Kramer, Russell Miller, and Alexandra Shlapentokh.

Arnold Beckmann, Benedikt Löwe (*eds.*). *Acts of the programme "Semantics and Syntax".*
Isaac Newton Institute for the Mathematical Sciences, January to July 2012.

Talk given at the SAS Satellite Workshop "The Incomputable" (Kavli Royal Society International Centre, Chicheley Hall, Newport Pagnell), 12 June 2012, 12:00–12:30.

From Intrinsic to Designed Computation with Turing's Unorganized Machines

Christof Teuscher

Portland State University, Portland OR, United States of America

E-mail: christof@teuscher-lab.com

Turing proposed unorganized machines and evolutionary search in a 1948 National Physical Laboratory (NPL) report entitled "Intelligent Machinery." These machines have very similar properties to what is today known as random Boolean networks, which have been used as models for genetic regulatory networks. In addition, the concept of (self-) assembling simple compute nodes that are interconnected in unstructured ways has gained significance with the advent of nano- and molecular electronics over the last decade. In this talk I will first present Turing's various original unorganized machines as a representative of intrinsic computation, extensions to them, and then relate the work to contemporary random Boolean networks, nano- and molecular electronics, and computing theory. I will illustrate that many of Turing's original ideas are more than ever current, influential, and deeply fascinating.

Arnold Beckmann, Benedikt Löwe (eds.). Acts of the programme "Semantics and Syntax". Isaac Newton Institute for the Mathematical Sciences, January to July 2012.

Talk given at the SAS Satellite Workshop "The Incomputable" (Kavli Royal Society International Centre, Chicheley Hall, Newport Pagnell), 12 June 2012, 11:30–12:00.

The Meta-morphogenesis of Virtual Machinery with "Physically Indefinable" Functions

Aaron Sloman

The University of Birmingham, Birmingham, United Kingdom
E-mail: A.Sloman@cs.bham.ac.uk

I use "meta-morphogenesis" to refer to the mechanisms and processes by which morphogenesis, especially morphogenesis of information processing functions and mechanisms, changes—over evolutionary, developmental and social time scales. I shall give a brief presentation of some of the ideas, including conjectures about how the development of virtual machinery in biological organisms can be compared with some of the complex, often unnoticed, developments in computing systems over the last six or seven decades including production of virtual machinery with complex internal causation as well as external and "downward" causal connections. Some of that virtual machinery has functions whose description requires language, e.g., talk of "wanting", "trying", "believing", "inferring", "introspecting", that cannot be translated into the language of the physical sciences (as currently understood). This fact could cause intelligent machines to become puzzled about their own consciousness and mind-brain relationships in the same ways as human philosophers and scientists have. In both cases well-designed tutorials in systems engineering may (for some individuals) help to remove the puzzles.

For more information, see [1, 2].

Bibliography

[1] A. Sloman. Meta-morphogenesis theory as background to cognitive robotics and developmental cognitive science. Presentation at the Dagstuhl Seminar on Mechanisms of ongoing development in cognitive robotics, February 2013.

[2] A. Sloman. Virtual machine functionalism. In preparation, 2013.

Arnold Beckmann, Benedikt Löwe (eds.). Acts of the programme "Semantics and Syntax".
Isaac Newton Institute for the Mathematical Sciences, January to July 2012.

Talk given at the SAS Satellite Workshop "The Incomputable" (Kavli Royal Society International Centre, Chicheley Hall, Newport Pagnell), 12 June 2012, 12:00–12:30.

Classifying Computably Enumerable Equivalence Relations

Andrea Sorbi

Università Degli Studi di Siena, Siena, Italy

E-mail: sorbi@unisi.it

We study computably enumerable equivalence relations (ceers) on the set of natural numbers ω, under the reducibility $R \leq S$ if there exists a computable function f such that, for every x, y, $x \, R \, y$ if and only if $f(x) \, S \, f(y)$. We prove, see [1], that the degree structure originated by this reducibility is a bounded poset that is neither a lower semilattice, nor an upper semilattice, and its first order theory is undecidable. We then study the universal ceers, i.e., the ceers R such that $S \leq R$ for every ceer S. We show that the uniformly effectively inseparable ceers (i.e., the ceers yielding a partition of ω such that every disjoint pair of sets in the partition is effectively inseparable, via a productive function that can be uniformly found from any choice of pairs of representatives in the equivalence classes) are universal. This theorem extends known results in the literature concerning ceers, see e.g. [2] and [4], and is a natural companion of classical results of computability theory, such as universality of creative sets, and of pairs of effectively inseparable sets; uniformity is essential here, since we prove that there are effectively inseparable ceers (i.e., ceers just yielding a partition such that every disjoint pair is effectively inseparable) that are not universal. We study also the halting jump operator on ceers introduced by Gao and Gerdes [3], defined as $x \, R' \, y$ if and only if $x = y$ or $\varphi_x(x) \downarrow R \, \varphi_x(x) \downarrow$, and show that a ceer R is universal if and only if $R' \leq R$ (answering an open question of Gao and Gerdes). Finally we consider index sets of some classes of universal ceers, and show for instance that the index set of the universal ceers and the index set of the uniformly effectively inseparable ceers are Σ_3^0-complete (the former answering an open question of Gao and Gerdes).

This is joint work with Uri Andrews, Steffen Lempp, Joseph S. Miller, Keng Meng Ng and Luca San Mauro.

Bibliography

[1] U. Andrews, S. Lempp, J. S. Miller, K. M. Ng, L. San Mauro, and A. Sorbi. Universal computably enumerable equivalence relations. Technical Report NI12020-SAS, Isaac Newton Center for the Mathematical Sciences, 2012.

Arnold Beckmann, Benedikt Löwe (eds.). Acts of the programme "Semantics and Syntax". Isaac Newton Institute for the Mathematical Sciences, January to July 2012.

Talk given at the SAS Satellite Workshop "The Incomputable" (Kavli Royal Society International Centre, Chicheley Hall, Newport Pagnell), 12 June 2012, 14:30–15:00.

[2] C. Bernardi and A. Sorbi. Classifying positive equivalence relations. *J. Symbolic Logic*, 48(3):529–538, 1983.

[3] S. Gao and P. Gerdes. Computably enumerable equivalence realations. *Studia Logica*, 67:27–59, 2001.

[4] F. Montagna. Relative precomplete numerations and arithmetic. *J. Philosphical Logic*, 11:419–430, 1982.

Definability Properties of Marker's Extensions

Ivan N. Soskov

Sofia University, Sofia, Bulgaria

E-mail: soskov@fmi.uni-sofia.bg

Marker's extensions of a structure are introduced by Goncharov and Khoussainov in 2002. The definition is based on earlier work of Marker. We shall discuss results on definability in Marker's extensions and prove that for every finite ordinal n, the $(n+1)$st Marker's extension of a countable structure A behaves as a Model Theoretic nth jump inversion of $A \oplus \varnothing^{(n)}$. We shall show that in the general case such kind of jump inversions are impossible for infinite recursive ordinals.

Arnold Beckmann, Benedikt Löwe (eds.). Acts of the programme "Semantics and Syntax". Isaac Newton Institute for the Mathematical Sciences, January to July 2012.

Talk given at the SAS Satellite Workshop "The Incomputable" (Kavli Royal Society International Centre, Chicheley Hall, Newport Pagnell), 12 June 2012, 15:00–15:30.

The Complexity of Computable Categoricity

Andrew E. M. Lewis

University of Leeds, Leeds, United Kingdom

E-mail: andy@aemlewis.co.uk

I will report on recent work with Downey, Kach, Lempp, Montalban and Turetsky. A computable structure is computably categorical if there is a computable isomorphism from the structure to any computable copy. It has been a longstanding question to decide the complexity of the index set of computably categorical structures, i.e., to establish what oracle is required to decide which computable structures are computably categorical. We have shown that the index set is Π^1_1-complete, demonstrating that computable categoricity has no simple syntactic characterization. As a consequence of our proof, we exhibit, for every computable ordinal α, a computable structure that is computably categorical but not relatively Δ^0_α-categorical.

Arnold Beckmann, Benedikt Löwe (eds.). Acts of the programme "Semantics and Syntax".
Isaac Newton Institute for the Mathematical Sciences, January to July 2012.

Talk given at the SAS Satellite Workshop "The Incomputable" (Kavli Royal Society International Centre, Chicheley Hall, Newport Pagnell), 12 June 2012, 15:30–16:00.

Modern Computation

Peter Wegner

Brown University, Providence RI, United States of America

E-mail: pw@cs.brown.edu

Alan Turing made important contributions to early models of computation in the 1930s and 1940s; but his tragic suicide in 1954 prevented him from contributing to its later evolution. Maurice Wilkes, who passed away aged 99 in November of 2011, informed me of Turing's death during my final exam week at Cambridge in June 1954, where I was studying for the first postgraduate diploma in computer science ever offered anywhere in the world.

Computing models developed after the 1970s have moved well beyond the Turing machine model. My talk will discuss my recent edited book on Interaction Machines [1] post-Turing later evolution of computing through personal computers, object-oriented programming and the Internet.

Bibliography

[1] D. Goldin, S. A. Smolka, and P. Wegner, editors. *Interactive computation - The new paradigm*. Springer-Verlag, Berlin, 2006.

Arnold Beckmann, Benedikt Löwe (*eds.*). *Acts of the programme "Semantics and Syntax"*. Isaac Newton Institute for the Mathematical Sciences, January to July 2012.

Talk given at the SAS Satellite Workshop "The Incomputable" (Kavli Royal Society International Centre, Chicheley Hall, Newport Pagnell), 12 June 2012, 14:30–15:00.

Incomputability in Economic Theory

K. Vela Velupillai

University of Trento, Trento, Italy

E-mail: kvelupillai@gmail.com

The origins of classical recursion theoretic and computational complexity theoretic formalisms in core areas of economic theory—game theory and rational choice theory—can be traced to the pioneering articles by *Herbert Simon, Michael Rabin* and *Hilary Putnam*, in the 1950s and early 1960s. From the outset, particularly in Rabin's work, the issues of unsolvability, incomputability and undecidability played crucial roles in the effectivized formalisation of problems in *playable* games, *satisfiable* choice sets and rational behaviour. At the frontiers of economic theory, these issues have now taken on some analytical and computational significance via considerations of the incomputability of game theoretic, welfare theoretic and general equilibrium characterizations of varieties of formally—non-constructively and non-effectively—demonstrated equilibria. In this paper, after a brief survey of the historical evolution of the subject of what I have come to call *Computable Economics*, an attempt is made to outline also the frontiers of the subject and identify directions for future research on incomputability and undecidabilty in economic theory.

Arnold Beckmann, Benedikt Löwe (*eds.*). *Acts of the programme "Semantics and Syntax".* Isaac Newton Institute for the Mathematical Sciences, January to July 2012.

Talk given at the SAS Satellite Workshop "The Incomputable" (Kavli Royal Society International Centre, Chicheley Hall, Newport Pagnell), 12 June 2012, 15:00–15:30.

Equilibrium and Termination

Vincent Danos

The University of Edinburgh, Edinburgh, United Kingdom
E-mail: vincent.danos@gmail.com

We present a reduction of the Post correspondence problem to the question of whether a continuous-time Markov chain has an equilibrium. It follows that whether a computable CTMC is dissipative (ie does not have an equilibrium) is undecidable, and more generally equilibrium can be seen as a form of sequential termination. We generalize this idea to a class of reversible communicating processes. Transition rates are derived from a formal notion of energy which increases exponentially with the size of the local history of a process. This second construction can be seen as a concurrent version of the Metropolis-Hastings algorithm.

Arnold Beckmann, Benedikt Löwe (*eds.*). *Acts of the programme "Semantics and Syntax"*.
Isaac Newton Institute for the Mathematical Sciences, January to July 2012.

Talk given at the SAS Satellite Workshop "The Incomputable" (Kavli Royal Society International Centre, Chicheley Hall, Newport Pagnell), 12 June 2012, 15:30–16:00.

Turing Machines vs. Diophantine Machines

Yuri Matiyasevich

Russian Academy of Sciences, St. Petersburg, Russia

E-mail: yumat@pdmi.ras.ru

Alan Turing introduced his celebrated machines by analyzing elementary steps of computational devices, real physical and abstract imaginary ones. Diophantine machines were introduced by Leonard Adleman and Kenneth Manders from quite different considerations—on the base of DPRM theorem about sets defined by Diophantine equations. The talk will be devoted to comparison and interplay of these two kinds of machines.

Arnold Beckmann, Benedikt Löwe (*eds.*). *Acts of the programme "Semantics and Syntax"*. Isaac Newton Institute for the Mathematical Sciences, January to July 2012.

Talk given at the SAS Satellite Workshop "The Incomputable" (Kavli Royal Society International Centre, Chicheley Hall, Newport Pagnell), 12 June 2012, 16:30–17:30.

Contributions of Emil Post to the Study of the Incomputable

Martin Davis

New York University, New York NY, United States of America

E-mail: martin@eipye.com

The talk will survey Post's work on unsolvable problems and degrees of unsolvability beginning in the 1920s. Connections with computer science will be emphasized.

Arnold Beckmann, Benedikt Löwe (*eds.*). *Acts of the programme "Semantics and Syntax"*.
Isaac Newton Institute for the Mathematical Sciences, January to July 2012.

Talk given at the SAS Satellite Workshop "The Incomputable" (Kavli Royal Society International Centre, Chicheley Hall, Newport Pagnell), 13 June 2012, 09:00–10:00.

Turing's Theory for Biological Pattern Formation

Philip Maini

University of Oxford, Oxford, United Kingdom
E-mail: maini@maths.ox.ac.uk

In his seminar 1952 paper, Turing proposed a mathematical model for biological pattern formation in which he showed how a system of reacting and diffusing chemicals could spontaneously generate spatially heterogeneous solutions. He hypothesized that this chemical pattern underlay the patterns that we see in many biological organisms. In this talk we will discuss his theory and its impact.

Arnold Beckmann, Benedikt Löwe (*eds.*). *Acts of the programme "Semantics and Syntax".*
Isaac Newton Institute for the Mathematical Sciences, January to July 2012.

Talk given at the SAS Satellite Workshop "The Incomputable" (Kavli Royal Society International Centre, Chicheley Hall, Newport Pagnell), 13 June 2012, 10:00–11:00.

Strong Jump Traceability

Rod Downey and Noam Greenberg

Victoria University of Wellington, Wellington, New Zealand
E-mail: rod.downey@vuw.ac.nz and greenberg@msor.vuw.ac.nz

Interactions between randomness and computability have been very fruitful in the last decade. Figuiera, Nies and Stephan [4] introduced a concept called strong jump traceability which was seen as a possible combinatorial characterization of K-triviality at the time. Though this characterization failed (Cholak, Downey and Greenberg [1]), the SJT reals turn out to have significant interactions with randomness such as, for instance, Greenberg, Hirschfeldt, Nies [5] and Greenberg-Turetsky [6]. Moreover, recent work of Diamondstone, Greenberg and Turetsky [2], has shown that these considerations apply outside of the computably enumerable sets, and, indeed, SJT is an intrinsically enumerable property.

Recent work of Downey and Greenberg [3], and then work in preparation of those authors with Diamondstone and Turetsky has shown that this interaction of randomness and computability can work very effectively the other way. Downey and Greenberg show that a longstanding question on pseudo-jump inversion can be solved using SJT sets under inversion, via the sets that think that the halting problem is SJT relative to them.

In the first lecture Downey will introduce the concepts of strong jump traceability, discuss its motivations and look at the techniques devised to handle the class. He will also discuss the class under inversion.

In the second lecture, Greenberg will discuss the results connecting SJT reals with randomness and benign cost functions, and the class of Demuth random reals. Given time he will also discuss the intrinsic enumerability of the class.

Bibliography

[1] P. Cholak, R. Downey, and N. Greenberg. Strong jump-traceabilty. I. The computably enumerable case. *Adv. Math.*, 217(5):2045–2074, 2008.

[2] D. Diamondstone, N. Greenberg, and D. Turetsky. Inherent enumerability of strong jump traceability. Submitted.

[3] R. Downey and N. Greenberg. Pseudo-jump inversion and SJT-hard sets. Submitted.

[4] S. Figueira, A. Nies, and F. Stephan. Lowness properties and approximations of the jump. *Ann. Pure Appl. Logic*, 152(1-3):51–66, 2008.

Arnold Beckmann, Benedikt Löwe (*eds.*). *Acts of the programme "Semantics and Syntax"*.
Isaac Newton Institute for the Mathematical Sciences, January to July 2012.

Talk given at the SAS Satellite Workshop "The Incomputable" (Kavli Royal Society International Centre, Chicheley Hall, Newport Pagnell), 13 June 2012, 11:30–12:30.

[5] N. Greenberg, D. Hirschfeldt, and A. Nies. Characterising the strongly jump-traceable sets via randomness. Submitted.

[6] N. Greenberg and D. Turetsky. Strong jump-traceability and Demuth randomness. Submitted.

Quantum Turing Test

Elham Kashefi

The University of Edinburgh, Edinburgh, United Kingdom
E-mail: ekashefi@inf.ed.ac.uk

A fundamental goal in quantum information processing is to test a machine's (or more generally nature's) ability to exhibit quantum behaviour. The most celebrated result in this domain, which has been also demonstrated experimentally, is the celebrated Bell Theorem that verifies the non-local nature of quantum mechanics. Could we generalise such approaches to verify that a given device is in fact taking advantage of quantum mechanics rather than being a disguised classical machine. Considering the exponential regime of quantum mechanics, the issue of efficiency of such tests are the key challenge from the complexity point of view. On the other hand, from the foundational point of view, it is an intriguing open question whether a fully classical scheme could verify any quantum properties of a larger system while being experimentally feasible. We present some recent progress towards this direction that has also surprising consequences on an entirely different open question, the existence of fully homomorphic encryption schemes.

Arnold Beckmann, Benedikt Löwe (eds.). Acts of the programme "Semantics and Syntax".
Isaac Newton Institute for the Mathematical Sciences, January to July 2012.

Talk given at the SAS Satellite Workshop "The Incomputable" (Kavli Royal Society International Centre, Chicheley Hall, Newport Pagnell), 13 June 2012, 11:30–12:00.

Injections, Orbits, and Complexity

Valentina Harizanov

George Washington University, Washington D.C., United States of America

E-mail: harizanv@gwu.edu

We consider natural relations on a computable injection structure $\mathcal{A} = (A, f)$, a structure with a single unary $1-1$ function f. The orbit of $a \in A$ is:

$$\mathcal{O}_f(a) = \{b \in A : (\exists n \in \mathbb{N})[f^n(a) = b \ \vee \ f^n(b) = a]\}.$$

Hence the injection structures are characterized by the number of orbits of size k for each positive finite k, and by the number of orbits of types ω and Z. We investigate the complexity of orbits, the complexity of the set of elements with orbits of a given type, as well as the complexity of $Fin(\mathcal{A}) = \{a \in A : \mathcal{O}_f(a) \text{ is finite}\}$. For example, we show that for every computably enumerable Turing degree $\mathbf{b}$, there is a computable injection structure $\mathcal{A}$ such that $Fin(\mathcal{A})$ has degree $\mathbf{b}$. For every Σ_2^0 Turing degree $\mathbf{c}$, there is a computable injection structure in which the set of elements with orbits of type ω has Turing degree $\mathbf{c}$.

Furthermore, we study how the number of orbits of certain types determines the exact complexity level of the index sets of the corresponding injection structures. While the index set of computable injection structures with finitely many infinite orbits is a Σ_3^0 complete set, the index set of computable injection structures with finitely many orbits of type ω or finitely many orbits of type Z is a Σ_4^0 complete set.

This is joint work with Doug Cenzer and Jeff Remmel.

Bibliography

[1] D. Cenzer, V. Harizanov, and J.B. Remmel. Effective categoricity of injection structures. Submitted.

Arnold Beckmann, Benedikt Löwe (eds.). Acts of the programme "Semantics and Syntax".
Isaac Newton Institute for the Mathematical Sciences, January to July 2012.

Talk given at the SAS Satellite Workshop "The Incomputable" (Kavli Royal Society International Centre, Chicheley Hall, Newport Pagnell), 13 June 2012, 14:30–15:00.

Ten Years of Triviality

André Nies

The University of Auckland, Auckland, New Zealand
E-mail: andre@cs.auckland.ac.nz

In 1975, Chaitin and Solovay studied sets of natural numbers with minimal initial segment complexity. They looked at sets where the prefix-free complexity of the first n bits is at most $K(n)$, up to a constant. In 2002, Downey, Hirschfeldt and Nies coined the term "K-trivial" for such sets. They came up with an easy "cost function" construction of a computably enumerable, but incomputable K-trivial, and showed that K-trivials are Turing incomplete.

This marks the beginning of an intense study of such sets. Nies, with some help by Hirschfeldt, showed that the K-trivials coincide with the low for random sets in the sense of Kucera and Terwijn. More coincidences followed, the most recent being that a set is K-trivial if and only if it cannot be cupped above the halting problem with an incomplete Martin-Löf random set (Day and Miller 2011, relying on a result on non-density of Martin-Löf random sets in Π_1^0 classes by Bienvenu, Hoelzl, Miller and Nies 2011). Despite all these coincidences, major questions about the class of K-trivials remain.

We trace the developments of the past and discuss these open questions.

Arnold Beckmann, Benedikt Löwe (*eds.*). *Acts of the programme "Semantics and Syntax".*
Isaac Newton Institute for the Mathematical Sciences, January to July 2012.

Talk given at the SAS Satellite Workshop "The Incomputable" (Kavli Royal Society International Centre, Chicheley Hall, Newport Pagnell), 13 June 2012, 15:00–15:30.

Enumeration Degree Spectra

Alexandra A. Soskova

Sofia University, Sofia, Bulgaria

E-mail: `asoskova@fmi.uni-sofia.bg`

The enumeration degree spectrum $DS(A)$ of a countable structure A is the set of all enumeration degrees of the presentations of A on the natural numbers. The co-spectrum of A is the set of all lower bounds of $DS(A)$. The talk is a survey on the relationships between the degree spectrum and the co-spectrum of A.

We will discuss also a jump inversion theorem for degree spectra and some applications of it.

This is joint work with Ivan N. Soskov.

Arnold Beckmann, Benedikt Löwe (*eds.*). *Acts of the programme "Semantics and Syntax".* Isaac Newton Institute for the Mathematical Sciences, January to July 2012.

Talk given at the SAS Satellite Workshop "The Incomputable" (Kavli Royal Society International Centre, Chicheley Hall, Newport Pagnell), 13 June 2012, 15:30–16:00.

Computing with Structure

Steven Ericsson-Zenith

Institute for Advanced Science and Engineering, Los Gatos CA, United States of America
E-mail: steven@iase.us

In this presentation we propose realizable mechanisms for computable logic founded upon a structural theory of logic, sensory characterization, and response potential in closed manifolds.

Briefly, the mechanics of differentiation, in which the mechanisms of sensory characterization play a role, upon the surface of a closed manifold characterize logical elements (signs) and naturally covary with the mechanical response potential of the structure. The manifold provides a natural, continuous, and unifying dynamics binding these elements. Inference is a transformation of the manifold.

We suggest that these mechanisms are observable in nature. In biophysics it is structure and the concurrency of action that are first-order considerations. It is the shape of single cells and multicellular membranes ("closed manifolds" in mathematical terms) that characterize sense and modify action potentials that produce behavior.

A generalization of the existing evidence suggests that symbols form directly upon the surface of these manifolds in cell and membrane architectures, the processing of which constrains biophysical action potentials associated with the structure. This close binding of symbol processing and action potential is naturally formed by the evolutionary process.

Symbolic processing in the biophysical system is profoundly efficient. Storage is free and the capacity for symbol representation is combinatorial across dynamic sensory manifolds. This simple efficiency suggests general engineering principles that offer significantly greater symbolic processing capability in biophysical architectures than previously considered.

In contrast, parallel computation as we understand it today is decomposable, a second order consideration of the Turing model. Parallelism can be semantically removed from computer programs with no discernible effect upon the results. Therefore it contributes nothing algorithmically, providing only performance semantics.

The parallelism that we consider here makes a difference. As in biophysical systems, structural parallelism is not decomposable without impact upon the results. It plays a role algorithmically, providing the mechanisms of recognition and memory in the surface conformations of the processing architecture. Large scale differentiation appears in the dynamics of these closed manifolds and result in measurable characteristic behavior suggesting new architectures for recognition and prediction.

Arnold Beckmann, Benedikt Löwe (eds.). Acts of the programme "Semantics and Syntax".
Isaac Newton Institute for the Mathematical Sciences, January to July 2012.

Talk given at the SAS Satellite Workshop "The Incomputable" (Kavli Royal Society International Centre, Chicheley Hall, Newport Pagnell), 13 June 2012, 14:30–15:00.

Two opposing views concerning the nature of Logic will concern us. The first, represented in the variety of models of computation considered by Alan Turing [1, 2], is the view that logical operation is the integration of symbolic elements. The second is the view, suggested by Rudolf Carnap [3], that the basic relation is "recollection of similarity" (recognition) and computable Logic is "differentiation from the entirety of sense," in which symbolic elements are continuously bound by the originating whole.

Our goal here will be to show that these two views, and the realizable mechanisms that they represent, are distinct and that their operation produces different results. In particular, the models of Alan Turing represent a metaphysical view in logic that has no capacity for the basic relation of Carnap and results in prohibitive storage and value distribution requirements.

To effectively construct such machines we require the development of a new computational logic, one that deals with differentiation, structural conformation, and related action potentials. We will outline our first steps toward such a logic.

This approach suggests a new pragmaticist foundation for logic (and potentially a new mathematics to be built upon it) since it eliminates the integration of traditional truth values in favor of symbolic differentiation upon closed manifolds and the transformation of the associated structure.

Bibliography

[1] A. M. Turing. On Computable Numbers, with an Application to the Entscheidungsproblem. *Proc. London Math. Soc.*, S2-42(1):230, 1936.

[2] A. M. Turing. Intelligent machinery, a heretical theory. *Philos. Math. (3)*, 4(3):256–260, 1996.

[3] R. Carnap. *The Logical Structure Of The World*. Open Court, 1928. ISBN:0812695232.

Turing, from the "Discrete State Machine" to the "Continuous Systems" for Morphogenesis

Giuseppe Longo

Centre National de la Recherche Scientifique, and École Polytechnique, and École Normale Supérieure, Paris, France

E-mail: longo@di.ens.fr

Turing's Logical Computing Machine of 1936 grounds its effectiveness (and success) on a fundamental split: the distinction of hardware and software. This idea was originally proposed as a purely mathematical abstraction. It later became the core structure on which the universality and the effectiveness of computing is grounded: a "rigid" hardware allows a "soft" (immaterial) program to run. After World War II, when dealing (again) with physics, Turing stresses the key physical aspect of his machine: it is a Discrete State Machine (a DSM, as he says). He then works also with completely different physical structures, for his analysis of morphogenesis (1952): the "continuous systems", as he calls them. And his action/reaction/diffusion systems will pave the way to a new insight into some physical (and biological) processes, where the "computation" lies entirely in a continuous dynamics of forms: no software, just plastic and ever changing "hardware" and its unpredictable evolutions, subject to the "exponential drift". By his two inventions, Turing set the basis for an understanding of the core ideas of the Theory of Computability vs. Bio-physical phenomena in two opposing ways, that I would like to summarize as follows: computing as an "always identical iteration of alpha-numeric re-writing rules" (1936) and of Biology as a "never identical iteration of a morphogenetic processes", (1952) far away from the Computable. How does the "exponential drift" relate to incomputability, which is always proved by reduction to Gödel's and Turing's diagonal methods, even in computability over continua?

Bibliography

[1] F. Bailly and G. Longo. *Mathematics and Natural Sciences: the Physical Singularity of Life*. 333 pages, Imperial College Press, London, 2011.

[2] G. Longo. Incomputability in physics. In *Programs, proofs, processes*, volume 6158 of *Lecture Notes in Comput. Sci.*, pages 276–285. Springer, Berlin, 2010.

[3] M. Buiatti and G. Longo. Randomness and multi-level interactions in biology. Ongoing work (arxiv.org/abs/1104.1110v1).

Arnold Beckmann, Benedikt Löwe (*eds.*). *Acts of the programme "Semantics and Syntax"*.
Isaac Newton Institute for the Mathematical Sciences, January to July 2012.

Talk given at the SAS Satellite Workshop "The Incomputable" (Kavli Royal Society International Centre, Chicheley Hall, Newport Pagnell), 13 June 2012, 15:00–15:30.

Hypercomputation, Physics and Computation

Mike Stannett

University of Sheffield, Sheffield, United Kingdom
E-mail: M.Stannett@dcs.shef.ac.uk

We present an introductory overview of research in hypercomputation theory, especially as it relates to the relationship between physics and computation. On the quantum side, we argue that a computational model of quantum motion exists, showing that if super-Turing computation is possible it must (somewhat paradoxically) derive from uncomputable properties of classical action. On the cosmological side, we review the work of Hogarth, Andréka, Németi et al, showing that realistic models of spacetime permit the solution of formally undecidable problems. Conversely, very simple computational considerations imply that closed timelike curves (CTCs), if they exist, can act as very low capacity information storage systems.

The material, which is based on a recent talk at the British Mathematical Colloquium 2012, will be presented in easily accessible form, and questions from the audience (especially those we cannot answer) are very welcome.

Arnold Beckmann, Benedikt Löwe (*eds.*). *Acts of the programme "Semantics and Syntax".*
Isaac Newton Institute for the Mathematical Sciences, January to July 2012.

Talk given at the SAS Satellite Workshop "The Incomputable" (Kavli Royal Society International Centre, Chicheley Hall, Newport Pagnell), 13 June 2012, 15:30–16:00.

Relativistic Computing Beyond the Turing Barrier

István Németi and Hajnal Andréka

Hungarian Academy of Sciences, Budapest, Hungary
E-mail: nemeti@renyi.hu

By relativistic computing we mean general relativistic (GR) computing. As pointed out in earlier papers of the present authors, GR makes it possible to physically compute the "uncomputable" (at least in theory). In particular, we will show that we can design a physical experiment carrying out of which can tell the experimenter the answer to a Turing incomputable question. Such a question is, for example, deciding any recursive enumerable but not recursive set of the integers. We will claim that our future generations may be able to carry out such an experiment. In the talk we will discuss how and why. We will discuss various kinds of such relativistic hypercomputers. Among others, we will discuss hypercomputers based on kinds of Lorentzian wormholes, their connections with Einstein's equation and accelerating expansion of the universe.

Arnold Beckmann, Benedikt Löwe (eds.). Acts of the programme "Semantics and Syntax". Isaac Newton Institute for the Mathematical Sciences, January to July 2012.

Talk given at the SAS Satellite Workshop "The Incomputable" (Kavli Royal Society International Centre, Chicheley Hall, Newport Pagnell), 13 June 2012, 16:30–17:30.

A Framework for Logic in Physics

Fay Dowker

Imperial College London, London, United Kingdom

E-mail: f.dowker@imperial.ac.uk

Mathematics and science, particularly physics, are so intertwined that it might be expected that physics will inform even foundational issues in mathematics such as logic. In this spirit, I will set out a framework for logic in physics due to Rafael Sorkin in which logical rules of inference are seen to be a special case of dynamical law. The framework incorporates the fact that the physical world is contingent: a meaningful proposition such as "The particle detector clicks within 10 seconds of turning on," is not in itself true or false but is either affirmed or denied by the physical world, after the fact. The framework accommodates classical and quantum physical theories and *anhomomorphic* logic. In a well-defined sense, it tolerates inconsistency and it is therefore tempting to explore what it might have to say about the Russell Paradox.

Arnold Beckmann, Benedikt Löwe (*eds.*). *Acts of the programme "Semantics and Syntax"*. Isaac Newton Institute for the Mathematical Sciences, January to July 2012.

Talk given at the SAS Satellite Workshop "The Incomputable" (Kavli Royal Society International Centre, Chicheley Hall, Newport Pagnell), 14 June 2012, 09:00–10:00.

P vs. NP, Phase Transitions, and Incomputability in the Wild

Cris Moore

Santa Fe Institute, Santa Fe NM, United States of America
E-mail: moore@santafe.edu

Theoretical computer science concerns itself with complexity classes and their relationships; most famously, the P vs. NP problem, of whether solutions are easy to find whenever they are easy to check. P and NP are roughly analogous to the classes of decidable and recursively enumerable sets, since membership in an RE set can be confirmed in finite time. Sadly, we learned from Baker, Gill, and Solovay that the diagonalization argument of Turing and Church cannot possibly prove that P $\neq$ NP. It was recently proposed that the behavior of random NP-complete problems near their phase transitions might shed some light on P vs. NP; but as I will discuss, 3-SAT and XORSAT have similar statistical properties, even though 3-SAT is NP-complete and XORSAT is in P.

I will end by commenting on incomputability in physics. It is easy to prove incomputability whenever we can engineer a computer out of tiles, atoms, or the like, but I suspect that many physical problems may be incomputable even when we cannot do this. In other words, I expect there are physical problems that are incomputable, but not Turing complete.

Arnold Beckmann, Benedikt Löwe (eds.). Acts of the programme "Semantics and Syntax". Isaac Newton Institute for the Mathematical Sciences, January to July 2012.

Talk given at the SAS Satellite Workshop "The Incomputable" (Kavli Royal Society International Centre, Chicheley Hall, Newport Pagnell), 14 June 2012, 10:00–11:00.

Interpreting Arithmetic in the Turing Degrees below Generics and Randoms

Richard A. Shore

Cornell University, Ithaca NY, United States of America

E-mail: shore@math.cornell.edu

We discuss how interpretations of arithmetic in the Turing degrees developed to characterize the theory of the degrees and of various ideals (including many principal ones) can be used to answer some questions about the theory of the degrees below generic and random reals.

It is an old result of Jockusch that for any two generic degrees $\mathbf{g}_1$ and $\mathbf{g}_2$ (i.e., there are $G_i \in \mathbf{g}_i$ which are n-generic for every $n \in \mathbb{N}$), $\mathcal{D}(\leq_T \mathbf{g}_1) \equiv \mathcal{D}(\leq_T \mathbf{g}_2)$. We denote the common theory by $\mathrm{Th}(\leq_T G)$. Jockusch asked if there is an $n < \omega$ such that $\mathrm{Th}(\mathcal{D}(\leq_T \mathbf{g})) = \mathrm{Th}(\leq_T G)$ for all n-generic $\mathbf{g}$. The same situation prevails for random degrees, i.e., there is a common theory $\mathrm{Th}(\leq_T R)$ which is $\mathrm{Th}(\mathcal{D}(\leq_T \mathbf{r})$ for every random $\mathbf{r}$ (i.e., some $R \in \mathbf{r}$ is n-random for every $n \in \mathbb{N}$). Barmpalias, Day and Lewis raise the same question for random degrees. They also ask if $\mathrm{Th}(\leq_T G) = \mathrm{Th}(\leq_T R)$.

We use the interpretations of standard models of arithmetic below 1-generics of Greenberg and Montalbán and our own methods for coding sets below an r.e. degree to answer all three questions in the negative. The basic structural facts needed about n-generic and n-random degrees for $n \geq 2$ is that they are relatively r.e. and the 1-generics are downward dense below them (Jockusch; Martin; Kurtz; Kautz; Barmpalias, Day and Lewis).

Arnold Beckmann, Benedikt Löwe (eds.). Acts of the programme "Semantics and Syntax".
Isaac Newton Institute for the Mathematical Sciences, January to July 2012.

Talk given at the SAS Satellite Workshop "The Incomputable" (Kavli Royal Society International Centre, Chicheley Hall, Newport Pagnell), 14 June 2012, 11:30–12:00.

Classification of Countable Structures and the Effective Borel Hierarchy

Julia F. Knight

University of Notre Dame, Notre Dame IN, United States of America

E-mail: Julia.F.Knight.1@nd.edu

Let K be a class of structures for a fixed computable language, with universe a subset of ω, and closed under isomorphism. Classifying the members of K, up to isomorphism, involves understanding and describing the different isomorphism types. We may use "Turing computable embeddings" to reduce the classification problem of one class to that of another class. The following definition is from [1].

Definition. A *Turing computable embedding* of K in K' is a Turing operator $\Phi = \varphi_e$ such that

- for each $\mathcal{A} \in K$, there exists $\mathcal{B} \in K'$ such that $\varphi_e^{D(\mathcal{A})} = \chi_{D(\mathcal{B})}$—we write $\Phi(\mathcal{A})$ for $\mathcal{B}$,

- for $\mathcal{A}, \mathcal{A}' \in K$, $\mathcal{A} \cong \mathcal{A}'$ iff $\Phi(\mathcal{A}) \cong \Phi(\mathcal{B})$.

Turing computable embeddings give rise to a pre-ordering $\leq_{tc}$ on classes. For many classes, this pre-ordering agrees with $\leq_B$, the pre-ordering given by Borel embeddings, see [2]. For Borel embeddings, it is standard to consider only structures with universe ω. For Turing computable embeddings, the universe is an arbitrary subset of ω.

We give a sample of results, locating some familiar classes under $\leq_{tc}$. In [1], it is shown that the class FPF of finite prime fields lies strictly below the class FLO of finite linear orderings, which lies strictly below the class of Q-vector spaces. The class FLO lies "on top" among classes of finite structures. It is tc-equivalent to the class of number fields. More recently, Ocasio and Knight have shown that the class of free groups is equivalent to the class of Q-vector spaces. In [2], it is shown that the class ApG of Abelian p-groups does not lie on top under $\leq_B$. There is a special class of graphs SG, coding families of sets, such that $SG \not\leq_{tc} ApG$ [4]. Recently, Ocasio [3] has shown that SG is tc-equivalent to the class of Archimedean ordered fields. The construction is interesting from the point of view of computability, and it also uses some model theory (*o*-minimality).

Arnold Beckmann, Benedikt Löwe (eds.). Acts of the programme "Semantics and Syntax". Isaac Newton Institute for the Mathematical Sciences, January to July 2012.

Talk given at the SAS Satellite Workshop "The Incomputable" (Kavli Royal Society International Centre, Chicheley Hall, Newport Pagnell), 14 June 2012, 12:00–12:30.

Bibliography

[1] W. Calvert, D. Cummins, J. F. Knight, and S. Miller. Comparing classes of finite structures. *Algebra and Logic*, vol. 43(2004), p. 666–701.

[2] H. Friedman and L. Stanley. A Borel reducibility theory for classes of countable structures. *J. Symb. Logic*, vol. 45(1989), pp. 894-914.

[3] V. A. Ocasio-González. Turing computable embeddings and coding families of sets. In S. Barry Cooper, Anuj Dawar, Benedikt Löwe (Eds.): *How the World Computes* - Turing Centenary Conference and 8th Conference on Computability in Europe, CiE 2012, Cambridge, UK, June 18-23, 2012. Proceedings. Lecture Notes in Computer Science vol. 7318, pp. 539-548, Springer 2012.

[4] E. Fokina, J. F. Knight, A. Melnikov, S. M. Quinn, and C. M. Safranski. Ulm type and coding rank-homogeneous trees in other structures.

Compact Closed Categories and Frobenius Algebras for Computing Natural Language Meaning

Mehrnoosh Sadrzadeh

University of Oxford, Oxford, United Kingdom

E-mail: mehrs@cs.ox.ac.uk

Compact closed categories have found applications in modeling quantum information protocols by Abramsky-Coecke. They also provide semantics for Lambek's pregroup algebras, applied to formalizing the grammatical structure of natural language, and are implicit in a distributional model of word meaning based on vector spaces. In particular, in previous work, Coecke-Clark-Sadrzadeh used the product category of pregroups with vector spaces and provided a distributional model of meaning for sentences. We recast this theory in terms of strongly monoidal functors and advance it via Frobenius algebras over vector spaces. The former are used to formalize topological quantum field theories by Atiyah and Baez-Dolan, and the latter are used to model classical data in quantum protocols by Coecke-Pavlovic-Vicary. The Frobenius algebras enable us to work in a single space in which lives meanings of words, phrases, and sentences of any structure. Hence we can compare meanings of different language constructs and enhance the applicability of the theory. We report on experimental results on a number of language tasks such as word sense disambiguation and term/definition extraction and show how our theoretical predictions are verified on real large scale date from British National Corpus.

This is collaborative work with Steven Clark, Bob Coecke, Edward Grefenstette, Dimitri Kartsaklis, Anne Preller, and Steve Pulman.

Arnold Beckmann, Benedikt Löwe (*eds.*). *Acts of the programme "Semantics and Syntax"*. Isaac Newton Institute for the Mathematical Sciences, January to July 2012.

Talk given at the SAS Satellite Workshop "The Incomputable" (Kavli Royal Society International Centre, Chicheley Hall, Newport Pagnell), 14 June 2012, 11:30–12:00.

Would You Please Stop Talking About the Church-Turing Thesis, Please

Mark Hogarth

University of Cambridge, Cambridge, United Kingdom
E-mail: mhogarth@cantab.net

The new and flourishing field of unconventional computing (hypercomputing) has prompted some to question the alleged truth of Turing's thesis. I am prompted towards a more radical view. I maintain that what these exciting investigations reveal is that there is no such thing as an 'ideal computer', and consequently Turing's thesis, which in essence asserts the equation of this ideal computer with the Turing machine, should be seen as a pseudo-claim. I have no special brief to be rid of the ideal computer or the Church-Turing claim. Rather, my view stems directly from a new picture of computability, which itself is motivated by an analogy with the concept of geometry. This picture will be sketched.

Arnold Beckmann, Benedikt Löwe (eds.). Acts of the programme "Semantics and Syntax".
Isaac Newton Institute for the Mathematical Sciences, January to July 2012.

Talk given at the SAS Satellite Workshop "The Incomputable" (Kavli Royal Society International Centre, Chicheley Hall, Newport Pagnell), 14 June 2012, 12:00–12:30.

Computational Complexity and Set Theory

Sy-David Friedman

University of Vienna, Vienna, Austria

E-mail: sdf@logic.univie.ac.at

I'll discuss two recent interactions between computational complexity theory and set theory.

What does it mean for a function on sets to be computable in polynomial time? In joint work with Beckmann and Buss [1] we use a set-theoretic analogue of the Bellantoni-Cook schemes of safe-recursion to answer this question.

Can set theory offer new approaches to problems in computational complexity theory? In joint work with Buss, Chen, Flum and Mueller [2] we provide a positive answer to this question by studying the natural analogue of Borel reducibility for isomorphism relations on PTIME classes of finite structures.

Bibliography

[1] A. Beckmann, S. Buss and S. D. Friedman. Safe-recursive set functions. In *The Infinity Project*, Centre de Recerca Matematica Document Series, 2012.

[2] S. Buss, Y. Chen, J. Flum, S.-D. Friedman, and M. Müller. Strong isomorphism reductions in complexity theory. *J. Symbolic Logic*, 76(4):1381–1402, 2011.

Arnold Beckmann, Benedikt Löwe (*eds.*). *Acts of the programme "Semantics and Syntax".* Isaac Newton Institute for the Mathematical Sciences, January to July 2012.

Talk given at the SAS Satellite Workshop "The Incomputable" (Kavli Royal Society International Centre, Chicheley Hall, Newport Pagnell), 14 June 2012, 14:30–15:00.

Structures and Isomorphisms in the Difference Hierarchy

Douglas Cenzer

University of Florida, Gainesville FL, United States of America
E-mail: cenzer@math.ufl.edu

This will include recent work on injection structures and on structures with functions f which are at most two-to-one. Such structures consist of orbits, where the orbit of a point a is the set of all elements x such that either $f^n(x) = a$ or $f^n(a) = x$, for some n. A central goal is to characterize structures which are computably categorical or more generally Δ_2^0 categorical. The universe of a structure may be a computable set, or a c.e. set, or more generally, an n-c.e. set, where an element may go into and back out of the universe multiple times. We also consider functions which may change a finite number of times, as well as isomorphisms which may change.

Arnold Beckmann, Benedikt Löwe (*eds.*). *Acts of the programme "Semantics and Syntax"*.
Isaac Newton Institute for the Mathematical Sciences, January to July 2012.

Talk given at the SAS Satellite Workshop "The Incomputable" (Kavli Royal Society International Centre, Chicheley Hall, Newport Pagnell), 14 June 2012, 15:00–15:30.

A Computability Theoretic Equivalent to Vaught's Conjecture

Antonio Montalban

The University of Chicago, Chicago IL, United States of America

E-mail: antonio@math.uchicago.edu

We find two computability theoretic properties on the models of a theory T which hold if and only if T is a counterexample to Vaught's conjecture.

Arnold Beckmann, Benedikt Löwe (eds.). Acts of the programme "Semantics and Syntax". Isaac Newton Institute for the Mathematical Sciences, January to July 2012.

Talk given at the SAS Satellite Workshop "The Incomputable" (Kavli Royal Society International Centre, Chicheley Hall, Newport Pagnell), 14 June 2012, 15:30–16:00.

The Halting Problem Revisited

Cristian Calude

The University of Auckland, Auckland, New Zealand
E-mail: cristian@cs.auckland.ac.nz

The talk will present the famous Halting Problem from different new points of view. In particular, a probabilistic solution to the problem will be given.

Arnold Beckmann, Benedikt Löwe (eds.). Acts of the programme "Semantics and Syntax".
Isaac Newton Institute for the Mathematical Sciences, January to July 2012.

Talk given at the SAS Satellite Workshop "The Incomputable" (Kavli Royal Society International Centre, Chicheley Hall, Newport Pagnell), 14 June 2012, 14:30–15:00.

Computability and Non-computability Issues in Amorphous Computing

Jiři Wiedermann

Academy of Sciences of the Czech Republic, Prague, Czech Republic
E-mail: jiri.wiedermann@cs.cas.cz

Amorphous computing systems can be seen as extreme cases of wireless communicating networks. They consist of a huge set of tiny simple stationary or mobile processors whose computational, communication and sensory part is reduced to an absolute minimum. In an airborne medium the processors communicate via a short range radio while in a waterborne medium via molecular communication. In some cases the computational part of the processors can be simplified down to probabilistic finite state automata and the system as a whole can still possess universal computational power with a high probability. Thus, the resulting amorphous systems belong among the simplest (non-uniform) universal computational devices since their functionality is fully defined by any of their processors and there is no need to describe the "architecture" of the system as a whole. An interesting question arises in the reverse simulation of amorphous computing systems by Turing machines. Namely, operation of certain amorphous computing systems also depends on abilities of their processors and those of their environment that are of non-computational nature. Therefore, it is questionable as to what extent the Church-Turing thesis covers the case of such amorphous computing systems.

Arnold Beckmann, Benedikt Löwe (eds.). Acts of the programme "Semantics and Syntax".
Isaac Newton Institute for the Mathematical Sciences, January to July 2012.

Talk given at the SAS Satellite Workshop "The Incomputable" (Kavli Royal Society International Centre, Chicheley Hall, Newport Pagnell), 14 June 2012, 15:00–15:30.

Trouble with Computation

Mark Bishop

Goldsmiths, University of London, London, United Kingdom
E-mail: m.bishop@gold.ac.uk

In 1980 John Searle first published a novel argument, which has become known as the Chinese Room Argument (CRA), that purported to demonstrate that "by itself, syntax is neither constitutive of, nor sufficient for, semantic content." If correct the CRA suggests that programs cannot produce minds. Clearly, the suggestion that syntactic manipulation alone is not sufficient for meaning or thought is significant—not just in the context of Artificial Intelligence (AI) but in the philosophy of mind in general, as many prominent theories hold that the essence of mind is computational. In the 31 years since the CRA was first published the importance of the argument has merited that it has been attacked (and defended) in strong measure. In this presentation I will suggest that the CRA remains the "elephant in the room" regarding AI and that even recent "cognitive" approaches to building intelligent machines do not escape its grasp; because the "trouble with computation" is that it does not take embodiment seriously.

Arnold Beckmann, Benedikt Löwe (*eds.*). *Acts of the programme "Semantics and Syntax".*
Isaac Newton Institute for the Mathematical Sciences, January to July 2012.

Talk given at the SAS Satellite Workshop "The Incomputable" (Kavli Royal Society International Centre, Chicheley Hall, Newport Pagnell), 14 June 2012, 15:30–16:00.

What Features of Living Systems Can We Simulate on a Quantum Computer?

Vlatko Vedral

University of Oxford, Oxford, United Kingdom

E-mail: vlatko.vedral@qubit.org

In my talk I will present recent results regarding the role of quantum coherence in living molecules. Living molecules are difficult to simulate even if
we assume that they are completely classical, but the fact that some of their
key properties could be genuinely quantum, leads us naturally to inquire
about the additional complexity of simulating them. I will briefly review
evidence for quantum biology and then sketch out how quantum computers could be used to further our understanding of the role coherence might
play in the energy and information transport processes in bio-molecules.
A question presents itself if all biological features could be simulated on a
quantum computer and, if so, would such a computer effectively be thought
of as being alive.

Arnold Beckmann, Benedikt Löwe (*eds.*). *Acts of the programme "Semantics and Syntax".*
Isaac Newton Institute for the Mathematical Sciences, January to July 2012.

Talk given at the SAS Satellite Workshop "The Incomputable" (Kavli Royal Society International Centre, Chicheley Hall, Newport Pagnell), 14 June 2012, 16:30–17:30.

Intensionality, Definability and Computations

Samson Abramsky

University of Oxford, Oxford, United Kingdom

E-mail: samson@comlab.ox.ac.uk

The aim is to talk about higher-type computation, and how to characterize various forms of computability in this setting. This will reference various developments in computer science, e.g., domain theory, the full abstraction problem, and game semantics.

Arnold Beckmann, Benedikt Löwe (*eds.*). *Acts of the programme "Semantics and Syntax"*. Isaac Newton Institute for the Mathematical Sciences, January to July 2012.

Talk given at the SAS Satellite Workshop "The Incomputable" (Kavli Royal Society International Centre, Chicheley Hall, Newport Pagnell), 15 June 2012, 09:00–10:00.

The Mathematics of Relative Computability

Theodore A. Slaman

University of California, Berkeley CA, United States of America

E-mail: slaman@math.berkeley.edu

Alan Turing had the remarkably prescient insight that understanding the means by which we work with things can be as important as, or even equivalent to, understanding those things. Equally remarkably, he combined a deep understanding of the abstract with pragmatic good sense. We will discuss some of the mathematical developments arising from his early investigations.

Arnold Beckmann, Benedikt Löwe (eds.). Acts of the programme "Semantics and Syntax".
Isaac Newton Institute for the Mathematical Sciences, January to July 2012.

Talk given at the SAS Satellite Workshop "The Incomputable" (Kavli Royal Society International Centre, Chicheley Hall, Newport Pagnell), 15 June 2012, 10:00–11:00.

The Computably Enumerable Sets: A Survey

Peter Cholak

University of Notre Dame, Notre Dame IN, United States of America
E-mail: `Peter.Cholak.1@nd.edu`

We will survey recent results on the computably enumerable sets and ongoing research projects.

Arnold Beckmann, Benedikt Löwe (*eds.*). *Acts of the programme "Semantics and Syntax"*.
Isaac Newton Institute for the Mathematical Sciences, January to July 2012.

Talk given at the SAS Satellite Workshop "The Incomputable" (Kavli Royal Society International Centre, Chicheley Hall, Newport Pagnell), 15 June 2012, 11:30–12:00.

On the Strongly Bounded Turing Degrees of C.E. Sets: Degrees Inside Degrees

Klaus Ambos-Spies

University of Heidelberg, Heidelberg, Germany

E-mail: ambos@math.uni-heidelberg.de

We consider two variants of strongly bounded Turing reductions: An identity bounded Turing reduction (ibT-reduction for short) is a Turing reduction where no oracle query is greater than the input while a computable Lipschitz reduction (cl-reduction for short) is a Turing reduction where the oracle queries on input x are bounded by $x + c$ for some constant c. Since ibT-reducibility is stronger than cl-reducibility and cl-reducibility is stronger than wtt-reducibility (where a weak truth-table (wtt-) reduction is a Turing reduction where the oracle queries are computably bounded in the inputs) we may look at the partial ordering of the computably enumerable (c.e.) ibT-degrees inside the cl-degree of a noncomputable c.e. set A and, similarly, at the partial ordering of the c.e. cl-degrees inside the wtt-degree of a noncomputable c.e. set A. In our talk we discuss some properties of these partial orderings.

Arnold Beckmann, Benedikt Löwe (eds.). Acts of the programme "Semantics and Syntax". Isaac Newton Institute for the Mathematical Sciences, January to July 2012.

Talk given at the SAS Satellite Workshop "The Incomputable" (Kavli Royal Society International Centre, Chicheley Hall, Newport Pagnell), 15 June 2012, 12:00–12:30.

Computation, Measurement and the Interface Between Physical Systems and Algorithms

John V. Tucker

Swansea University, Swansea, United Kingdom

E-mail: j.v.tucker@swansea.ac.uk

Edwin Beggs, Felix Costa and I have developed a theory of combining algorithms with physical systems based upon using physical experiments as oracles to algorithms. The theory has two broad applications:

1. exploring the role of physical technologies in boosting computations (Turing's original motivating idea for oracles) and

2. exploring the influence of computers on performing experiments and measuring physical quantities.

The talk will introduce and survey the current state of our theory.

Power: In a series of papers we have shown that adding physical equipment as an oracle can boost the power of algorithms beyond the Turing barrier. For specific examples of physical system(mechanical, optical, electrical) the computational power has been characterised using non-uniform complexity classes. The power of the known examples vary according to assumptions on precision and timingbut seem to lead to the same complexity classes, namely P/log* and BPP/log*. Recently, we have developed axiomatic specifications of experiments that suggest these classes arise naturally and widely.

Limits to measurement: When an experimenter applies a experimental procedure to some equipment, due to its systematic nature, the experimental procedure can be thought of as an algorithm that governseach step in the experiment and processes the data. Indeed, in practice, many experiments are controlled by software. Inspired by Turing's 1936 and 1939 analysis, we have proposed the idea that:

"The experimenter following a systematic experimental procedure can be modelled by a Turing machine, and his or her interaction with equipment can be modelled as an oracle device connected to the Turing machine via an interface that governs the initialisation and operation of physical equipment."

Arnold Beckmann, Benedikt Löwe (*eds.*). *Acts of the programme "Semantics and Syntax".* Isaac Newton Institute for the Mathematical Sciences, January to July 2012.

Talk given at the SAS Satellite Workshop "The Incomputable" (Kavli Royal Society International Centre, Chicheley Hall, Newport Pagnell), 15 June 2012, 11:30–12:00.

We are creating an algorithmic theory of measurement that enables us to analyse some basic questions about measurement, including:

1. What are the costs in time to perform measurements to a given accuracy?

2. What are the limitations to measurements imposed by equipment and experimental procedures?

3. How computable and complex are measurements?

How Hard is Proving Hardness? Logic Approach to Barriers in Complexity

Antonina Kolokolova

Memorial University of Newfoundland, St. John's NL, Canada

E-mail: `kol@cs.mun.ca`

In spite of much work over the years, the main questions in complexity theory such as P vs. NP remain unresolved. Is this question solvable at all? Is P vs. NP independent of some logical theory? Indeed, on a meta-level, there are several results that state that certain classes of techniques, including Turing's celebrated diagonalization, cannot be used to resolve these questions. Such results we call the "barriers" of complexity theory.

In this talk, we will survey some of the main such barriers (Relativization, Natural Proofs, Algebrization), and talk about how knowledge of such barriers helps evaluate (and, so far, discard) proposed proofs of P vs. NP. We will talk about the logic basis for such barriers, where a barrier means an independence of a logic theory.

Arnold Beckmann, Benedikt Löwe (*eds.*). *Acts of the programme "Semantics and Syntax".*
Isaac Newton Institute for the Mathematical Sciences, January to July 2012.

Talk given at the SAS Satellite Workshop "The Incomputable" (Kavli Royal Society International Centre, Chicheley Hall, Newport Pagnell), 15 June 2012, 12:00–12:30.

Randomness and Classes of PA and DNC Functions in Computability

Antonin Kučera

Charles University, Prague, Czech Republic
E-mail: kucera@ksi.ms.mff.cuni.cz

Some levels of randomness and properties of PA and DNC classes from the point of computability will be presented. Among others, it will be discussed what information can be extracted from objects of mentioned types, especially with a connection to c.e. sets.

Arnold Beckmann, Benedikt Löwe (*eds.*). *Acts of the programme "Semantics and Syntax".*
Isaac Newton Institute for the Mathematical Sciences, January to July 2012.

Talk given at the SAS Satellite Workshop "The Incomputable" (Kavli Royal Society International Centre, Chicheley Hall, Newport Pagnell), 15 June 2012, 14:30–15:00.

Definable Relations in the Turing Degree Structures

Marat M. Arslanov

Kazan State University, Kazan, Russia

E-mail: Marat.Arslanov@ksu.ru

I will consider classes of n-c.e. sets and degrees which are definable in the language of the n-c.e. sets $\{\subseteq, \cup, \cap, 0, \omega\}$ and in the language of the Turing degrees $\{\leq_T\}$.

Arnold Beckmann, Benedikt Löwe (eds.). Acts of the programme "Semantics and Syntax".
Isaac Newton Institute for the Mathematical Sciences, January to July 2012.

Talk given at the SAS Satellite Workshop "The Incomputable" (Kavli Royal Society International Centre, Chicheley Hall, Newport Pagnell), 15 June 2012, 15:00–15:30.

The Hierarchy of Equivalence Relations on the Natural Numbers Under Computable Reducibility

Joel David Hamkins

City University of New York, New York NY, United States of America

E-mail: jhamkins@gc.cuny.edu

I will speak on the computable analogue of the theory of equivalence relations on the reals under Borel reducibility. The Borel theory has been enormously successful in clarifying the hierarchy of classification problems arising throughout mathematics. The computable analogue, meanwhile, appears to be particularly well-suited for an analysis of the c.e. instances of those problems, a rich context with many natural examples, such as the isomorphism relation on c.e. graphs or on computably presented groups. In particular, every equivalence relation on countable structures has its natural restriction to the c.e. instances, which may be viewed as an equivalence relation on the indices of those c.e. sets. Specifically, one equivalence relation E on the natural numbers is computably reducible to another F, if there is a computable function f such that nEm if and only if $f(n)Ff(m)$. This reduction notion has been introduced and studied independently by several different researchers and research groups. In this talk, I will describe recent joint work with Sam Coskey and Russell Miller that fills out parts of the hierarchy. An abundance of questions remain open.

Arnold Beckmann, Benedikt Löwe (eds.). Acts of the programme "Semantics and Syntax".
Isaac Newton Institute for the Mathematical Sciences, January to July 2012.

Talk given at the SAS Satellite Workshop "The Incomputable" (Kavli Royal Society International Centre, Chicheley Hall, Newport Pagnell), 15 June 2012, 15:30–16:00.

How Computer Science Helps to Bring Quantum Physics to the Masses

Bob Coecke

University of Oxford, Oxford, United Kingdom
E-mail: coecke@cs.ox.ac.uk

We present computational aspects of quantum theory in a computer science dress and show how this not only helps towards novel quantum technologies but also allows for a more intuitive presentation of the theory which doesn't require a background in mathematical physics. In particular, the language that we will use closely resembles flowcharts. We also illustrate how this research is transcendental with respect to disciplinary boundaries and has helped in solving problems in other areas, most notably, natural language processing.

Bibliography

[1] J. Aron. Quantum links let computers understand language. *New Scientist*, 2790:10–11, 2010.

[2] B. Coecke. Quantum picturalism. *Contemporary Physics*, 51(1):59–83, 2010.

Arnold Beckmann, Benedikt Löwe (*eds.*). *Acts of the programme "Semantics and Syntax"*.
Isaac Newton Institute for the Mathematical Sciences, January to July 2012.

Talk given at the SAS Satellite Workshop "The Incomputable" (Kavli Royal Society International Centre, Chicheley Hall, Newport Pagnell), 15 June 2012, 14:30–15:00.

Classifying the Theories of Physics

José Félix Costa

Instituto Superior Técnico, Lisbon, Portugal
E-mail: fgc@math.ist.utl.pt

We suggest that the Turing machine is a good model of a scientist, both in the task of monitoring (let us say) measurement experiments in Physics and in the task of establishing physical laws from those measurements, providing mathematical support of concepts in the philosophy of science.

Is the physical law computable or rather non-computable? We show that, in our model, once the observed phenomenon departs from pure randomness, a law of physics can be Turing machine computed from observations, regardless the computable or non-computable character of the observed phenomenon. Then we suggest that the price of such derivations is the disunity of science, a generic non-unification theorem.

To state and prove the above mentioned results, we have included in our previous model of a scientist conducting an experiment in Physics some concepts of computational learning theory, generalising the known computational EXplanatory classes EX, EX^n and Behaviourally Correct classes BC and BC^n to non-computable functions.

Then we revisit Popper and Kuhn theses in the new PREDictive PRED-identification paradigm and prove our formulation to be sound with respect to a notorious case study in the history of science.

Arnold Beckmann, Benedikt Löwe (eds.). Acts of the programme "Semantics and Syntax". Isaac Newton Institute for the Mathematical Sciences, January to July 2012.

Talk given at the SAS Satellite Workshop "The Incomputable" (Kavli Royal Society International Centre, Chicheley Hall, Newport Pagnell), 15 June 2012, 15:00–15:30.

Author Index